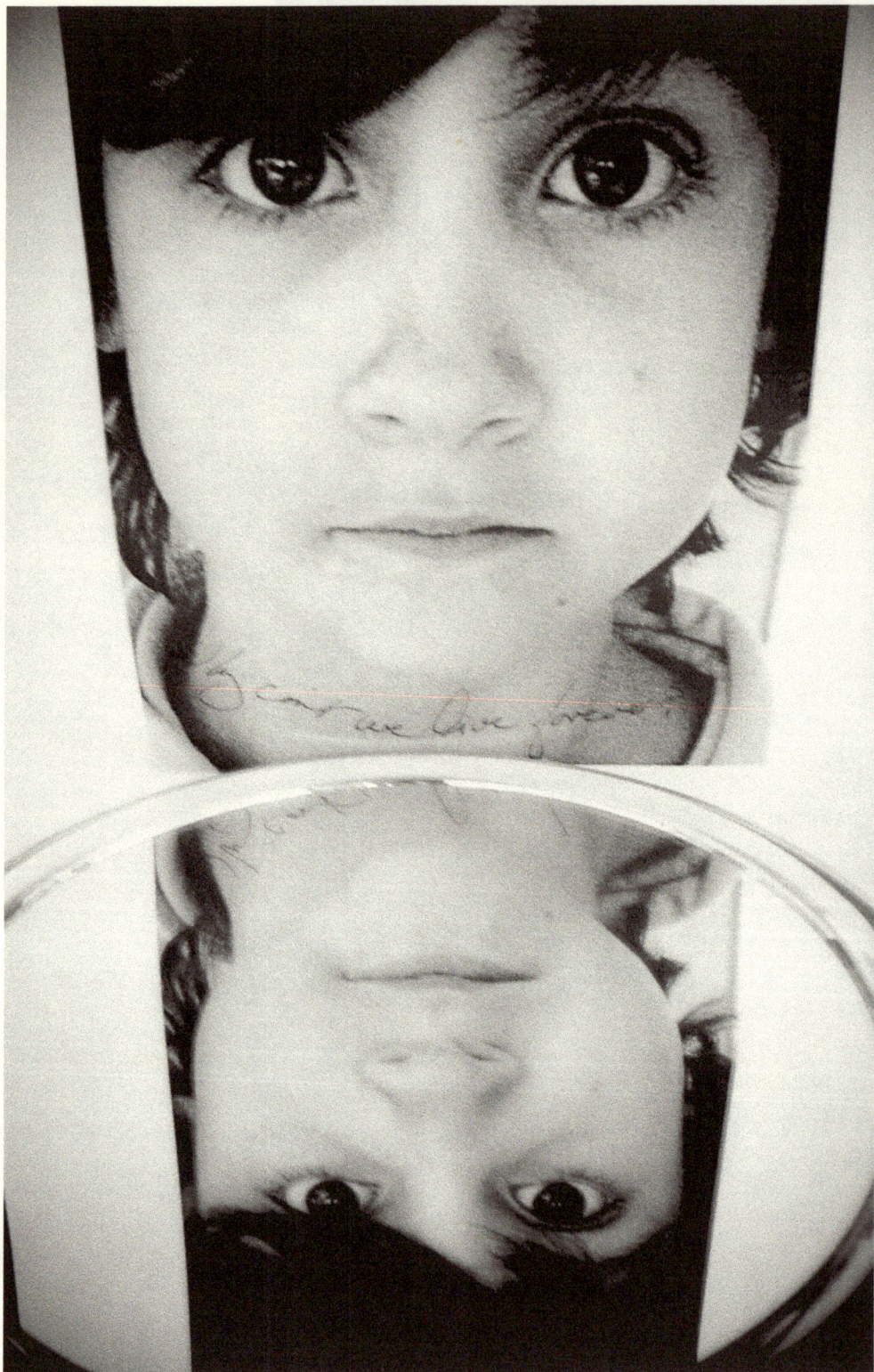

DARING TO REPAIR
What Is It, Who Does It & Why?

WISING UP ANTHOLOGIES

ILLNESS & GRACE, TERROR & TRANSFORMATION
2007

FAMILIES: THE FRONTLINE OF PLURALISM
2008

LOVE AFTER 70
2008

DOUBLE LIVES, REINVENTION &
THOSE WE LEAVE BEHIND
2009

VIEW FROM THE BED
VIEW FROM THE BEDSIDE
2010

SHIFTING BALANCE SHEETS:
Women's Stories of Naturalized Citizenship & Cultural Attachment
2011

COMPLEX ALLEGIANCES:
Constellations of Immigration, Citizenship, & Belonging
2012

DARING TO REPAIR

What Is It, Who Does It & Why?

Heather Tosteson & Charles Brockett
Editors

Wising Up Press
Decatur, Georgia

Wising Up Press
P.O. Box 2122
Decatur, GA 30031-2122
www.universaltable.org

Catalogue-in-Publication data is on file with the Library of Congress.
LCCN: 2012952328

Wising Up ISBN-13: 978-0-9827262-7-3

TABLE OF CONTENTS

II. PARENTHOOD

III. ROMANCE

IV. MARRIAGE

V. BEREAVEMENT

VI. EXPANDING INTO THE HUMAN CONDITION

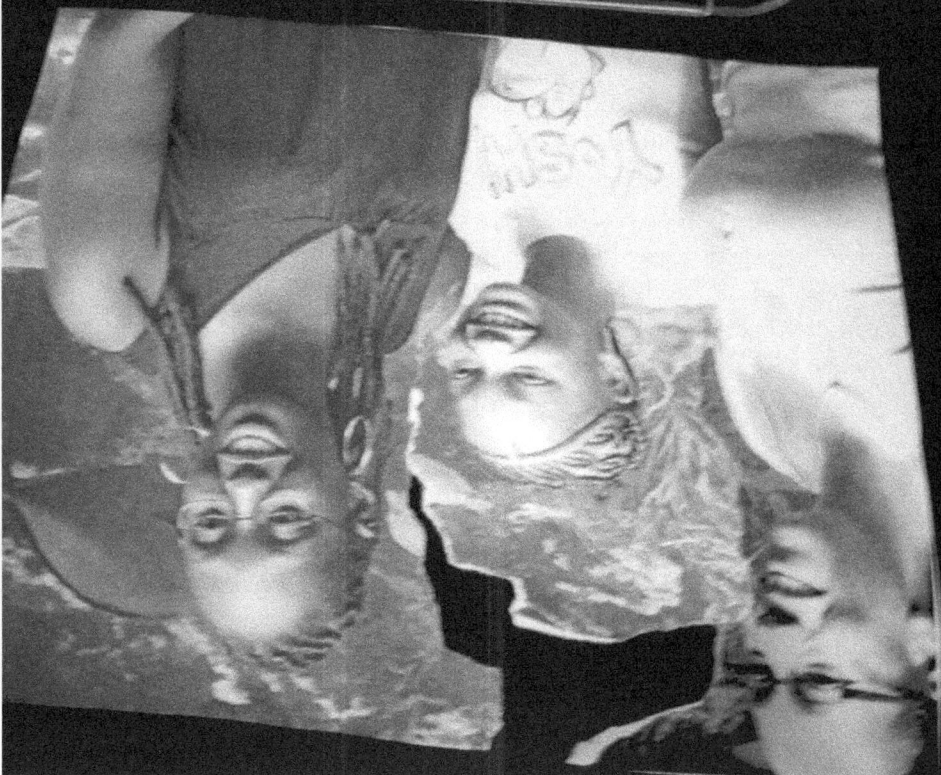

HEATHER TOSTESON

INTRODUCTION: WRITING TO REPAIR

What IS Repair in Human Relations?

We tend to select topics for our anthologies that resonate with us personally—and which we would like to explore with others because they are common challenges, essential for healthy, resilient relationships . . . and difficult to stay with comfortably. Repair is one of them for me—perhaps because it requires such patient good faith, accountability tempered by self-acceptance, and a firm sense of proportion and time, none of which, even at sixty-one, are my most reliable virtues (although they are my husband's). Repair also requires attunement, a taste for the subjective worlds of others, an ardent desire for things to turn out 'right,' a flexible and inventive freedom to re-imagine that 'right' in a way that makes room for changing insights, realities, and stories, and tenacity that verges on the quixotic, all of which, for better and worse, are intrinsic to me.

But what *is* repair? In the *Concise Oxford English Dictionary*, it is defined as "1. restore (something damaged, worn, or faulty) to good condition. 2. set right (a rift in relations)." Its root is the Latin "*reparare,* from *re-* 'back' + *parare* 'make ready'." In the two definitions, we hear some of the tensions we experience with repair in human relations. What *is* it that we are making ready? And ready for what? What is this *thing* that is damaged, worn, or faulty? What thing has a rift in it? Is it just a hairline fracture? A shattering? A molten mess?

Whatever we are able to do with it now, to repair means something was once whole, functioning, that now is not. It may well be something whose wholeness or functioning we recognize only in retrospect, perhaps only when it is too late. When we agree to try to repair a relationship, we are agreeing first of all to know it as *not* the seamless, intrinsic, seemingly reliable thing it was before. Repaired, a relationship may be good as new, but it will not, by definition, be new. It may function better than before, but its vulnerability (to damage, wear, or fault) is now part of our understanding of it.

Repair, if we undertake it, also means that we are committing ourselves to live in a world that is not all about new beginnings, right steps, happily-ever-afters. It's not just about our best selves or the best selves of those we choose to live with. Even knowing that, we are going back for more, redefining what a good ending, or a good relationship, or a good self, is in the process.

But what was that relationship? A shared goal that people needed to conform to and couldn't or wouldn't? A resonant affective flow that has been blocked or channeled elsewhere? A shared reality that has been shattered? What planet did you come from, we wonder when we no longer feel we have any common ground. What does repair have to do with separate solar systems, expanding universes?

This metaphorical play has an important purpose, for how we imagine what a relationship is has a lot to do with how we imagine what repair is both needed and possible. To ground us in the particular, I share one from my relationship with my husband (my third and, if either of us has anything to say about it, my last).

This is a story about *Our Baby*. My husband and I have been married for almost fifteen years now. The marriage is a keeper and both of us are keenly aware of our good fortune in finding each other—and the mutual tenacity that kept us coming back, seeking new ways to connect, over an issue that astonished us with its ferocious intensity for years: our children. I don't mean ours, of course. I mean the two he fathered and the one I mothered to adulthood. Although our children were young adults when we met, we fell in love with the (essentially single) parent in each other. We identified with the challenges and rewards of the role. We saw ourselves reflected there. Wouldn't we have done it better together, we wondered. However, second, or third, marriages have, for everyone concerned, complex histories of powerful attachments, painful and often devastating ruptures, ours perhaps more than many. So, although we identified with each other imaginatively, the reality was something very different. The ruptures my son and I had experienced and the ruptures my husband and his children had experienced intersected poorly. They didn't cancel each other out, they magnified each other. All the ambivalences that our children 'should' have directed toward others found their way toward us (and why shouldn't they, since we, the historically turn-to parents, were the ones who were inexplicably changing). But we were so well-intentioned, so undeserving! I don't think our children (all off making their own mistakes, building their own lives) gave us much thought most of the time and certainly had no idea how ferociously, often, and long we fought about them: *their* rights, *their* expectations, *their* behaviors, *our* expectations of each other in getting them to reflect the same appreciation of us in these time-honored, quasi-heroic parental roles that we had reflected back to each other in our courtship. I wasn't willing to accept a bit part (for myself or my son) in my husband's old family drama (especially that of villainess, wicked step-mother), and he was just as unwilling to do the same (for himself or *his* children) in mine. Thank goodness, I think now, that we all insisted on existential acknowledgement—and gave it to ourselves (with irreconcilable rupture stories) for years.

However, eight years in, our children all married or in live-in relationships, one day, mid-fight, I looked at my husband and said, "I'm sorry. I cannot be the person you want me to be in relation to your children. I don't *want* to be her. Perhaps we should just stop trying to bring these worlds together. But the one thing we both need to accept is that this is *our* madness, just ours. Not theirs."

I found I was crossing my arms, looking down at them as if they held a small infant. I started instinctively rocking back and forth to quiet her. I looked at my husband (we're both baby freaks), lifted my eyebrows, and brought *our* offspring to him. He took her from me with equal care. And there we were. Attuned. Amused. With a very different story. A metaphor that worked miraculously for us. For *that* beautiful child, so invisible to everyone but us, carried so much of both of us in her innocent little face and body—all the guilt and helplessness we had felt and still felt as parents over not being able to protect our children from our actions, the actions of others, their own temperaments, their own choices, our hopes, our limitations, our heart-breaking knowledge that time runs in only one direction and there was no undoing what has already been done, not the deaths, the abandonments, the divorces, the crazy ways we'd tried to make it right, the crazy ways we hadn't. *And* she was our great hope as well for she also contained what was best in us. For through all those experiences we had learned, we had built skills, we had never lost sight of the goodness, the vitality, the sheer us-ness, we had also brought into being and helped nurture in a way that enlarged and enriched our own lives immeasurably. We were good-enough parents, each of us, and for once, miraculously, at our advanced ages, we could be so together. I put my arms out to take her back, but my husband was contentedly sitting on the wicker armchair, humming softly.

Why Does Repair Matter?

In attachment theory, human connections are seen as a constant matching and mismatching process, as essential as they are messy. The capacity to attune to each other is core to our feelings of attachment (safety), intimacy (love), and also our sense of basic shared humanity (intersubjectivity). The developmental psychologist Ed Tronick, who has studied the attachment behaviors of infants extensively, describes why connection with others is so core to us at any age:

> *When connection is made with another person, there is an experience of growth and exuberance, a sense of continuity, and a feeling of being in sync along with a sense of knowing the other's sense of the world. With disconnection there is an experience of shrinking, a loss of continuity, a senselessness of the other. Feeling disconnected is painful, and in the extreme there may be terrifying feelings of annihilation.*

Tronick goes on to describe, as many developmental psychologists and neuroscientists do now, a view of human beings as open systems, ones that are constantly developing into higher states of organizations, and whose complex self-organization, both physiological and psychological, develops most fully through relationships with others. The infant learns how to regulate physiologically as well as emotionally and socially through the responses of the mother; the mother, as well, discovers a new pattern of organization for herself through this resonance. Infants become aware of themselves, develop a state of consciousness, which includes all the systems of their body and experience, but with their mothers infants also develop what Tronick calls a dyadic state of consciousness. "As a consequence," Tronick writes, "the coherence and complexity of each individual's sense of the world increases."

We are larger and more resilient individually through these dyadic relationships, this shared consciousness. But this shared consciousness is messy, ever changing, and periodic disorganization in favor of growth is frequent and frequently destabilizing. This destabilization can be profound for these states of consciousness are an "individual's private, continuously changing knowledge of the world and their relationship to it." They have a purpose, "an impelling certitude about the way the world is." "They are the meaning the individual has for being in and acting on the world in the present as he or she moves into the future." No small stuff, that. These states of organization give us our reason for being and the means to act on it.

When we are young, our states of consciousness are being enlarged, stabilized, by shared states with others. They are also being destabilized, brought to conscious awareness, when they are *not* shared, when growth is slowed down or disorganized by extensive mismatches and ruptures, and the capacity to grow is limited to the individual alone.

In infants, the periods of mismatching make up as much as seventy to eighty percent of the time of an interaction, and mismatches in attunement can happen as many as four to ten times a minute. So, should we take that oscillation as the norm? Is what we talk about as attachment really eighty percent the experience of *de*tachment? Or should we, as Tronick does, see that oscillation itself as the source of both resilience and continuity? Tronick argues that rather than being passive, infants from a very early age begin to learn how to manage their interactions with their caretakers, whether actively seeking a matching attention and intention or avoiding it, signaling to the caretaker the level of stimulation that engages, the level that is aversive. The mother, in turn, is signaling availability, responsiveness to shifting states of interest, a matching of energies and actions that reflect an understanding of the inner state of the child. This constant process of cueing, mismatching, cueing, matching is what builds a sense of continuity and agency in both mother and child, a sense that our worlds can mesh, separate, mesh again.

If mismatching is so common, not only in infants but also in adults, why does the discontinuity hit us with such force? Why do we act as if mismatch *isn't* the way it is supposed to be? It has to do, of course, with the importance of that state of hopeful enlargement, what it makes possible for us as individuals and pairs—at any age. Repair can be seen *as* that, a re*pair*ing of sensibility, a re*pair*ing of energy states, emotions, objects of attention, shared intentions and shared meaning.

But if discontinuity and rupture are so painful to us, why is repair so difficult? Why do we, as often as not, resist doing it—instead placing the responsibility for re-establishing connection on our partners?

Why Is Repair So Difficult for Us?

Jonathon Haidt, in *The Happiness Hypothesis*, devotes a chapter to the question of why we find it so difficult to see the log in our own eye, while we can't stop criticizing our neighbor or spouse for the speck in his. He describes how persistently we all are biased in our own favor. We compare ourselves unreasonably positively with those around us, rarely if ever feeling we are anything but above average. We provide ready and generous rationales for our lapses of judgment or behavior but impute far less positive motives to the actions of our neighbors. We see the bias in our brother, sister-in-law, or a political candidate's self-assessment, but seem constitutionally unable to apply the same criteria to ourselves.

Haidt explores the role of "naive realism" in the deep-rooted tendency to see the best in ourselves as objective truth:

> *Each of us thinks we see the world directly, as it really is. We further believe that the facts as we see them are there for all to see, therefore others should agree with us. If they don't agree, it follows either that they have not yet been exposed to the relevant facts or else that they are blinded by their interests and ideologies. People acknowledge that their own backgrounds have shaped their view, but such experiences are invariably seen as deepening one's insight. . . . But the background of other people is used to explain their biases and covert motivations . . .*

Haidt goes on to nominate naive realism as the greatest obstacle to harmony, in particular because it easily expands into group prejudice. Another major obstacle to repair is our tendency to see our own acts of aggression as justified. Haidt discusses the findings of social psychologist Roy Baumeister on human aggression from the perspectives of both the perpetrator and the victim, in particular Baumeister's troubling finding that almost all perpetrators of violence feel they are not doing anything wrong and have reasons for their aggressions, "which usually involve retaliation for a perceived injustice, or self-defense." Haidt goes on to remark that the greatest contributors to aggression that Baumeister identifies, inflated self-esteem and moral idealism, are qualities that we as a society reinforce.

There are other reasons that we tend to think in black and white in moments of distress, to favor our own view above all others. The cognitive psychologist Daniel Kahneman discusses how sensitive we all are to the halo effect, the tendency, when we like someone, to ascribe positive motives to their actions, to like everything about them. And, on the flip side, when we dislike someone to be unable to see anything good about them, their appearance, actions, or motivations—and, in our naively realistic way to believe these perceptions are objectively true.

Kahneman also discusses our deep need to see patterns, especially through story, to provide coherent, plausible (to us) explanations for whatever is happening to us. He introduces the idea of two selves, "the experiencing self, which does the living, and the remembering self, which keeps score and makes the choices." The remembering self provides much of the content for our stories. Our current affective state provides its motive and drives its meaning. We look for confirmation of our current gut instincts, thinking we are reviewing all the evidence. In the case of emotional rupture or breaks, we're usually feeling cut off and furious and looking for a good reason why, and, especially, what this cut off may mean for our future. If we're feeling hurt, someone must be responsible—and it is least likely to be us! It is the *other* person who needs to reform. We are justified in our own behavior, or our outrage at the other's behavior.

One reason, then, repair is so difficult is that ruptures are usually upsetting to *both* parties. *Both* parties are likely to be remembering only the bad, not the good experiences, and the intensity of the negative experience, however brief, holds more sway than years of positive interactions. That's just the way our minds work. We organize by threat. We collapse time. At times like this it is almost impossible to create a more balanced story for ourselves or by ourselves because we truly don't remember the counterbalance—all those years of calm, those hundreds of small acts of kindness. And our partner, equally busy remembering the bad, can't either.

Unfortunately—or fortunately—repair, like connection, takes two world views. Repair is impossible if we can't see the impact of our behaviors on another as clearly as we can see the impact of their actions on us, but to see the impact of our actions on others, especially when it differs greatly from our own idea of ourselves, can deeply disrupt our sense of ourselves and of the world. One reason we often can't has to do with how deeply painful, almost unmanageable, shame is to most of us. Shame is the immediate application of the negative side of the halo effect to our most visceral self. It's not our actions we judge, it's our whole being. Shame does not make us empathize, it makes us either helplessly withdraw or attack. It shatters our naive realism, which is, in Tronick's description, also a state of consciousness, the source of both our reason for being and our ability to act on it.

Guilt, on the other hand, which is more strictly focused on behavior, is less disorganizing and does allow for empathy and also a feeling of agency. We feel less helpless before it. If we did something wrong and know it, then we can probably do something right as well.

But two problems arise here. We often *don't* feel guilt for what has hurt another. We feel guilt where we feel we have failed to meet our standards—not necessarily where we have failed to meet theirs. I'm reminded of a time with my own son when this became very clear to both of us. This was a period in his adolescence when I was rather obsessively reviewing my own flaws as a mother. He too was making a list of my failings. But when I apologized for the items on my list—divorce, moving him four times in three years, job loss, depression—he shrugged. He couldn't have cared less. When he shared *his* list of my failings—asking him to keep his room clean, fussing when he got paint on his new clothes, limiting television, embarrassing him by saying hello to his friends on the street—I, for the first time in months, didn't feel a twinge of guilt. We were, ludicrously, right back where we started—and not, for we both saw the humor in the mismatch. I gratefully accepted his list as the gracious pass it was, and saved my own for a later day of reckoning, bound, I was sure, to come.

Another reason that guilt, a recognition that we have hurt someone, doesn't inevitably lead to repair is that the other person may not be willing to continue the relationship, whatever amends we are willing to make. Repair may mean very different things to each person. Neither party may have any idea how to repair what has cracked, dented, rusted, bent, ripped, or dissolved. The affective interplay that is at the heart of the relationship may not be there. Mismatch follows mismatch, despite good intentions, each time making both parties feel more and more hopeless and helpless. Our stories of the reasons for rupture or rift may be irreconcilable. We may not have a shape for the story of repair that is culturally, individually, or jointly acceptable— the roles it would put us in feel too far from what we are willing to know of ourselves, or of life itself.

What Does Writing, Narrative in Particular, Have to Do with Repair?

James Pennebaker has studied the health effects of expressive writing since the 1980s. Subjects in his experiments were asked to write for fifteen to twenty minutes a day for three or four consecutive days. Half of them were told to write on unemotional topics, the others were to write about a traumatic experience. Those who wrote about highly emotional experiences showed improved immune function, reductions in blood pressure and elevations of mood. There are various explanations for why people might find writing helpful for both physical and mental health. What Pennebaker discovered was that "*having* a coherent story to explain a painful experience was not necessarily as useful as *constructing* a coherent story." In fact, people can often become mired in their stories of trauma, repeating them obsessively.

When Pennebaker and his colleagues returned years later to analyze in greater depth why writing about trauma had positive effects for some people, they observed that when people developed their stories by changing perspectives, usually beginning in the first person, then taking alternative perspectives, then switching back and forth, there were greater health benefits: "In other words, healthy people say something about their own thoughts and feelings in one instance and then explore what is happening with other people before writing about themselves again."

There are several ways that writing out a story of rupture can assist us in repair. The first is simply that it acknowledges the reality of the rupture and its impact on us. Karl Tomm and Trudy Govier, in an interesting article on the role of acknowledgement in repair, write: "Acknowledgement is essentially a relational phenomenon: people acknowledge when they express their knowledge *to* someone. There is always a 'to' element, even when the acknowledgement is to oneself, as distinct from another person. Thus, there must always be a receiver when something is acknowledged." The presence of a receiver changes the experience for the speaker: "Overall, the vividness of a specified reality is enhanced and the degree to which the same knowledge is held in common by both speaker and listener is increased."

The very act of writing can be an existential acknowledgement to the writer that this rupture, so visceral, so difficult to contain, so isolating, has really taken place. Writing about it is also one way of bringing the experience back into communion, into connection, with ourselves if not yet with anyone else, for writing always assumes an audience (even if it is our own next, wiser self).

As we describe the details of our experience, reconstitute it in some way, we can slow down the strong emotions and physical reactions of rupture so that we begin to see the actions a little more clearly, but not in a way that triggers unbearable shame or reactive anger. As our own first reader, we are able to take a slightly different position toward our experience, one that assumes in its listening posture that we are like other people (for better or worse) and we know it. We can revisit these events in slow, reflective time, which is the time that external repair, as well as inner repair take, so our expectations about time, about process, perhaps become more realistic. We work, as storytellers, under the assumption that there is meaning in these events and it is within our power to find it.

But to move beyond a simple self-justifying protest cry or the obsessive, ruminative story that locks us in grievance and doesn't heal into some more responsible, inflected, generous and implicating story, we need to be able to shift perspectives, to begin to see the other participants' points of view as being as valuable as our own, to understand our own motives and actions in new, not always comfortable, ways. Rupture and disruption involve two people (at least), repair does too. Those different perspectives need existential acknowledgement as well.

The assumptions of story itself help us here, for interesting stories assume multiple characters and multiple, often conflicting, intentions, goals, passions and beliefs, which to be credible must have value in themselves and in their differences. As effective storytellers, we have to stand away from our original interpretations in order to describe these different sensibilities, different realities to readers who do not automatically see what we see. We begin, without noticing, to take the reader's third perspective, to see with their eyes, have a wider field of vision. We begin to impute to the other characters the same range and value of intentions and motives as we grant ourselves. The story requires this expansion and we begin to rise to the expectation, to open our hearts to new possibilities in both cause and consequence, not only for ourselves but also for others. We grow in complexity, inclusiveness, and coherence—and invite others to meet us there.

What You Will Find Here

All this discussion of the reparative effects of stories is, however, wonderfully abstract—and that is why anthologies are so grounding as well as expanding. For in the stories and poems and memoirs here we will find people at all stages on this continuum of repair. Some rant about it, despair of it, feel complicit or graced, or astounded. Let's listen. We can learn from

every one of them.

We have organized the sections developmentally, moving outward to relationships of increasing mutuality and complexity.

Adult Children

We began this anthology with this section because so many of the submissions we received concerned writers (of all ages) working out their relationships with their parents in ways that were heartfelt, and in which the writer often felt interpenetrated but reactive and fundamentally blameless. The primary repair here was often to accept and forgive the parent for his or her limitations, and to accept the consequences of those ruptures on their own development.

These writers yearn to have an effect on their parents, but puzzle the effects their parents still have on them. Caridad Moro, for example, describes herself when younger rejecting her mother's offers to help "because I think it should cost her/something to help me." Thomas Stevenson, in his poem "Tender Vandalism," describes his reaction to his father as "the repulsion proper to polar opposites," but then goes on to describe how the same man he detests can also disarm and transport him.

Arhm Choi exploring the fear she had of her abusive father, describes herself and her sister "sucking back into our small mouths/the air we let him take." In her other poems she describes the approach-and-avoid with which she tries to both accept and reject his impact on her. Rachel Raimondi, in "Dealing with Dad," receives the apology she never expected and must now wonder how it might change the story of her life. Lori Rottenberg and Terry Cox-Joseph explore their complex relationships with their mothers. "Somehow in the act of letting go, we came together," Cox-Joseph writes, while Rottenberg says, "she beats inside me/like a trapped moth." Marian Mathews Clark, in her memoir "Getting There," describes her father's quiet, steady concern for her, even in his nineties asking, in relation to his possible death, "Would you be all right?"

Don Thackrey in his wry sonnet "Coming to Know Pa" describes his changing relationship with his father as he himself ages: "I didn't know my pa until he died./Alive he seemed a natural force, like frost/." In "Polaroid," Martha Gies, instead of needing to distinguish herself from her mother, learns to claim as her own some of the qualities she most loved about her mother, including hospitality and free attention.

Parenthood

Parenthood is more bittersweet, torn between perspectives. The poet Paul Hostovsky writes in his poem "Visitation," "I make him the best lunches though./I mean I made his mother/a lousy/best friend."

Georgann Turner's "Talking with Sophie" describes with deadpan humor the splendid resilience of both this foster-become-adoptive mother and her teenage child: "Sophie has had a lot of character building experiences. She will not peak in high school."

Rose Burke in "Waiting for Sunrise" describes being reunited with the son she gave up for adoption, the wonderful relationship she developed with his adopting family, and the complex decision she would make again—but also how with the help of this welcoming family, this repair, she is able to redefine who she is, participate in a new story where she remains the reserved and private person she is but is also a mother and grandmother with love that is finally free to flow.

Mary Wheeler in "Pom Poms and Circumstance" captures the interplay between affection and distance, a constant exercise in repair, a mother feels watching her son, so often a stranger to her now, graduate.

Bill Denham in the poem "Do You Remember, Dad?" assumes responsibility for "a truth to which I must now bear witness/since words are so elusive/to your damaged/mind."

In the short story "Repair" I explore the lasting effects of abuse—and love, the rupture and repair they occasion in a family over several generations.

Romance

The first two entries here, written by our youngest writers, Caitlin Buckley and Sophia J. Nolan, both explore important sources of maturity and responsibility, choices that bring new, fully adult selves into being. In Buckley's "Ignorant Bliss," a young woman takes responsibility for her actions and makes choices that will have irreversible consequences for her. In Nolan's "No Reservations," a college student integrates the reality of rape into her physical relationship with her current boyfriend. Repair, for her, involves being met in this disturbing place. Any invitation out of it that doesn't acknowledge the reality of this trauma doesn't repair her sense of what the world can faithfully hold.

Michele Markarian in "The Dream of Bob" reflects back on her high school romance and the freedom she has now in middle age to recognize love in its many forms. Carol Tufts, from a similar distance, explores a similarly ambiguous relationship with a mentor. Marta Tveit's elliptical and evocative dialogue opens up the question of how we repair and how we stay connected when we can't, perhaps, accept ourselves.

Marriage

The poems and stories in this section range in place and tone but in all there is a density of commitment, a sense of the multiple choices, the oscillations of intimacy and distance, forgiveness, acceptance and accountability, that go into a lasting relationship. Melanie Reitzel's oblique and poignantly poised prose poems reflect both intimacy and the mystery of otherness. Many of us will find ourselves using the suggestions found in Bari Benjamin's funny and apt "The Importance of Follow-up Questions."

Patricia Barone's sharply observed "Moving Day Restaurant," explores the fine line between repair and repetition compulsion in two divorced participants in a therapy group who are encouraged to revisit issues similar to those in their failed marriages in the hope of different outcomes.

Tim Myers captures the loyal bemused resignation of long marriages in his poems, saying in "At a Certain Point in a Marriage," "So much comes between them—necessities/of living, and of this life they've made/together—even the breakfast table, here now/as they sit on either side of it."

William Henderson, in "Scar Tissue," explores his grief at the loss of a passionate gay relationship and his commitment to his children born into a celibate, heterosexual marriage. It is a meditation on resilience in families, however atypical their structure, and wounds that don't repair.

Wendy Jones Nakanishi begins her thoughtful memoir, "I once believed what had been broken could never be repaired." In an essay expansive in scope and generous in tone, Nakanishi muses on her parents' difficult marriage in rural Indiana and her own successful marriage to a Japanese farmer with a gift for repair. Janet Lunder Hanafin's "At Last" evokes the intricate commitments of marriage, the layering of rancor and generosity.

Bereavement

In her poems, Judith Goedeke explores the lasting costs of early maternal loss, how intense inconsolable bereavement both separated her father from her and finally reunited them, and the lasting, life-giving gift a dying mother gave, "inviting us into the safest place in the whole world."

Beth Lefebvre describes in "The Widower" the slow repair process, sometimes frozen or imperceptible, of a biker mourning his wife, a process his friends and family are drawn into whether they want to be or not. There is something valiant in his insistence, "This is my pain, my grief." He isn't asking to be relieved of it.

Eve Mills Allen in "China Rose on the Floor" describes the delayed depression she experienced after the loss of a beloved granddaughter: "I made sure everything was perfect. A new crisp pink linen dress covered the tiny body in the white satin casket. . . . I set myself upon the tasks at hand like a soldier deployed in a war-torn country. There was no time to think about what *happened,* only time to make sure everything and everyone was all right." Except for her. Repair, she learns, begins there.

Wendy Brown-Báez in "A Good Day" describes how the relationship she has with her homosexual husband, which she describes like salt and chile, challenges her back into life a year after the death of her son by suicide: "He is my life raft and in return, I believe in him, his dreams and determination, his ability to force me to live. And yes, to move on."

Elaine Taber describes the death of an ex-husband, a second sequence of reconciliation and repair, and Isabelle Bruder Smith elegantly describes the slow process of recovery and equilibrium after loss.

Expanding into the Human Condition

In this section the selections branch out beyond questions of repair that are intimate, familial, interpersonal, beyond questions of choice and character to questions of conditions and structures—poverty, racism, war, physical differences, disease.

Parsing Responsibility

Paul Hostovsky's poems in this section explore the impact of prejudice, his aunt's and his own, of which he writes, "And I loved being wrong—"

Willy Conley in his story "Sifting Dirt" explores the tension between deaf parents with a hearing child about what world he will belong to. "Not now!" the wife protests. "First, what? he understands us, must!—you, me— our language—before too late." To which her husband responds, "Do you want him to look stupid?" And then is forced to consider the validity of both their questions, where repair lies for him, for them.

R.E. Hayes in his story "Gait" describes well the back and forth
that goes on inside the narrator as he tries to parse out the roles of racism,
wounded self-esteem, and real questions of responsibility and social efficacy
in his job: "Still, he felt put upon, his sense of self deeply wounded and in a
way he couldn't articulate, it affected his innocent sleeping son."

Fruits of Illness

Andy Weatherwax's moving collection of poems explore the impact
of developing Parkinson's in his thirties as both a personal journey and an
invitation into the human condition. In his poem "My Teacher" he writes, "I
am of the nature to grow old, to fall ill, to die/ everyone I love and all I hold
dear/is of the same nature."

In Russ Allison Loar's "Complete Honesty," his narrator is brought
up short in his ruthless attempt to make himself a completely honest man
when his dying father-in-law asks him a question.

Evelyn Sharenov's "Deliverance" describes how a recently divorced
lawyer repairs his sense of life and expectancy by taking in an old friend dying
of AIDS: "Karma or grand gesture? I don't care. It just seems like the right
thing to do." At the end of the story, he seems at one with his world, both
social and elemental; as he says, "alone but not lonely."

Social Currents, Inner Selves

In her poem "Sometimes an Angel," Mary Kay Rummel writes
"There was a time when I was holy/and a time I was not." Her poems explore
the intersection of history and personal development, the movements of the
1960s, Vatican II, war protests, intimate distances, all looked at now with the
immediacy of mortality and the bemused detachment of age.

Adrian Ross Scanlan explores in "Drops of Water" a similar
intersection of social concerns and inner development twenty years later
as an anti-nuclear activist and aspiring writer: "Believing I had no story
worth telling, lacking the experience that births voice, my silence felt more
immovable than changing the world."

In "Sunset Red" Dianne Mierzwik, growing up, and aging, in an
increasingly feminist world, develops a humorous and sometimes acerbic
dialectic between changing norms and laws and the pragmatics of a woman's
category defying personal experience.

In "Mama's Hair," Weihua Zhang comes to understand her

relationship with her mother not only as it was intertwined with her mother's troubled marriage, but also with her mother's ambitions and with the great social events in China in both their lifetimes.

Amends and Mismitzvahs

Susan Chernilo's story, "When Trying Is All You Can Do," describes the attempts at repair a recovering addict now living with AIDS makes with her grandchild and her daughter, and a social worker's attempt to maintain some balance between hope and attrition in a system she has no hope of deeply changing.

Jim Pahz's humorous memoir, "Good Intentions," explores some of the more dubious rewards of altruism—and introduces us to the lovely neologism, mismitzvah.

We hope that you will feel, after reading these works, that your own stories of repairs, attempted, accomplished, stumbled upon, will find good company here. We hope you will share them, and these, with others. For the one thing that becomes clear is that repair is nearly as natural as breathing, nearly as necessary.

BIBLIOGRAPHY

Haidt, Jonathon. *The Happiness Hypothesis: Finding Modern Truth in Ancient Wisdom.* New York: Perseus Books, 2006.

Hughes, Daniel A. *Attachment-Focused Family Therapy.* New York: W.W. Norton, 2007.

Kahneman, Daniel. *Thinking, Fast and Slow.* New York: Farrar, Straus, and Giroux, 2011.

Pennebaker, James W. *The Secret Life of Pronouns: What Our Words Say About Us.* New York: Bloomsbury Press, 2011.

Tomm, Karl and Trudy Govier. "Acknowledgement: its significance for reconciliation and well-being." *Hope and Despair in Narrative and Family Therapy: Adversity, Forgiveness and Reconciliation.* Eds. Carmel Flaskas, Imelda McCarthy, and Jim Sheehan. New York: Routledge, 2007. 139-149.

Tronick, Ed. "The Inherent Stress of Normal Daily Life and Social Interaction Leads to the Development of Coping and Resilience, and Variation in Resilience in Infants and Young Children." *Resilience in Children.* Eds. Barry M. Lester, Ann S. Masten, and Bruce McEwen. *Annals of New York Academy of Sciences.* Vol. 1094, Dec. 2006.

Tronick, Ed. *The Neurobehavioral and Social-Emotional Development of Infants and Children.* New York: Norton, 2007.

I
ADULT CHILDREN

CARIDAD MORO

PERSPECTIVE

My mother does not like escalators
moving ladders she calls them
and in an attempt to enlighten me
she speaks of *Abuela Panchita*
who took a tumble in *El Encanto*
the only store in Havana
to have one at the time.

Folklore or no
I think
her downright dumb—

       because we are in Miami
       because I am thirteen
       because should the escalator break down
       I can walk my way to rescue.

I prey on her pride
shame her into a ride
mutter *Chicken*
beneath my breath.

Years later,
in the first apartment
I can barely afford
she offers to decorate
her favorite thing to do
so I find her offer tainted—

because there is no sacrifice
because without sacrifice, it's merely fun
because I think it should cost her
something to help me.

Still, we pick out colors,
cover my nicotine stained walls
with Miami Vice Aqua and Pepto Pink
to the beat of Donna Summer.

When it comes time for edges
taller than either of us
she climbs each rung
and I realize how little
fear has to do with reason—

because she is still afraid of heights
because she is trembling and terrified
because she is painting
saying *For you, mija, for you.*

COMING OUT TO MAMI

The cushions were beige,
dinner-partied, lived-on,
scrubbed clean as bleach would allow.

She spoke of remodeling,
zero percent interest at Rooms To Go,
how what couldn't be replaced
could be reupholstered.

We scoured fabric stores for bolts of cloth
dark enough to mask my stains,
strong enough to handle the strain
of starting over, as if perfect
squares of Enchantment Twill
could contain the messiness of living.

At home I slid scissors across material
she pressed into my hands.
She watched as I struggled for straight lines,
as I wept over jagged edges
I could not control.

She taught me to conceal irregularities,
to pin them down
beneath the sting of a staple gun,
smooth new skin over battered innards,
cushion after cushion reassembled,
both of us sure
I too could be remade.

THOMAS J. STEVENSON

TENDER VANDALISM

Sitting in the tumbledown Pictou Island Church,
waiting to humor our Lord and Savior,
theological debate breaks out
between my girlfriend
and my father. The lofty way
he speaks to her—like that
my trunk is jammed full of fists; my head,
a cloud of startled canaries; my hands
as if inflamed by thistles
ache to crack his wicker limbs
at joints and points of weakness
and grind his bones to powder,
fit to be spread on a playing field.
For years, I have felt this space
between us—though empty
it carries a charge
and the repulsion proper to polar opposites.
I would not begrudge the bulge
of the whole world between us.
So how is it
that when he cracks the ghosts of his lips
to sing the psalms in a broken, reedy baritone
whose range is overstretched
by the most humdrum melodies,
how is it
that I am disarmed
and transported, trussed in a body
no bigger than a potato sack
to a wiry pair of arms,

garnished with dark hair, a familiar
flannel-clad headrest that bobs gently
as its owner marches up and down the hall
in a manner he has learned
from his first bagpipe lessons?
Folk-songs and standbys—"Waltzing Matilda,"
"Goodnight Irene," and a detailed number
about a doomed whaling voyage—issue
from no particular direction, their words
escaping and being recaptured
with a regularity that seems to promise sleep.
One thought occurs to me by way of reply:
parents mark the freshly-poured concrete of their children
before it has a chance to harden. I protest this tender vandalism.

ARHM CHOI

THE ROAD'S EDGE

My father's riding down the ribbon of road
with his head out the sunroof window.
The wind pushing his face, his lungs bloom.

At 53 he's getting his first lesson in flying,
shirt collar whipping around his neck
mouth half open like a loose fist.

His Volvo is packed with cigarettes,
one bottle of water.
I wonder what his attention tastes like
and shyly lick the rim.

He has been stutter, stop
and go since I've been here. He
taught me how drunk drivers
like pounding the gas along with their wife

but I'm in the driver's seat now
with all this reckless speed at my feet.
If I wanted, I could snap his neck
send it careening down the mountain.

Instead, I reach to hold his hand
hardened by twisting cheap lids
off bottles of vodka.

Every three months
the skin on the body
is entirely remade. In three months
I will have never touched him.

MEMORY

His knees buckle
in a drunk pigeon walk.
Mom hides in the side room
nursing little sister
though her breasts have seized.

I could've locked the door faster
but he's inside
pulling us to the couch—
only horrible daughters
aren't happy to see their dad.
If I could smell,
his breath would be the rank
of burnt sugar.

He holds our shoulders too tight—
we make our faces pebbles
that fervent thumbs
can rub smooth. Dad
is too much water,
hungry to erase edges.
Call the cops again,
and I'll kill you.

I dial the phone while I pretend to pee.
We hid one in the blanket closet
just for nights like this.
He leaves before the cops arrive,
the river of him
slashing sideways
as he walks out the door.
We'll be ready next time.

Mother in the side room
breasts still dry
baby still hungry
and we two
sucking back into our small mouths
the air we let him take.

WHATEVER IT IS WE HAVE FAITH IN

It is finally springtime.
Whenever the ground shakes

I close my eyes
like my daddy taught me.

I could fall madly for the woman
in my bed and I'm trying to stay here

on this soft shoulder, this robin
egg room with windows open,
trying to ignore my instinct to hug
my knees and stuff my ears.
My lover's song
swears to not leave me
in fractures but
I want
to love
so open
I could break.

While lilacs hum and cherries burst
and dark gets left behind,
I lift my hands up to her face
widen my neck to her teeth
and let one in
who could make me lose
the name
to all my gods.

RACHEL RAIMONDI

DEALING WITH DAD

A ringing telephone before 7 a.m. on a weekday is never a good sign. I'm not the type that gets that many phone calls, so it's certainly important. Definitely not just a little early morning chit-chat session. This phone call means business.

And when it's a family member, it's even worse. A family member that you barely speak to on the telephone? Well, something pretty bad has to be going on.

I dried my hands off from the shower and answered. A pit sprung in my throat. Don't get upset, I attempted to convince myself. Someday you will have to be a grown-up and face the music about a lot of things. You can't keep crying about everything.

"What's doing?"

Uh, "what's doing" with me? I'm not the one making early morning phone calls here, buddy. But instead of starting with him (anyone who does better be prepared for combat), I replied with "Just getting out of the shower. What's wrong?" Better to just cut to the chase here.

He cleared his throat. The pit grew. My god, he was preparing for some sort of speech. This was certainly something, definitely not nothing.

"I know how you feel. And I'm not trying to pressure you into anything. I understand. But if I were you, I'd consider going to visit with Dad. Very soon."

"Okay." How else was I supposed to reply to this?

"He's got pneumonia. Doctors are saying it doesn't look good. I mean, it's up to you. I just wanted to tell you. I thought you should know what was happening. You probably won't regret seeing him, but there is a good chance that you'll regret not having seen him."

"Okay. Thanks for calling."

"I'm going tonight. You can come with me then if you want. Call me later."

"Will do."

The day progressed. Phone calls, emails, price proposals, customer inquiries, customer grumbles; I had everything that day to keep me occupied. It was business as usual. Each day at the office, I can't wait for it to be over. Go home, relax, not have to talk to anyone. But today was different. Today zipped by. Actually went by so quickly that I didn't have time to really mull over the morning phone call. I love to go back and forth trying to make decisions; weighing pros and cons, picturing possible scenarios in my head and seeing how I'll deal with them. And here it was, a rather important thing to deal with and I was incapable of finding the time to go over it in my head. I was going to be totally mentally unprepared.

I headed to my brother's house directly after work. I felt numb, yet terrified. I'm not sure it's possible to feel nothing and fear at the same time, but it's the only way that I can describe it.

His wife was home and coming along with us. I was glad for the buffer. If there was ever a pair of siblings who barely knew each other, yet were frequently in each other's faces, it was us. She would keep it from being uncomfortable. I can't speak for my brother, but I knew that for me, I definitely needed that.

The car conversations ranged from the mundane ("I hate this weather") to the serious ("Will he know we're there?"). I tried to remain the cool, talkative and unaffected person I had told myself for years that I would be when this time came. Instead, I was more petrified than I had ever been in my entire life. And it pissed me off that he could make me feel this way. The phrase "how dare he?" repeatedly flowed through my thoughts.

I hadn't been inside a hospital in years. In fact, I tried to stay out of them as much as I could. I hated being around people who were in pain and sad. I didn't understand it all and couldn't relate to them. Things that I cannot comprehend tend to scare me. And who would want to scare themselves like that on purpose?

We had to take the elevator up. One of the giant ones where you can fit what feels like forty-five people. It was only us three in ours, but luckily between us, there was enough tension to fill up the rest.

The doors opened.

"You know, as much as I want to deny that I have any of Dad's traits, there's one thing that as hard as I try, I can't get rid of." I cleared my throat. Just thinking about it almost made it happen. "I cry about everything."

My brother turned around. "Yeah, you're telling me."

I was surprised. I'd seen him upset before, but it was very rare. Did he really possess that trait like I did or was he just saying it to try and make me feel better about myself?

We turned the corner and looked for his number. I wanted to run back and wait outside. Not like it would matter; me being there at all. I could walk away and no one would be any wiser. But instead of doing that, I walked straight with my head high, not looking back.

The man lying in the hospital bed was not my father. Perhaps in part he still was, but I was shocked how a change in appearance could affect a person so much. I knew that it had been a long time since I had seen him and of course, I was not expecting him to look fantastic, but I suppose you can never fully prepare yourself for something that you have no idea about.

I gave it about 2.5 seconds before I rushed out of the room, clutching my purse with white knuckles while I tried to compose the warm tears and shortness of breath as I whispered, "Holy shit, holy shit, holy shit" in threes over and over.

Neither my brother nor his wife came out to comfort me. They'd seen him the last five years, so the deterioration I was currently dealing with was probably not as real to them as it was to me. And I was a big kid; I should be able to deal with this. And lastly, who decided to wait this long to visit? That was certainly all me and it was only right that I dealt with the repercussions on my own. I didn't blame them for just leaving me be. I reentered the room a few minutes later.

My father was always a big man. Well, at least in my lifetime and what I could recall of him. Who knows, perhaps in my years up until age three, he was as trim as those faded photos my mother has portray him to be. But not to me. Never. Let's be honest, anyone who knew me, knew that when I used the term, "the fat man," I was talking about my father.

The being in front of me was not my father. I was fairly sure that it wasn't even half my father. This man was three-quarters the size. Where was the beer belly? His hair was cut close to his head, almost a buzz cut. And it was whiter than I had remembered. Where was that salt-and-pepper mop of hair that always looked out of place no matter how many brush strokes or hair products were put in it? And the beard. Never in my life had I seen a beard on him. Not even in pictures before I was born or from his childhood. Who was this guy?

But the eyes. The piercing blue eyes. The kind of blue that no pair of contact lenses could make. The kind that sucked and locked you in immediately, tranced by their lightness. They were kind eyes, puppy dog sad eyes all the time. And those eyes were just the same. No amount of aging or sickness or lack of life could change your eyes. They always survived. And they were staring straight at me, piercing their way into me. They knew who I was. I was half of them.

I stood at the end of the bed, unable to move any closer, scared to move farther away. The eyes stayed on me. Studying, wondering, perhaps flashing remembered moments of me to their owner.

"Do you think he knows who I am?" The million dollar question, folks.

Shrugs.

"Do you know who that is?" My brother asked.

The head nods yes, but the eyes stay fixed on me. Did they really know who I was? Or was the nod just an act of courtesy? Did I look fragile enough to crumple if I were to be told no? Or did the eyes immediately recognize their kin and register to the brain?

Small talk begins. Well, not on my end. I cannot even approach the bed any further than at its foot.

My brother talks about work. My sister-in-law shows pictures on her cell phone and chats about her children; his grandchildren. I still remain quiet. I'll be damned if my father even recalls what I do for a living. And kids? Well, I could sit there all day and tell him about all sorts of kids. But none my own.

He's attentive. I'd been told that he was pretty out of it and didn't really understand or know what was going on around him, but this guy here really seems to know "what's doin'." He's even trying to speak. They're mostly grunts, but if you get really close to him, you can sort of decipher what's being said. Small, inane phrases are relayed back to me as I stand awkwardly wringing my hands. Have you ever tried to avoid eye contact with someone whose eyes are boring holes through your head? It's not easy. It was as if he knew I was there to see him and expected me to look. Those eyes said, "Look at what I've become. This is what my life has amounted to. This is what you wanted. Your life has got to be better than mine." I was fairly sure that if I left the room again, his eyes would follow me into the hallway. Might even jump off of his face and into my purse to go home with me.

It's clear that my lack of attention and unwillingness to join in conversations is now making everyone else uncomfortable. Hand and eye gestures indicate that I must speak or do something. I clutch my heart in my chest and trade places with my brother at the side of the bed. As you may have guessed, his eyes follow me.

"Um . . . " I search for words, but nothing of consequence comes to me. "So, I'm here." I speak as if I'm six years old again, presenting myself to someone who, for all purposes, is a stranger to me.

Eyes search me. Not for recognition, I can tell. It's for something else. A light? Acceptance? Money?

I become more nervous as he just stares and I avoid glancing back at him. For some reason, the idea of locking a gaze with him petrifies me.

He starts making noises; sort of how a person with allergies would try to clear their throat on a dry, early day in May.

"Is he trying to talk?" I ask my brother and his wife. They look as dumbfounded as I do. He'd nodded his head and grumbled some words before, but there was nothing like the lead-up that was coming on at the moment.

Another grunt. Okay, he is definitely trying to talk. I lean in sideways, close to his mouth, trying to forget that all I can picture in my head is his creepy, ashy hand grabbing my hair and yanking it out of my head. I watch too many scary movies to not expect the worst from an old man lying in a hospital bed. For all I knew, he'd already gone zombie and was looking for brains. Specifically mine.

It's sort of inaudible and I'm big on telling myself that things are exactly not what I think they are, but the words that are finally released sound distinctly like, "I'm sorry."

The three of us look at one another in disbelief. In turn, we look at my father with the exact same expression on our faces.

I say it just to be sure. "Did he just say 'I'm sorry'?"

"I think so."

I step closer to my father than I have been the entire time that I've been standing there. Scratch that; closer than I have been in years. I bring myself to touch his arm. But only lightly.

"Thank you. I can't tell you that it's okay because it's not. But thank you. I appreciate it."

We leave some time later. My father's apology is, of course, the hot topic. We're all dumbfounded.

The constant jokester, my brother tells jokes and we laugh. Laugh away what was a really big moment for me and a slightly large moment for him.

"I seriously cannot believe Dad told you that he was sorry, this might change your whole life." He laughs.

I don't return the laugh. "I know."

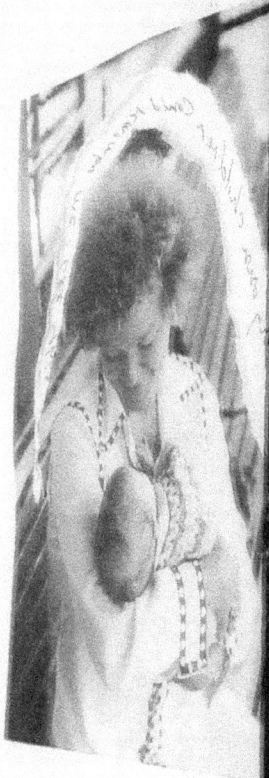
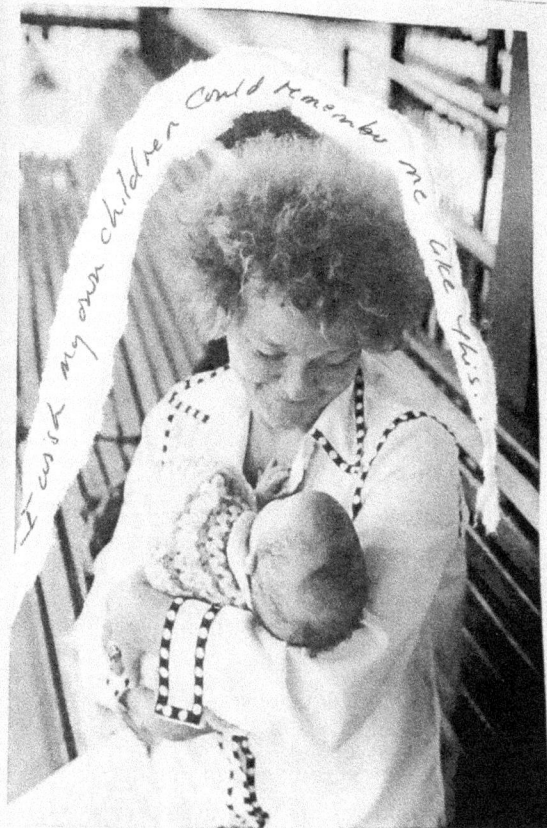

LORI ROTTENBERG

ENCHANTRESS

An earlier generation opened
this black path
through layered rock.
Though they parted the mountain
to make my road home effortless,
the Thruway's exposed walls
remind me of the blasts needed
to make such escape possible.

As I exit into the valley,
the gristly muscles
of the town's edge squeeze
me in their unwholesome grip—
leering rural billboards,
bulging neon gas stations,
adult book stores and strip malls,
headstone sales and hair
salons in roadside houses—
the only clues that it could be different
the occasional ruined farm opening
an emerald stream into the landscape,
the wasted architecture
of a once-fine homestead,
the violet mountains that hold us
in their distant hug.

It changes but is always the same,
this accidental place that swallowed us whole,
this place whose backroads I first paced

then drove away from as fast as I could.
Yet no matter how far I stretch away, I always snap
back to the crisscrossing web
of New York routes 208 and 52.
Even when I come with reinforcements—
my sane man,
my golden babies—
it isn't enough to stop
the eager dread of being home.

          *   *   *

The girls see it right away:
She is enchanted, she transforms paper into dolls
and gives them their own scissors and crayons,
wands for the weekend.
She shows her collections,
she enlists them
in the conspiracy of her toys:
just-a-buck finds in every cobwebbed corner,
dolls she is resurrecting, empty
boxes to mail all she will never sell.
She shows me semi-precious
beads she strings for dolls' fragile
wrists and necks, how she repaired
a mouth here, fixed an eye there.

She eats candy for breakfast, sleeps till noon.
She turns on overhead lights
with a tiny plastic hand that stretches
towards the sky. She keeps it near
the chair, avoiding real movement
whenever possible.
My daughters gulp her presence; they race
into her crowded bedroom, hoping
she will awaken for an audience.

The cats rule, they lay on tables,
drugged by treats and hypnotized
by the lull of TVs murmuring
in every room. We start
to do the same, each day
a little less pulled to the light;
our eyes begin to adjust
to the dark, our bodies become torpid and limp.

I see how they begin to grow
to her, they stop wanting
morning's light or afternoon's wind,
clamor only for her paper magic
performed in half-lit rooms,
touch her bottles and creams and potions,
finger her spare jewels and dolls
and strange tools, all she animates
with her failing breath.
I start to panic:
this is how I, too, was led.
I want to gather them to me,
explain how you can die
from a diet of chocolate,
how funhouses inhabited by glamorous ghosts
can trap you forever,
why my firm and boring love is also necessary.

       *   *   *

Saturated with TV and too much
chocolate, flattened by the strain
of warding off her spells,
I am bled
of my humor and drama,
become numb in the face
of all she is:
too much and never enough.

I start to pace my old routes,
invent reasons to take
walks, plan unnecessary
outings, anything to feel
the sun's fingers and see people
and know what is real
until her magic no longer
holds me.
Strengthened, I spar with her over the right
way to live; I win neither battles nor wars,
and she retreats at night
to her cramped and darkened den.

But at the end
when she hobbles bravely
onto the driveway to see us off,
her skin yellow,
her eyes unused to the sparkle of day,
her frame bent and weak, blowing
kisses and waving like the little girl
she has always been,
my heart dissolves its protective armor—
my mommy,
my mommy,
my mommy . . .

How cruel I am to save myself,
bring my babies back to their golden world.
I hack off the valley's sad grip, easily cleave
the mountains open again,
head for my chosen place.
But even as I put the certainty of miles between us
she casts her final enchantment:
she beats inside me
like a trapped moth;
I carry her forever
in webs of pity and love.

THE REST

I've pointed out the fault lines,
the cracks where I almost fell in;
I've documented the depths of pits and crevasses,
the murky sludge that almost trapped me.

Now it is time to draw the rest
of the landscape that is you—
to tell of toenails painted sparkly green and purple,
the clothes, always new, always young,
the dangly earrings in the shapes
of animals and hearts.

Now it is time to paint the wild bloom
of our homes:
daylily yellow, wet jungle green, iris purple,
deep latin teal, trumpet-vine orange.
Is there a color you did not sample?
Only beige would never do.

Now it is time to label the bridges
of words you built to lead us over the dark
ravine of our childhood, the bricks
of gold-leafed leather classics I don't know
how you paid for, the sly, loony
magazines you subscribed to—
Mad, National Lampoon,
Games, Psychology Today,
Fantasy and Science Fiction—
a froth of ideas, showing me to look
for other paths when the center didn't seem right.

Now it is time to catalog the soundtrack
of our journeys, the pesky distinction
you made between hearing and listening,
the wall of mercilessly eclectic vinyl:
the rockers and the balladeers,
the jazz, opera, and classical,
Sondheim and Beatles and Van Halen
and Carly Simon,
musicals you belted in your smoke-ruined voice
with your eyes closed, always impressed
with the cleverness of words, hippie songs
with curse words resting beside
Stravinsky, Gershwin, Beethoven, Prokofiev,
all collected and known and revisited
like a 19th century library.

Now it's time to tell of the creatures of your land:
prides of cat, torn rabbits and birds,
abandoned school guinea pigs bereft of personality,
who each found your beacon in a tangled world,
pity for the weak spilling out of you like light.

I write the postcards
about the vertical walls we somehow
climbed together,
about the lost canteens and malfunctioning tents,
about the miserable shivering nights,
because bad travels always make for good stories
when you are warm and safe and dry,
but know I always carry the rest,
the shoes that somehow covered
my feet and the warm
food that maintained me,
the tools you gave me for a life
of thinking, of loving;
I am heading for those places
you never dreamed to touch,
and I will bring you with me
with the invisible rappelling cord that will bind us
always.

TERRY COX-JOSEPH

REDEFINING

As my belly stretches, I prepare nots to define our love:
I will not call you names,
shout that I wish you'd never been born,
smash martinis onto glass vanities.

I will not laugh at your tears,
share your secrets with my bridge club,
sneak through your dresser drawers
in search of disgust-filled diaries.

I will not yank you from your warm bed
at midnight to sort siblings' laundry,
peel out of the driveway at 3 a.m.
and weave down the icy highway
to my mother's while you sob
at the back door.

I will not promise you new contact lenses but
give you a hangover.

Tiny pink fists and toothless smile redefine me.
I am not locked into genetic inevitability.
I will embrace you, stare into your eyes,
inhale the scent of your snowdrop scented hair.

No longer do I say "I will not"—but
"I will" love you.

IN HER IMAGE

We prayed so hard to have you, my mother once said.
I wanted to be the one they longed for but knew
she wished to re-create the toddler whose scuffed
shoes and fuzzy toys were packed away forever.
Nature combined DNA, ensured two X chromosomes,
dark hair, brown eyes, identical bone structure, genes
in my sister's image, whisper of creation, fingertips
in the Sistine Chapel, so close, my great-grandmother
couldn't tell us apart. My mother's eyes swept over
all of us, yearning searchlight, but we returned
unfamiliar gazes—blue irises here, blonde hair there,
freckles in the wrong place. The neighbors' dog
was run over so they bought a new puppy—
our squirming bodies, rumpled blankets mere diversions.
I imagine my mother's cry deep inside my cells—*No,*
I don't want that one, I want the one I lost—
I want her back—but heredity negated her prayers,
offered similar phenotype in temporary deceit.
Like a snowflake inside her I was unique.
It must have been hell to stare at me all those years
and worse, when my teenage angst necessitated
protective distance. Our heartbeats never synchronized,
grew fainter in dissymmetry of loss.

MAKING PEACE

Somewhere between rage and control
we found common ground

not that we apologized
or melded our philosophies
or went to counseling, God forbid.
No, we formed a truce over the phone
in the space that connected
diagnosis and radiation
tracheotomy and therapy.

Somewhere between laundry and a living will
you asked how the kids were doing and really listened
and I asked how you were doing and understood.
You wore yourself out in those fragile moments
phone too heavy, life too heavy,
you had to put it down,
sink back among the pillows
puffed around you like peach and pink clouds
get-well cards strewn about your lap.

I never did figure out where you found the strength
but somehow in the act of letting go
we came together.

MARIAN MATHEWS CLARK

GETTING THERE

It's 3:40 in the morning. Once again, I can't sleep, so I crawl out of bed and wander into the kitchen. I flip on the light and glance around, then groan, remembering, when I see bits of cabbage afloat in the clogged sink. Earlier, at dinner, after I'd stuffed cabbage leaves down the disposal, the water wouldn't drain. I reach under the sink and pull out the stair-step gizmo taped to the disposal.

Twenty years ago, when I was married, I prided myself on the fact *I* was the one who always "fixed" the disposal. But now, I've not had any luck. When I insert the tool, it does its circular whirl without resistance and the disposal emits its normal growl. So I grab the plunger, fit it over the drain, shove down hard, then yank up with a snap. The suction slurp sounds loud enough to uncork a sewage line, but those cabbage leaves hold fast. It's clogged, and that's that.

Before April when my father died of pneumonia, I would have told him about the broken disposal during our daily conversation. Though he lived 2000 miles away, in Oregon, and at ninety-three was in no condition to fix things, he still liked talking about machinery. Often, he would ask me, "How many miles does your car have on it now?"

I'd cringe, vow to myself I'd check that darned odometer before our next call, then confess I didn't know. Yes, my broken disposal would have grabbed his interest. He would have said, "Well, the dickens. That's too bad."

As I stare at the floating cabbage, I long to hear "the dickens." That and the "Good bye, sweetheart," he started saying at the end of our conversations after my mother died. Sometimes, when our talk was winding down, I'd say, "I love you bunches." He'd reply, "I love you even more bunches," and I'd tell him, "You're a bunch ahead of me this time." And then he'd laugh.

When I return to bed, it's 4:27. I close my eyes, do my "breathe in, breathe out," mantra and start to relax, till I think, "The condo board meeting's at my place this week. I'll have to fix a snack. But what will it be?" I think about my mother who loved working with food and envy her.

My father worried about my kitchen skills. In fact, once he asked me if not knowing how to cook had caused my divorce. When I said, "No. Mel liked to cook. We were just growing in separate directions," he frowned, perplexed. My divorce was confusing to him, period. "If Mel and you are still friends, why couldn't you stay married?" he wondered.

My father was married to my mother for fifty-nine years. They loved each other and made things work. Till death did them part. I stare at the ceiling. With no children, siblings or spouse, I ponder if anyone I love will be with me at the end.

My friend, John, in Maryland calls the next morning. We call daily. We're not "involved," though used to be—sort of. We've agreed we're more than friends, but with his move last year, it couldn't be more, even if it were. I envy people whose lives are free of "sort-of"s and "not-any-more"s but contain consistent commitment forever.

When John asks me what I'm doing, I tell him my sink has turned on me. "What if I just pour Drano into the cabbage water?" I ask him. "Do you think that would do it?"

"First tell me about the layout under your sink," he says. He can fix anything.

I groan.

"Don't be negative," he says. "Just look under the sink and tell me what you see."

I study the layout. "There's a pipe a couple inches down from this round metal thingy at the top of the disposal."

"Does the pipe lead to the trap?"

I run through all the "traps" in my repertoire and see nothing under the sink that looks like any of them. "The pipe from the disposal leads to a pipe under the other sink that goes straight down to a loopy pipe," I tell him.

"The trap," he says.

"Yes, the trap," I say.

"Better not use Drano," he says. "But it sounds simple to fix. How is the pipe attached to the disposal?"

"With some kind of bolt thing."

"I'll bet the cabbage is trapped at the sleeve of that discharge tube," he says. "If you had a channel lock, you could remove the clamp."

I don't ask, "And what might a channel lock be?" but envision twisting off the clamp with a large scary-looking tool and water spewing all over the kitchen. I think of my downstairs neighbor, wondering where that gush is coming from and why her ceiling is caving in. "It sounds way too hard," I tell him. "I'll just call the repair number on the disposal."

"It's not hard at all," he says. "I wish I were there. I'd fix it in no time. I like fixing these kinds of things."

"If wishes were fishes," I tell him and don't add, "Well, if you hadn't moved, you *would* be here." The fact I want to say it tells me I'm not quite over his leaving and he hasn't quite achieved the platonic friend status. "But getting there," I tell myself.

My father, in his last months, told me repeatedly he couldn't sleep. He needed to move back over the eleven miles of winding mountain road to Mist, Oregon, where he'd lived for eighty-five years. Where he'd been a logger and a saw filer in the mill, with words like gang saws and chipper knives and board feet of lumber as his daily vocabulary. Where he and my mother had lived out their married life, until her heart problems necessitated their moving closer to the hospital.

"I can't sleep in this place. I think it's the altitude," he told me.

"You mean the Amber?" I said, referring to the assisted living facility I'd moved him into a few months before. I hoped it wasn't yet another way that that facility was unsatisfactory when compared to the rental house where he and my mother had lived for four years after leaving their home in Mist. And where he'd lived for the last three years since her death.

"This side of the mountain, period," he said. "I'm going back to Mist to stay with Betteen and Alvin for a few nights to see if I sleep better." Betteen and Alvin were his aging sister and brother-in-law.

"Who'll lift your legs up into bed at night?" I asked him.

"I don't need help," he said.

"You can't get in bed by yourself after you go to the bathroom," I told him. "That's why I started hiring people three years ago to stay with you at night. Remember?"

"Betteen or Alvin will help me," he said.

"Dad," I said, trying not to sound as frustrated as I felt, "Aunt Betteen just got out of the nursing home with a broken arm. And Uncle Alvin has heart trouble." I didn't remind him they were 89 and 92.

"I can't sleep here," he said. "I haven't slept well since your mother and I moved over the mountain. I always slept well in Mist."

"Well, you can't stay with Aunt Betteen," I told him, then thought about how, when I was a child, he'd let me climb aboard his slippered feet and walk me to the bathroom in the night.

"I'll talk to the people in the Amber and see if we can't think of a way to help you sleep better," I told him. "And I'll be there in just a few more weeks for Christmas. I can't wait to see you. The time will go fast."

As soon as I hang up from talking to John, I call the 800 number on the side of the garbage disposal. I promise myself that when my disposal is fixed, I'll make a list of service places for *every* emergency. I resolve to make this list every time something goes haywire.

After going through a phone tree, whose options include fixing, buying and selling every appliance made, the voice finally says, "Choose seven for repair centers in your area." I wonder what part of the country I've called. When the human answers, he isn't unkind but asks questions that seem to have nothing to do with locating the service center nearest me. For instance, he wonders, "What's the model number?" As I ask him to hold and I kneel by the sink, I mutter to myself that I knew somebody would ask for that stupid number, and I should have found it before I called. I scan the white sticker covered with 115 volts and ½ HP and 1 PH and 6.7 amps and S/N ME 50100648 and the 800 number. I'm about to give up when I spot "Model" and bend my neck at an angle I hope it'll recover from to see 5-38.

"Oh, um hm," he says, when I tell him, then wonders if I've tried using the service wrenchette or a plunger.

I tell him, "I tried the plunger and even the stair step bar under the sink."

There's a pause. "Yes, the service wrenchette," he says and finally relinquishes the number and community of the nearest repair center. To my relief, it's only fifteen minutes away.

I hang up, mad at the generic systems he represents—all the systems I dealt with as my father grew older and more confused about the world that at one time made sense to him. Phone trees without an option for what you need. Companies that prey on the elderly and vulnerable. Service workers who don't know and don't care.

Protecting my father from those systems after Mother died was one of my biggest challenges. I was forever telling *Reader's Digest*, "DON'T SEND ANY MORE OFFERS TO MY FATHER" who insisted he hadn't bought anything and was only entering their contest and couldn't imagine why he'd received their "un-free" book. How could they not be on the up and up? He'd subscribed to their magazine for years. One of his caretakers and I made a pact to intercept and throw out the "dangerous" contest mail, but we felt guilty. After all, filling out those forms gave him something to look forward to.

And all the cheaply made free gifts he received—the watches he showed me and the tiny plastic bags of "gems" he proudly bestowed upon me whenever I flew out. The things that kept him going. And that kept the caretakers and me trying to figure out what the fine print said and what he really owed. Those damned companies, never giving up, sending all their crap. And my father, looking forward to the mail, trying to keep cheerful in the wake of losing Mother, assuring me every time I called, "I'm doing pretty good."

When I call the Repair Center, I'm relieved to connect with a real woman who promises she'll have their serviceman phone me at 7 a.m. to let me know when he's coming. It'll be sixty dollars for the visit and thirty minutes of service. It seems like a lot, but I tell myself this is a family business, not a big company. And she's a real person with a genuine voice. She reminds me they're not plumbers, and I don't ask what happens after thirty minutes.

John calls in the evening, and when I tell him the garbage disposal people will charge sixty dollars, he says, "Good God. I know I can walk you through fixing it. I'm sure there's just cabbage caught at that discharge sleeve. You said the disposal made its regular sound, right?"

"Yes, and the self service wrenchette makes a complete turn," I tell him. I wait for a word of praise for my terminology, but he only says "hm."

"I know there's nothing in the disposal itself," I tell him.

"How do you know that?"

"Because I reached down and checked."

"Did you make sure it was turned off?"

"Of course," I tell him. "I'm not stupid."

"Well don't reach into the disposal," he says, then offers again to walk me through the process. I don't want to pay sixty dollars, but feel anxious about taking the disposal apart. I envision putting the pipe back in, screwing in the bolt, turning on the water and watching it seep out around the bolt. Drip drip. And no matter how tight I would twist the bolt, there would always be a leak. The sink would never be the same. Suddenly it makes me sad to think of setting its demise in motion. "That's all right," I tell him. "Thank you, though."

That night, I'm tired and go to sleep quickly. At 4 a.m. something wakens me. I get out of bed, still with a light step for someone in her sixties. Actually, it's a light step for fifty or forty. The difference is that at younger ages, I wasn't thinking, "It's a light step." I just stepped. I miss just stepping.

I kneel by the window that faces out on the wall of the next condo. I think of my father's bedroom window in the assisted living facility and him, unable to sleep. I wonder what he thought about, lying there. Did he worry about dying? Did he enjoy the row of firs on the hilly incline and did it make him think of the forest where he'd grown up? Was that comforting? Or did it simply make him miss his valley more?

After I'd told him he couldn't stay with his sister, he said he was going to buy a trailer and move back over the mountain. When I'd reminded him that the Mist Store had burned the year before, removing the only establishment in the town of fifty people, and that he didn't have a car or driver's license and no one to take care of him, he wondered what I would think about returning to Oregon and being his caretaker. "I'll pay you whatever you're making," he said.

I thought about my friends in Iowa and the advising job I loved at the university. I'd go crazy, leaving my life behind. After my divorce, it'd taken me a while to feel connected. I told him. "I can't move back, Dad." He didn't say, "You mean you won't," though I wondered if he was thinking it.

I stretch to see the pond and the trees across the water. After my father moved into the Amber, I pointed out his trees to him on several occasions. "That row of trees is really pretty, isn't it," I'd say, sounding falsely perky even to my own ears. He would nod with little enthusiasm. I tried to comfort myself that at least he usually wasn't sitting up in bed where, instead of trees, he would have seen a wall of cement blocks.

A logger friend of my father's tried to dissuade me from moving him to an assisted living facility. At the point I made the decision—when my father was falling frequently and the complex caretaking system I'd set up was breaking down—his friend said, "Your father won't last a year in that place." Those words haunted me when I got the call, the morning before I flew out to be with him in his last hours. The caretaker who phoned me said, "Marian, he couldn't wait for you to get here. The hospital just called." She was crying.

"Oh no," I said, crying, too. "Do you think he knew I loved him?"

The next morning I have my alarm set for earlier than usual. But the garbage disposal man doesn't call. When I call the company, the woman apologizes, saying she'll be sure to have him call in the evening to set up a time. He must have gotten held up.

I hang up, irritated. "I wish people would do what they promise," I say aloud, then have to laugh. I sound like my father, a man of his word. Even to the end. The Christmas before he died, he tried to warn me he wouldn't see me again. He called me into his bedroom where he'd been taking a nap. "I want to talk to you," he said.

I sat by his bed, dutifully, but with apprehension. He'd never liked talking things over. "All right," I said.

"If I died after you went back to Iowa, would you come back?"

"Do you mean for the funeral?" I said, trying not to panic.

"Yes," he said. His voice was weak.

"Well, of course," I said. "But I don't want you to think that you're not getting better. I can tell, even since I got here a week ago, that you're gaining strength after your embolism. You know, not many people survive those. You're doing very well."

He nodded without conviction. "Would you be all right?"

I wanted to say, "No, I wouldn't be all right. I don't want you to go. I'll be alone in the world, my biggest fear. You can't die." But I couldn't say that. Wasn't I always the one who said people needed to communicate? To tell each other the truth? So I hesitated, to figure out what that was. "I don't want you to die," I told him. "I would miss you terribly. But I have friends who would help me. I would be all right." We sat in silence for a few moments in the growing dusk. I tried to keep my sniffs quiet. But then he looked at me. "Do you have a cold?" he said.

Before I turn off the kitchen light for bed, I look at my sink. The sixty dollar an hour garbage disposal guy's coming at 8 in the morning, and I make a last stab at clearing the clog. I use the plunger, the wrenchette, and a few curses. But nothing. I stare at the metal drain, beneath which lies the disposal that with its mysterious jaws eats my garbage. A simple device compared to rocket ships and computers. Yet it has me totally flummoxed.

Why didn't I learn about the physical world from my father when I had the chance? All his years in the woods had taught him heights and weights and machines. He kept us afloat in our isolated community when the electricity went out for days, or when the pumps broke. As an only child, I fell heir to being his helper, but never paid attention to how things worked; I just did what he told me. I pulled up the buckets of dirt when he and I dug our well; I held tools for him when he fixed the pumps; I helped him gather the winter wood. I even helped him log a little, with him setting chokers and me driving the cat.

Yes, he tried his best to pull me into his world, but nothing he said could convince me of its value. On one occasion, he asked me how many gallons of water our dishwasher pumped a minute. When I was clueless, he said, "What will you do when a teacher asks you that question?" I shrugged and said, "Tell her I don't know," then walked nonchalantly out of the room.

But I couldn't help but feel I'd let him down.

My fight with the garbage disposal has left me tired, and again, I fall asleep quickly. But I wake an hour later, wide-eyed, restless. I think about how I used to sink to the bottom of sleep and stay there for the entire night. What's down there now that's stopping me?

I wonder if all the frightening events we encounter through the years drift down into our psyche. My gentle cousin, Dwight, who drowned at twenty-five, just when he'd found a job and had his life in order. Drift down. Handsome Frankie Checkmonic, who died in a logging accident, leaving beautiful Eleanor a widow at thirty. Drift down. My friend's son who came through the Gulf War unscathed, then died in a motorcycle accident. Drift down. Drift down. Drift down.

For years the stories lie scattered in our minds. There's plenty of "unstoried" territory we bypass on our way to sleep. But year after year, stories fill the space, and finally there's a chink-less layer we can't squeak through. So we close our eyes, sink into shallow sleep until we smack into the wall of drowning cousins and dead loggers and motorcycle victims who bounce us back to the surface with a jolt. It strikes me that my father's death closed the gap.

I look out into the night and see the overflowing dumpster, ripe for the garbage men whose beeping and cranking will wake me before morning. If I'm not already awake, that is, from a passel of newspapers hitting the condo door below my window.

I think of growing up in Mist where the only night sounds were the coyotes, erupting in a unison of yips. It was oddly comforting, waking to their eerie voices, knowing they were at home out there in those dark woods while I was nestled safely under my blankets. My father had listened to their sounds for eighty-five years. No wonder in those last months he wanted to go home.

I toss right, then left and know I won't get to sleep, so I finally crawl out of bed and make my way to the kitchen. I flip on the light, and glance into the sink, then do a double take. The water has drained. I turn on the faucet and the sink fills again, but I know something has loosened. I grab the plunger, push down, release with a sploosh, and again, push, release, sploosh. The sink drains. I flip the disposal button; the water runs down the drain and keeps going.

I smile at the empty sink and think about what I would say to my father if we still had our daily conversations. I wouldn't tell him about the repair guy who didn't show up or the fact I'd discovered the drained sink during my nocturnal wanderings when I couldn't sleep, or the conversations with my kind-of-friend friend. Those things would only worry him.

No, I would tell him, "I used the wrenchette and plunger, but those didn't help. You see the water wasn't flowing through the trap, and as I didn't have a channel lock, I couldn't remove the clamp. But the cabbage loosened miraculously by itself and now the water's back to running at its usual 2.5 gallons per minute." And my father would say, "The dickens," and I could tell by his voice that he was proud of me. And I would say, "I love you bunches," and he could tell by mine that I'm all right.

DON THACKREY

COMING TO KNOW PA

I didn't know my pa until he died.
Alive, he seemed a natural force, like frost,
But in his death he showed a human side
That drew forth family grief for what we lost.
The farm fell hard on me, the oldest son;
I was surprised to feel unhinged, alone.
I knew the land, the stock, what must be done;
Why did I need his vision? I had my own.
Years passed. My gestures, voice, and thoughts became
Increasingly like his. At first, I tried
To change the self I wanted to disclaim,
But no: I was Pa's son, and satisfied.
On mornings when I shave, I sometimes see
A wry amusement as he studies me.

MARTHA GIES

POLAROID

I was never going to be one of those people who, upon the death of a parent, begins fighting with her family over the possessions of the deceased. So I was thrown into a state of confusion to find myself, in 1999, staring across my long refectory table at my sister who, as I mentioned one by one the ten or a dozen items belonging to our mother that I hoped to have, either challenged me directly or stared with abstracted and impenetrable disbelief. Nearby, our brother sat silent, a survival technique he'd perfected way back in the fifties, growing up in a household with sisters.

We'd waited to have this meeting after the funeral, which my brother and sister had been content to let me, the eldest, plan; and after my brother, designated executor by mutual agreement, had taken a look at Mother's finances which—no surprises there—had been depleted in the last two post-stroke years of her life by doctors, therapists and the best assisted living facility we could find. My sister, the youngest, was, technically, already in possession of Mother's things, as they'd been stored for two years in the basement of her house.

My brother and sister had finished dividing up the furniture between them, none of which I needed in my apartment, where too much space was already claimed by my long table.

There had been a few warm moments of *fraternité* before we reached this impasse: the three of us share a dark humor and can be made to laugh much harder by each other than by anyone outside the family. And we also love soul, the music we listened to as white kids growing up in the civil rights era; at some point we may even have talked of finding a Saturday night to go dancing.

But when the conversation turned back to the business at hand, I'd get stonewalled by my sister. At the final tally, I had been conceded a ring and a pair of earrings, along with two of the many gifts I'd bought for my mother over the years.

My sister had lived quite separated from the family, clear across the country, from 1969 until 1986; and after that, though back in the region, had strictly rationed her visits. Hence, her disbelief that so many of these lovely items had come from me. I did end up getting the colorful jacket I bought Mother in Guatemala, and also the large framed pencil sketch of a hop dryer, identical to the one on her father's hop ranch, that I'd bought from the artist in 1979. It had hung above Mother's fireplace for years.

But I was not allowed to have the beautiful glass tumblers, each a different pastel shade, that I'd carried in my lap on the flight home from Prague. Flabbergasted, I was determined not to start a fight.

The worst loss on my side of the table was Mother's sterling silverware, to me a remembrance of the formal dinners—I'd wager 150 of them—that she and I had prepared together and hosted over the years. We loved to serve roast duck or my mother's favorite, leg of lamb, and we each had our special recipes for soups, salads and desserts. The original slow food hostesses, we played a game of seeing how long we could keep a lively dinner party at table, eating their way through half a dozen courses.

Entertaining gave us such pleasure that we produced our dinners not only at her home and—albeit without the silver and crystal—at my apartment, but sometimes, most ingeniously, at the motels we rented on our annual trip to Ashland for the Shakespeare Festival. In fact, when we bought our tickets, we always kept one evening free for a dinner party.

After I read Pablo Neruda's memoirs, I began to keep a book of guests and menus, an idea I took from his story about the three French ladies who lived in the wild Chilean forest by the sea. My brother and his wife were at many of these dinners, but my sister's name does not appear because she was either living at a great distance or, when in town, she turned us down.

One night, I recall, Mother and I were sharing a last-minute cocktail as we made a final check of the table, set with goblets for wine and water and the multiple spoons and forks that gleamed against the white linen tablecloth. Roses, candles, the works. As we stood back to admire it all, I announced, "When you die, I want the silverware."

"Why not?" she replied with a shrug. "But with the way the price of silver has shot up, I'll have to give the other kids the house and the car."

Obviously, this is where we get our sense of humor. Even so, she was then in the full bloom of health, else I never would have said such a thing.

"No problem," I said.

"So what's wrong with the crystal and the china?" she demanded.

"You're going to live long enough to break all the crystal," I predicted. "And I've never liked this brown stoneware you call *china*."

"It can get a little loud," she conceded. In fact, a fork would scrape shrieking against one of those brown plates. "But you should have the sterling, Martha." She turned serious for a moment. "I don't think either of the other kids care a hoot about setting a table."

But now, when I claimed the sterling, I got only this skeptical stare. My sister lacked all possible context for my request: a nurse, she had come to Mother's aid after the stroke, but by then, of course, the dinner parties had ceased.

For the first year or two after Mother's death, I thought often of the silverware. Looking back now, I can see that my inability to simply let it go was a substitute for my deeper feelings of loss. Yet those feelings came out as anger, not every day, of course, but certainly whenever I tried to set a nice table with my own flatware or whenever I found myself at my sister's house surrounded by furniture, vases and other effects that had been in the family for years. There was never any sign of the sterling and I had to imagine it had either been sold or boxed away somewhere; in any event, my sister's little round table only seats two people, unless it is pulled into the middle of the kitchen and two more chairs be found.

My preoccupation faded, of course, though it never went away entirely.

Then one day, as I was looking through some of my old photographs, I found one of my mother, just before the dinner guests arrived. It had been taken at an auto court just outside Ashland, where we were staying for a week of plays. When I lifted the album's clear plastic to better inspect the photo, I laughed to see the white bed sheet—suddenly I remembered borrowing an extra one from the manager—that we'd used to cover an old wooden picnic table that sat in the oak grove just outside our cabin.

Mother stands at the head of the table, dressed in a white caftan and half a kilo of costume jewelry, and though the photo is grainy for being backlit by the late sun, I can easily make out the table setting: the Melmac plates, their yellow daisy design blistered with old cigarette burns, the paper towels we'd used as napkins, the mismatched stainless, the green plastic bowl (is that a dog bowl?) in which we'd floated a huge, yellow chrysanthemum, and the brown cardboard salt-and-pepper set, standard grocery store issue.

Within days, I had made a color enlargement of the Polaroid and carried it to the framer, a sweet Sri Lankan man who not only promised not to laugh at the degraded image, but indulged my choice of an elaborate double mat and an ornate gold frame. Thus enshrined, I brought it home to my office where it served as a daily reminder of what one true thing I really wanted to inherit from my mother. I could see that the sterling had nothing to do with it: I wanted her gift for genuine hospitality and the pleasure she took in each guest, and I wanted to express it the way she did, standing there at the head of the table with that glorious megawatt smile.

Last month on my birthday, I hosted a formal dinner party for eight at my apartment, and my sister came. I felt such a giddy happiness all that evening at table and, later, at the door downstairs where we all hugged as the guests took their leave for the night. Afterwards, I stood alone there in the dark foyer and observed a moment of gratefulness, for my sister's presence, and for our mother's great warmth, and for what she hoped to bequeath to me.

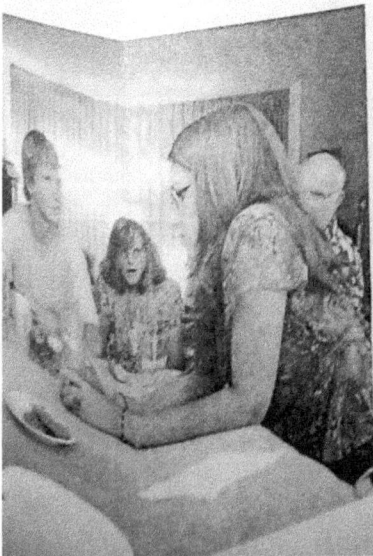

II
PARENTHOOD

PAUL HOSTOVSKY

LADDERS

Leaf-muck on the one hand,
a great view on the other.
All things being equal
I like it up here where the air
is clearer, and my thoughts
are clearer, and this old
ladder creaks and sways
under me like a boat, my son
text messaging his girlfriend
with two thumbs and a foot
on the bottom rung. My anchor.
I can almost see his mother
clear across New England (God
bless her) in her own house now
with her own leaf-muck clogging
her downspouts and gutters.
As Rainer Maria Rilke would say,
you can't lean a ladder up
against another ladder
just because you're in love
and want to make something out of it.
What you need is a solitude
as big as a house to sit in
the middle. But we were young
and in love and in a hurry and we
took a running start—all the doors
in the house flinging open as we flew
through it and out toward each other,
my ladder in my hands and her

ladder in her hands . . . And we
kind of mucked it up on the one hand,
but on the other we ended up with
these two solitudes in autumn
and this son with a cell phone
calling up to me now, asking me what
it's like up here, wanting to have a turn.

VISITATION

I make him the best lunches though.
I mean I made his mother
a lousy
best friend.
I mean I made her a little
miserable.
So she kicks me
off the team
for being what she calls
a lousy team player.
I concede I am a lousy team player.
I never coached little league
or basketball
or soccer and I only
make it to a handful of his games.
But I make him the best lunches,
a sandwich to beat all sandwiches
every single Thursday
and every other Monday,
which he takes with him to school
in a brown paper sack
in a pouch on the abdomen of his backpack,
a sandwich to make his friends say
a little ruefully,
a little wistfully,
"Man, your mother makes the best lunches,"
when really it's his father
who engineers these miracles,
these visitations

of the angel of lunches,
these mothers-
of-all-lunches every
single Thursday and every
other Monday when I have him,
when he sleeps over and I have another
chance to make it
right.

GEORGANN TURNER

TALKING WITH SOPHIE

Sophie hunches over her fries at McDonalds, snarfling and runny-eyed, temporarily deaf in one ear, half-staff eyes a bit wobbly. We've just seen the doctor and I don't want to take her back to school. We've stopped for lunch before we go home so she can rest.

Sophie is seventeen. She's got dark hair, pale skin, lots of freckles, a crooked smile that lights up the room, gorgeous blue eyes, what my family always called Black Irish. I adopted Sophie and her biological sister Grace from the foster care system. Grace was placed with me when she was eighteen months old. Sophie was placed with me ten months later, when she was one. Their adoptions weren't final until several years later. Sophie has had a lot of character building experiences. She will not peak in high school.

"Grace's getting moved to the state hospital today," I tell her. "The lithium's not working. She's swelling up like a puffer fish. But at least she'll be there for a long time so they can take their time figuring out what's going to work. Too bad about the lithium though, cause it really seemed to get rid of Sydney." Grace is eighteen. Sydney is the hallucination that tells Grace to set the house on fire, slash her wrists and jump off the roof. We really hoped to see the back of Sydney.

Sophie glances at me. She's not wanted to talk about Grace, not wanted to know what's going on with her. And she feels a little guilty about it. She says, "I know it's not Grace's fault what's happening to her but I'm not ready to deal with it yet. I know at some point I'm probably going to have to take care of her or something, but I don't really want to have to do anything right now." She dips a fry in some catsup.

"I know. You don't have to do anything right now. You don't have to deal with it. You have to take care of yourself. You have to get an education. You have to grow up. Besides, your dad and I are taking care of Grace."

I touch her hand. I make eye contact. I want to make sure she knows that I mean it. "It's OK to take care of Grace by having her be in the hospital. If you ever do decide to take care of her, it doesn't mean you have to have her in your home. It doesn't. That's not even the best way to take care of her. She feels safer in the hospital. She's happier there. She doesn't have to make so many choices. Making your own life crazy isn't required." I run my hand over her hair, my thumb over her over-plucked eyebrow. I make sure she's hearing this. I want her to get this part. I will tell her this more than once.

"You know, what happened to her is mostly because of the alcohol, not the drugs. Even drinking one drink in a pregnancy can do serious brain damage that you can't fix. And Grace was pickled during your birth mom's whole pregnancy." Pay attention to this part, too, I'm thinking.

"How come I got lucky?" She takes a sip from her soda. Her voice is hoarse.

"Your birth mom was in rehab for a lot of her pregnancy with you. She did really well in rehab. It would've been great if she could've stayed there. You didn't end up with any kind of learning disabilities or brain damage." You dodged a bullet.

Sophie looks at me from under her long dark lashes. "Except for the holes I put in with the ecstasy." She looks for a response. I close my eyes for a moment and draw a breath.

"Yeah, except for those," I say. We munch fries and think about lucky breaks and close calls.

"Each tab of ecstasy burns a one millimeter hole in your brain," she chirps.

"Learn that in rehab?" I ask, raising one brow. Note to self: Google that statistic.

"Yup." She chomps on her cheeseburger. I dip my fry in salt.

I knew about the ecstasy, not about the holes in her head.

"Grace has the kind of brain damage that means she can't learn from experience. You know how when you were little if you stole a candy bar and I got mad at you and you went back to the grocery and you saw a candy bar and said to yourself, I really want that candy bar, but you'd remember that you got in trouble last time? Grace would just think that she wanted a candy bar."

"Yeah, she'd just take it. Is that why she kept stealing my clothes?"

"Yeah. Plus, she's the perfect victim. She doesn't know when someone's a good person or not."

"So she'll just go with any guy who comes along."

"Exactly. Your birth mom was probably a lot like Grace, only without a family. She grew up bounced around in foster care. It was sad. She didn't have a chance. She had a lot of kids. She started having kids when she was really young. And she had three little boys after you by the time your adoption was final."

I'm grateful Sophie will let me talk about Grace. She's been very angry. Grace's behavior scared her. A lot. I'm glad she's opening up a little.

"You know, the first time I ever met you was at a McDonalds," I tell her.

"Really?" she says, dipping another fry into catsup, suppressing a cough. She takes a sip of her drink. "You know I can't eat chicken nuggets ever since I saw that movie in class about how they treat the chickens. It's really gross."

"Yeah. That's why I buy you free-range eggs. Happy chickens. Just one bad day." I sip my iced tea and look out the window at the clouds beginning to drizzle. She smiles.

"So tell me about meeting me."

"You were four months old. I just wrote about it in a story."

She looks up at me, eyes wide.

"I brought Grace for a visit with your birth parents." Grace and Sophie have the same biological mother. I'd just become Grace's foster mother.

"Do you think she has the same bio dad?"

"I don't think so," I say. "You look like your bio dad. She looks more like your bio mom."

"Yeah," she says, "I think so too. I think we must have had different fathers."

"Probably. I used to take Grace for some of her visits. That time we met at McDonalds, too, and you were there and you were four months old. You were in a car seat, bald as a coot. I was playing with you while your parents played with Grace. I made you a promise then. Not out loud, but a promise that when you got taken away I would come find you. And I did. Eight months later, you were with me."

Sophie was her birth mother's eighth child, Grace her seventh, each one removed because of abuse and neglect, each one placed in foster care. There was no reason to believe that this time things would be different.

And they weren't. When Sophie was nine months old, Child Protective Services found her living in the back of a stolen Ryder moving van several hundred miles away with her birth mother, her twelve-year-old sister, another twelve-year-old girl and a registered sex offender. Both adults were using methamphetamines and the mother was pregnant. Again. Three months later Sophie was placed with me as her foster mother.

"Did you take me on my visits?" Dip. Chomp. Sip.

"No," I said. "After a few months you had a different social worker. She and I didn't get along very well. She didn't want me to take you on your visits."

By this time Sophie's birth mother was in rehab again, and the new social worker was deeply committed to family reunification. She believed that Sophie's mother would succeed in rehab and Sophie's attachment to me was a bad thing. She wanted Sophie to be removed from my home and placed in a different foster home until she could be reunited with her birth mother. "There's a fun story there. Basically, your dad and I had to hire a Rottweiler of a lawyer, your attorney was fired, your social worker was taken off your case after the judge yelled at her in court, and we got to keep you. It was touch and go for a while. I was really scared I would lose you."

I took a deep breath. "Here's what happens. A baby forms an attachment to its mother even before it's born, during the pregnancy. Then after it's born, the attachment continues. If the baby is removed from the mother and placed in foster care, the baby has no idea what happened to the person who was their whole world, the person who kept them alive. All they know is they could die, and they don't even know what die means, it just means terror. Then someone else takes care of them for awhile, maybe they see their mother again, then the mother disappears, and someone else shows up and the baby tries to get attached to them, and then this attachment is torn up, then the baby is moved again and pretty soon the baby has experienced what must feel like constant terror over and over. And they stop attaching. They give up. And they do die. They die inside."

By now my breathing is ragged. I am right back where I was every week when I had to hand a screaming Sophie to a stranger who'd take her to visit her birth parents. And half the time they didn't even show up. And Sophie wouldn't know if she'd ever see me again. Or if she would ever see them again. I knew how much damage this was doing to her. I knew what reactive attachment disorder was. So did the social worker. Or she should have.

Sophie's still listening so I keep going. I tell her that bad as what birth parents do, what foster care does is even worse. They know better, and they do it anyway. For children who are older, who have language, visits are not as traumatic. But for babies who don't know that every act is not permanent, who don't have language, whose life experiences have taught them the Hobbesian truth that life is nasty, brutish and short, the process of these visits, done the way they are, is brutal. And it doesn't have to be that way.

The month before Grace was placed with me I got Ben. Ben was two years and one week old. Exactly. Ben had bright red hair, pale blue eyes and a thousand freckles on his nose, a chattering chipmunk of a toddler. He was not biologically related to Grace and Sophie. He was the biological brother to Violet, a baby I'd met at the local hospital where I'd been rocking drug-addicted babies in the NICU, the Neonatal Intensive Care Unit. Which is how I'd ended up being a foster mom in the first place. I was supposed to adopt Violet. She was the only one I didn't end up with, though we're still in touch.

I always took Ben on his visits with his biological parents before his adoption was final. (Ben's birth mom was in rehab with Grace and Sophie's mother.) We had the visits at Violet's foster home. She had lots of foster brothers and sisters and Ben always liked to play with them. He wasn't too interested in his biological parents, and he still isn't. But the important part was, he knew at the visit that he'd be coming home with me; he knew what would happen next. The visit didn't throw his whole world into turmoil.

"When Grace came home from her visits, the ones I didn't take her on," I said, "she beat her head against the sidewalk. I had to hold her tight, pin her arms to keep her from hurting herself. When you came home from your visits, you'd fling yourself to the floor and scream until you were hoarse, until you lost your voice. I'd pick you up and rock you, sing quietly to you until you'd calm down, until you'd start to breathe normally again. You always had night terrors after visiting day." These visits went on until parental rights were officially terminated. Grace and Sophie were both almost three years old when court-ordered visits finally ended.

Tears begin to well in my eyes. I've gone back seventeen years in an instant. I'm as angry and upset and helpless as I was then. I'm embarrassing Sophie in public. "I'm sorry," I say. "I used to be this crazed about foster care all the time."

"I'd like to find out more about my siblings," Sophie says. "I'm curious about them. My mom, not so much. I don't think much good could come from meeting her. But I'd like to find out more about my dad. He looks like some kind of Mexican in the picture I have of him."

"No, he's not. He's kind of a Black Irish guy. You look like him. He never did go into rehab. He might not still be alive. I can call the social worker. Her name is Carol. Do you want me to call her and find out what I can?"

"Yeah. I'd like to know about my siblings. About those three boys."

Sophie and I finish our fries. We crumple up our papers and toss them into the trash. We refill our drinks and head for the door. "Drink up your water," I say.

"I hate water," she says.

"I know." She drinks her water.

"When you were little I asked Carol to put a note in the file with the family who adopted the boys," I tell her, "and they weren't interested in having any contact." She looks disappointed. "But the boys were very little then. It's been a long time. The parents might be more open to it now. And the boys will be teenagers now. They might want to have contact with their siblings. I'll call Carol when we get home."

As we leave the restaurant, I take Sophie's hand. It's warm from her fever. Her cheeks are red and she coughs. I squeeze her hand and she squeezes back. The rain drizzles on our heads. We walk to the car and go home.

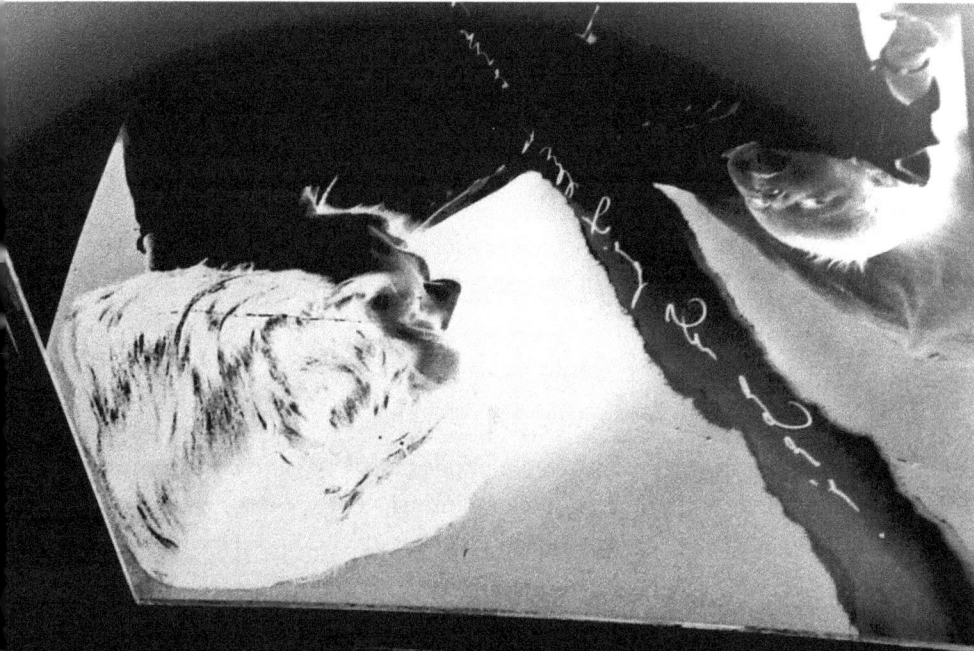

ROSE BURKE

WAITING FOR SUNRISE

Annoyance flashed when the phone rang. I was already late and had just dashed into the house for my appointment book. *I don't have time for this*, I thought, but, at its insistence, I picked it up.

"Hello."

"Is this Rose Smith?"

"Yes," I replied, wondering who would be using my maiden name.

"The Rose Smith who gave her son up for adoption?"

My heart paused before pulsing out an eager *yes*. A kind voice told me she has met my son Dave, that he is a fine young man, that he works in the States.

"Are you willing to have contact?" she asked.

"Oh yes, definitely!" My voice was calm but my heart was shouting. *He still has the name I gave him!*

She explained the process. He will send a letter and a picture which will be forwarded to me. I am to send my reply to their office with my picture and a completed release of information form. Then we will be able to communicate directly.

"Oh no!" I exclaimed, "I will be away the next two weeks."

"Not a problem," the voice replied, "his letter will be waiting for you when you get home."

But there wasn't a letter waiting; not the next day or the following week. Excitement turned to fear. Each night I would go to bed in 1999 but would toss and turn through 1971. I relived the interview with Adoption Services. The worker had said *you will abuse the baby*. No, I was sure I wouldn't, but she had insisted. *You will not mean to, but you will.* The hospital was so real; I was to name my baby but not see him. I saw myself walking alone down the corridor and around the corner to the nursery to see my son. I asked the nurse to bring David to my room for his next feeding and

she did. It was the only time I held him; it didn't work a second time. They
summoned the worker to reassure me I was doing what was best for my baby,
to make sure I did not change my mind. In 1971 a baby needed two parents.
I couldn't take care of a baby; I had no younger brothers or sisters, had never
even done any babysitting, and worst of all, I didn't think I had any maternal
instinct. I had never even played with dolls.

I was discharged the next morning, my breasts leaking and my arms
heavy with their emptiness. Those who had suspected I was pregnant never
asked; those who knew never mentioned it. A silence of shame enveloped me.
Whenever I formed the words to reveal my secret, tears would choke their
flow and I remained silent, keeping my shield firmly in place. My husband
knew about the son I had given up for adoption but I kept even him from
this very private place.

Finally the letter came, and it was long. It is beautifully written and
my son is handsome. He was raised in a loving family and has always known
he was adopted. He wrote *it is like being told that you really have a third eye in
the back of your head, you've just never been able to see it. God give me strength,
I'm now opening that eye. We are in a very unique position that we may see
similarities that can only be through a maternal connection.* I sensed his desire
to know the past and read no reproach behind his words.

Joyfully, I wrote back. I told him that my experience is different.
*There is a part of my life and emotions that are in a separate room. There is a
window in the door but it is covered with frost. Sometimes I would go to the door
and melt a hole in the frost and peek in, but I never had the courage to enter. Now
the door is being opened.* I told him about my family and that I would answer
all his questions as honestly as I can. I told him that I wanted a relationship
but I would never put pressure on him to move beyond the point where he
is comfortable.

Then I waited and waited, but a response never came. I wrote a
second letter but still there was no reply. When I could wait no longer, I
called Post Adoption Services. The worker was so sure everything was fine she
gave me my son's phone number. "Are you sure it is OK," I insisted, "I told
him in my letter that I would not put pressure on him, that everything would
be on his terms."

When I called, he sounded pleased to hear from me. He was very
busy at work but would write soon. I learned that his parents now lived
only about twenty minutes from me and that he planned to come home at

Christmas. My heart leapt at the news. *I will meet my son at Christmas time!* Later, I realized that he had not told me his parents' first names or their address. There were dozens of MacDonalds in the city.

Still no letter arrived. At night, I rethought all my decisions and long withheld emotions rose to the surface and seeped from my sleepless eyes. Had I said something wrong in my letters? Maybe I shouldn't have called. If he didn't call when he was home I would have no way to reach him. Would he look at me and only see the successful person I showed the world? Would he understand how different attitudes and beliefs were in 1971, that I had been a different person then, insecure and believing myself to be completely incapable of giving him what two loving parents could? Would he believe that I had done what I had been convinced was best for him? Would he be able to forgive me? And behind it all there was another accusing voice: *Are you sure your decision was what was best for him or was it really what was best for you?*

Finally the time arrived and he did call; joyful anxiety and fear flooded me as I waited. Then he was at my door and I felt the connection with our first long hug. We sat at the kitchen table and he just listened as my words and tears poured out. I was drained; he looked happy and his hug when he left felt strong and sincere. In bed that night, I replayed our meeting and then slept the best I had in months.

The next day I met his parents and I was welcomed warmly as we celebrated Dave's birthday. The cake had not turned out as planned and they joked that his cake would be my job from now on. They told me how pleased they were that we were connecting and proudly brought out pictures of our son as a child. Dave looked on with a slight smile but did not reveal much; I expressed my pleasure but did not reveal much.

I joined them again for breakfast the next morning and then he was gone, back to his job in Pennsylvania. I felt the emptiness and loss I had never before allowed myself to feel. As I stayed to talk with his parents, a new branch of the family tree was budding, but it was too soon to know if it would thrive. It was surprising how comfortable and natural it felt as we talked, adoptive parents and birth mother, and even more so when we decided that in May we would drive to Pennsylvania. "Driving that far together," I quipped, "will either make or break our friendship." We laughed, but a little hesitantly.

They invited me for lunch the following week and, as I worked nearby, it soon became routine to stop in a couple of times a week. We also talked by phone and it was as if we had always known each other. Our common bond was our son; the son who did not write, or call, or say much about how he felt about our meeting. They told me about every phase of Dave's childhood and how, even then, he had been reserved and felt no need to reveal his feelings. He just presumed everyone knew. They told me repeatedly how happy he was when he came home after meeting me, how they were sure he was overjoyed to have me in his family.

All his life, Dave's parents had encouraged connection with his birth mother, so he effortlessly shifted from having one Mom to two and was content. It was not so easy for me; while he was growing up I was judging myself harshly. Now I was prepared to answer all his questions but he didn't ask any. I had expected to be judged but received only acceptance, the balm I needed to continue my emotional journey.

I told my co-workers about my son, I told my friends and family members who hadn't known and each time it felt more real. I felt more real. The drive to Pennsylvania that first spring took me further. My heart grew a little lighter each time Dave made introductions. *These are my two Moms.* I could hear the pleasure in his voice and everyone was welcoming but each time I heard *birth Mom* I still felt the familiar stab of self-accusation, *you gave your son up for adoption.* It was a wonderful visit, and home again I received my first Mother's Day call.

I met Dave's five brothers and sisters and each welcoming embrace pulled our families closer together. My mom met Dave and his parents, and her joy released more pain. Soon Dave's mom was joining me to visit mine and during each two-hour drive I would reveal a little more. Thin layers were peeling away like the skin of an onion and I would need to give up the wheel as tears blurred my eyes. As she validated my experiences and feelings, I became more comfortable with who I had been and who I had become. And as she shared anecdotes about Dave's childhood, I started to feel like I was his mother too.

Our families blended, visits with Dave became natural and I was included in his wedding. Friends would say how he looked like me, and then how much we were alike. He became my mirror of re-evaluation. If the traits I had fought against were also in him, and I did not raise him, they must not be flaws; they are just who we are. There were little things and big things that people pointed out and I would see myself with fresh eyes. Once, conversation turned to driving quirks that frustrate my husband, and I admitted that prior to changing lanes I not only check my mirrors to ensure it is clear, but also wait for any cars to catch up and pass before pulling over. Dave's wife looked at him and started laughing; we even drive the same.

When they had their first child, a son, their world changed and so did mine. They are wonderful parents but the first months were so difficult as they adjusted to sleepless nights and all the demands and responsibilities of an infant. They have a home, stable income, experience and a wonderful support system, and still it is an amazingly difficult job to provide for the needs of a helpless infant. For the first time I truly knew in my heart that I had made the decision that was right for my son when I had given him up for adoption. I could not have given him what my grandson needs and is receiving.

Echoes will always remain but from the moment I met my son I felt the guilt leaving me, making room for new feelings and perceptions. As they took root and were nurtured, a new me was emerging. I will always be reserved and hesitant to share personal details. That is who I am, but now I am also a mother and a grandmother with love that is finally free.

MARY WHEELER

POM POMS AND CIRCUMSTANCE

The momentous long-awaited day arrives. Flocks of college graduates in flowing robes of glory parade into the auditorium, mortar boards proudly crowning their heads. Clutching a wadded Kleenex and camera at ready, the mother tears up as the ceremonial tune of Pomp and Circumstance fills the auditorium. Her graduate blends into the black sea of robes below. She scans the flock in vain searching for her son. The audience hushes with expectant listening as the keynote speaker commences.

This morning I have fourteen pieces of advice for our graduates. Why fourteen, you're wondering? Because David Letterman has already coined the Top Ten, and I don't want to get in trouble with him. Eleven makes us think about Chapter Eleven and the last thing we need is any hint of bankruptcy during this celebration. Twelve sounds like a twelve-step program; we certainly don't want to go there! And thirteen is an unlucky number. So here you go. Fourteen pieces of advice from me, a former graduate many years down the road of life.

The Graduate

Slouching in the last row along with others whose last names begin with "W," he cranes his neck to get a better view. He had planned on zoning out through the ceremony; instead, he elbows his neighbor and smirks with a *this guy is cool* thumbs up. Sitting up straight the graduate pays attention.

The Mother

Advice! She had been giving her son advice his whole life, but never really felt it had been well received. Her words of wisdom seemed as effective as nailing Jello to a tree. Always in search of new pearls of wisdom, she grabs for her journal to capture the speaker's wisdom.

#1. Don't fear failure.
It's through our mistakes that the true lessons of life are learned. Behold the wisdom of the turtle. He only makes progress if he sticks his neck out. . . . The next several years you ought to seek adventure over ease . . .

The Graduate

The graduate nods in agreement. He had stuck his neck out long ago in high school, declaring his goal. *"I will be a doctor."* Science had come easily to the graduate, the periodic table memorized alongside football plays overnight. Organic chemistry and genetics had been a breeze, and the acceptance letter into medical school had just arrived in the mail. Ahhhh, it feels good to be a man with a plan. The graduate sighs and beams.

The Mother

Yes, her son had been an aggressive turtle. In sports and academics. Prideful tears dribble down her face as she contemplates the road her son is claiming.

The only thing she knows about *organic* is vegetables.

Allowing her mind to wander, the mother wonders exactly how many times has she sat in such bleachers supporting and cheering on her son? Countless sporting and school events—there she has planted herself among the throng, watching her son perform over the years. She smiles, silently entertaining the thought that scientists determine the age of trees by cutting open their trunks and counting their rings. What if every time she had sat in the bleachers she had grown a ring on her bottom? How many would there be by now? 1,000? Perhaps that's why her derriere has become so enlarged?!

 # 5. Check your ego at the door.
It's not all about you. When you walk into any situation, think about the other people there. Put yourself in circumstances where you can pour yourself into serving others. Embrace humility. You will miss out on a lot of the world's best things if you make yourself the center and most important thing twenty-four hours a day.

The Graduate

Doors. He had walked through many doors since leaving home four years ago. Doors to classrooms, doors to dorms, fraternity and sorority houses, doors to bars and doors to places his parents had no idea about.

His ego? Intact. Critical to be competitive, on top of his game. College had taught him the importance of eye-contact, firm handshakes and social graces.

Serving others? Yeah, he had been on church mission trips in middle school. The memory of that poverty made him squirm. No time to serve others now.

Embrace? Well that word *embrace* puts a smile on his face as he re-lives a number of recent embraces with several hot babes over the past four years. Lots of doors, lots of embraces to fill his memory bank for a while . . .

The Mother

She hopes he's listening. Her son is a product of the *Age of Entitlement.* Kids these days . . . It's all about me, me, me, and me again. How she detests self-centered attitudes. Since he's left for college, she has poured herself into all kinds of volunteer service opportunities. Absolutely, generosity is the secret of life.

This speaker is spouting all kinds of wisdom. Once again she surveys the field of graduates below hoping to find her son leaning in and listening with fervent attention.

#10. Life is tough. Shakespeare was right when he wrote, you will suffer the slings and arrows of outrageous fortune . . .
Keep three words at your core:
faith, family, friends.

The Graduate

How much longer? Shakespeare, Schmakeshere—the graduate had relied on Cliff Notes when assigned Hamlet in high school . . . and faith?

Faith is on his back burner. Like his belly button, he knows he has one, but doesn't give it much thought.

Maybe someday.

Now, friends on the other hand . . . Just the mention of friends ignites a flurry of back and forth texts. Friends had become everything to him these past four years. His fraternity brothers are the guys who know him, understand him, and whose secrets are locked in an iron-clad code of brotherhood.

Family?

They're here. Somewhere. They always are. He smiles.

The Mother

Using her zoom camera lens as binoculars, she scans the scene of black robes where the end of the alphabet must be sitting. She wants to see his face—see his reaction to the wisdom from the sage on the stage. Does her son know, *really* know about the reality of the slings and arrows of outrageous fortune? What is medical school going to be like? She quickly calculates that by his next graduation she'll have yet another ring on her bottom and will qualify for senior citizen rates at the movies.

And where is he on the subject of God? Either God is everything, or God is nothing. You can't be half-pregnant. You either believe or you don't.

When was the last time they talked about faith? About any matter of the heart?

Oh how she longs to be the kind of mom he needs, who knows what to say, when to talk and when to be silent. Their relationship has grown distant over time. It stung to think about it. Looking left and right, she wonders if any of the other mothers in the crowd feel the same.

She says a silent prayer that the family will function as his soft landing place in the days to come. Certainly there will be slings and arrows. He has to know that no matter what tomorrow brings, he has a family that will be there.

#14 Examine yourself in the mirror daily.
Take a good look at what you see. Look yourself in the eye and say, "I like me." Be clear about your values, the people you admire, your aspirations. If you want to fly with the eagles by day, you can't run with the turkeys at night.

The Graduate

He looks at his watch and feels the itch of his robe irritating the back of his neck. Rubbing his chin, he prides himself for no knicks with the razor this morning after last night's late party. Shaving is when he gets his mirror examination, which these day is hardly daily. He's grown used to the grubby stubble look. This necktie is for the birds.

Speaking of birds . . . Eagles? Turkeys? He likes all kinds of people and has become an ornithologist as a result of attending this huge university . . . all kinds of fowl in his midst. And all kinds of foul fowl too. College has taught him to spread his wings, knowing sometimes he's at liberty to cackle with chickens, while other times he must be a wise owl and retreat to the library in order to get into medical school.

He steadies his hand on his right leg which now has that nervous twitch thing going on. His flock of buddies is about to change, as he knows no one else attending the same medical school. New birds to meet—new skies to fly.

The Mother

Self-examination. How many times has she quoted Socrates? *The unexamined life is not worth living.* She thinks about the scads of journals and scrapbooks she's maintained all these years, recording his first words and steps, a lock from his first haircut, and all of his report cards along the way. She'd written letters to him every Mother's Day and every birthday telling him of his adventures and cute antics. Now gazing down at her muffin top, her hands automatically rub her once-pregnant belly, remembering the dilemma of what to name him. *Practice reciting the first, middle, and last name in a formal slow voice as if he were crossing a stage at graduation.* The experts had said a name needs to be strong, crafted for all seasons of life. Once a cuddly baby, this very same boy is officially a man, twenty-two years old and over six feet tall. He can no longer, and has long ago not wanted to, sit in her lap and tell her about his day. His hair has gone from blonde to brown and now has a receding hairline. When did that happen?

Once again, the mother peers left and right, wondering what the other mothers have been thinking about during this keynote address. More than half of them seem to be lost in their cell phones. Seeing this she recalls the advice from the student panel at parent orientation four years ago: *You want better communication with your child? The answer is three words: Learn to text.*

So she joins the other moms, reaches for her phone and does . . .

Hey! We're under the American flag, third row up from the railing.

In a flash, he responds.

Yeah, I know. xoxo

He looks up and waves. She waves back.

That's all she needed.

A connection.

The Kleenex was shot now, stripped of any absorbency, just a wet wad in her hand. The calling of graduates was beginning. She could relax as the amplified graduate names A-V were announced slowly and formally—first, middle, and last. It was a gift to simply be, to breathe, to hold her husband's hand and to rest assured that the camera would do its duty to document this day and others soon to come.

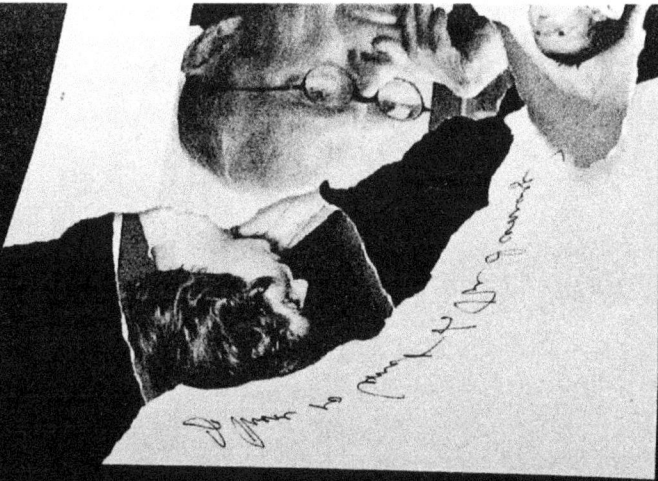

BILL DENHAM

DO YOU REMEMBER, DAD?

I

Nicholas, were I to stand before you,
        as if before god,
        and look steadily into the mystery
        of your deep, brown, eastern eyes,
        I would hear in my heart the question
        your chaotic mind could not speak
        but which your heart eternally poses:
        "Do you remember, Dad?"

"Yes, I remember, my son,
        those tiny seizures each time
        your infant hands reached out,
        stopping you in mid-act,
        your hands and eyebrows trembling,
        your senses scrambled.

And, I remember,
        on hands and knees,
        cross-pattern crawling,
        laying down pathways in your brain
        and endless hours of behavior mod
        as you screamed out your anger
        and intolerable frustration,
        as on that day in Manoa valley.
        You must have been two and a half
        and we had always wanted you
        to be a part of our family,

to join in with your big sisters
and it looked like you could,
at least on this day.

We got home from Makapu,
parked our old black and white
Buick Roadmaster in the garage
and all got out to go inside,
with a friendly, 'Come on, Nicholas,
let's go inside,' but you wouldn't move.
So I said to you, 'Come on in
when you're ready, Nick,'
and left you there to make it on your own,
knowing that you could,
if you would.
And I remember your screams,
piercing the neighborhood,
long into the afternoon, as inside,
we pretended to be
'a normal family.'"

II

"But, do you remember, Dad?"

"Yes, I remember, my son,
        when you and I were together,
        just the two of us,
        and you were five
        and the world *was* beautiful
        and I was teaching you to read
        with labels on everything
        and we milked the goats together
        and walked in the woods
        and you rode your exercise bike,
        the one I had made for you,

and stood on your tiptoes
to take a treat from off the shelf.
Yes, I remember.

And I remember
the long, long letters
(*lost now forever*)
painstakingly pecked out
on my old Smith Corona portable,
carefully detailing our lives
on the farm, for the others:
all the progress we had made, you and I,
and all the small, daily joys of being there,
like watching the goats come home
each evening as they emerged,
single file, into the clearing behind the house,
Manney leading the way, her bell tinkling,
all their sides so distended,
wide, beyond belief,
from a whole day of browsing
the mountain sides above our home,
their bodies gently rocking side to side
with each forward step,
reminding me always of a fleet of ancient sailing ships,
coming into view over the horizon,
heavily laden, rocking slowly
side to side as they moved
through gently rolling waves
toward safe harbor.

Oh, yes, I remember,
how beautiful the world was
and how I loved to write
those letters, late at night,
when you were asleep."

III

"But, do you *remember,* Dad?"

"Yes, I do remember, Nicholas,
        I can't forget, for from that black hole,
        defying all gravity, images do escape,
        rising, they come to me without warning
        or any particular feeling;

        they just come, over and over:
        that room—the bare floors, loft and ladder
        and your face, always your face, Nicholas.

        Images I'll carry into eternity,
        unchanging and everlasting,
        images that speak a truth,
        a truth to which I must now bear witness
        these many years later,
        so that all may know, as best as I can tell it,
        what your experience has been,
        since words are so elusive
        to your damaged
        mind.

This much I know, Nicholas:
        in the stark isolation and secrecy
        of that old Appalachian farm house,
        behind closed doors, where none could see,
        far away from society,
        a violation took place.

        I see you there, Nicholas,
        isolated and alone,
        our child, our child of special needs.

I don't mean I see you isolated and alone
because of your damaged mind
and your already fragmented sense of self
though that certainly set you apart.

I mean I see you literally isolated and alone,
removed from whatever warmth and nurture was there
and placed in solitary confinement
by me,
by your mother and by two other willing adults,
all of whom were charged with your care.

No voice spoke up.
No one said, 'Wait! Hold on!'
We simply put you in that room all alone,
away from us, away from your sisters,
not for half an hour or even half a day.
Oh yes, Nicholas, I do remember,
we put you there for one whole day
and then for two, then three and maybe four.
I don't know.

We covered the windows
so you couldn't see out;
we covered your hands,
sewed your sleeves shut,
so you couldn't suck your thumb;
we covered our own heads with brown paper sacks
so you couldn't see our faces
when we fed you portions
of protein powder and goat's milk
three times a day;
and we gave you a piss pot;
that's all.

Oh yes, Nicholas, I remember.
      There was a rationale;
      there's always a rationale.
      But in the end, it didn't work—
      whatever it was we said we were doing.
      So we let you out and went blindly on
      with our deeply troubled lives
      for decades yet to come."

IV

"As I imagine standing before you, Nicholas,
      your eyes, your deep, brown, eastern eyes
      do not accuse, they merely ask:
      'Do you remember, Dad?'"

"And I respond: yes, I do remember that time, my son.
      And though in my imagination
      your beautiful eyes
      do not accuse,
      I must stand before you now,
      as if before God
      without excuse or equivocation,
      to speak the unspeakable,
      to say, straight up,
      I was there!
      I did that!"

HEATHER TOSTESON

REPAIR

Cora

Daniel Gordon's mother, Cora, a vivid woman well on her way to ninety but looking a decade younger, closes both her soft hands around his left one and speaks in a slow, comforting voice.

"Our Father who art—"

"in heaven," Daniel begins to recite with her, a slight smile on his lips as he comes to "hallowed," which, with his drugged enunciation becomes "hollowed." His eyelids flutter slightly as if he heard himself and wants to see if she did too.

"be thy *name*, the kingdom *come*, thy will be *done* on earth as it is in *heaven* . . ." Cora's voice strengthens and deepens as she relaxes into the familiar, incantatory rhythm.

Cora releases her only son's hand, spreads it flat on the sheet, careful to keep it away from the ominous mounds of his legs, which she has told her daughters, "The mother in me refuses to see. As a nurse, I can fill in all the details." But that isn't true. She can't imagine what has happened to her son's body, how all the flesh has fallen away from his face and his ribcage, so he looks gaunt as her own father at eighty wasted cadaverous by emphysema— and then this lower body of his that keeps swelling as if with elephantiasis, blackening as if with plague. It's just Kaposi's and the lymphoma, she knows. But she still doesn't want to see and he doesn't want to show. There's no question of final judgment. He's doing his suffering here, poor boy.

Daniel has been sprawled across death's hearth, with occasional Lazarus-like arisings, for three years now. They are all so tired. After a quarter of a century, he's come back to them and they have welcomed him like the prodigal son, she and his father, his sisters, his ex-wife and her partner, his daughter and her children. Why, they have all been wondering for months now, doesn't he bid them a final good-bye and head on to that permanent welcome, more extravagant than anything they can provide here in Merced, or this life for that matter. Cora would go first if she were invited, but Daniel is their leader, the most chosen in that next world where the least of them comes first. She's tried to explain it to him—but the eyes that have blazed at her, the fierce clarity that dissolves his morphine haze instantly, have silenced her every time. That and the very shape of his skull, how the ears jug out, the cheeks sag, the nose every day is more dominant, the lips smaller, more embittered. Just like her father.

Cora opens her well-worn Bible and begins: *The Lord is my shepherd, I shall not want.* The thin page is cool, rippled. *He maketh me to lie down.*

Daniel smoothes the sheet around his hands in slow, sensuous circles; then, his palms slightly elevated, he continues the circles, as if he were a blind man reading the hands of his clocks with his palms.

Daniel

Though I walk through the valley of the shadow of death . . .

Cora keeps trying to press the waves out of the onion skin. Daniel's younger sister, Janie, fifty-one, but with a voice still light as a prepubescent girl's, joins her mother.

Thou prepareth a table for me—

Like her brother, all Janie's mass has come to rest below her waist. If the accrued flesh were self-worth, nothing would be able to rock her now. But Janie remains the baby of the family, needy as a one year old in her soul. "Oh Mama," she cries, as if help could finally come from that quarter. There had been too many of them, that was the simple truth of things. Five in ten years. Too many to feed. Too many to tend to. No body to blame. Daniel doesn't begrudge his parents their passionate bed play—even if it did bloom with foolish regularity into another hungry mouth and another set of blue eyes, bright and unblinking as those on the rim of a scallop's shell, to haunt his mother's post-partum psychoses. But Daniel no longer has energy to think about this.

Now that his mother and his sister's voices have subsided, his arms rise and fall as if he is trying to calm troubled waters or rile becalmed ones. His arms are thin, but sure, buoyant. As his arms move of their own mysterious volition, the waters of his consciousness tremble and calm, tremble and calm.

"There is nothing to fear, Daddy," Daniel's daughter Daniela said to him over the phone that morning. "I saw the truth in Nana's face just last week." Her maternal grandmother has taken half the time he has to die. No one needs to remind him. "There is peace on the other side."

"You too," Daniel had thought bitterly at the time. "Sloughing me off like an old skin." But now he hears his daughter's voice, light as his sister's, light as her own when he left her, at ten, to her own dreams.

"Left her for *your* own dreams, you fuck," he hears his ex-wife Sandra say. "Be honest for once. You never did anything for anybody else."

"Except Jésus," he had said. Ending with those words, quite intentionally, all the good will that had allowed her to offer him a bed in his sickness and him to accept it.

The ludicrous knock-down-drag-out over the marijuana in the garden was an afterthought, an excuse. It was just mentioning his dead lover's name that lit the fuse.

"It's just like it always was. You haven't changed at all. You always put your drugs over your family," Sandra screamed at him, her partner Kelly standing blinking, helplessly hand-wringing, at her side. He winked at Kelly, keeping his options open—but just for a second.

"Can't you take a moment and try to see each other's side?" Kelly asked.

Sandra turned on her. "Are you, in *my* house, daring to turn against me? Two years we've kept him—I always knew it was a mistake—and this is how he paid us back. He *lied* to me."

"You're right," Daniel had said. "I'd say anything to get free room and board."

"What made you stop?" Kelly asked him point blank as she helped him pack to move in with his resigned, aging parents an hour's drive south. They had always hated Sandra, blamed his own homosexuality on hers. (She, on the other hand, blamed his on the foreign exchange student his parents innocently hosted when he was fifteen, his first adolescent tryst.) Sandra's shocking generosity these past two years had tenterhooked his parents between gratitude and hardened rancor.

"What made you stop saying anything to get what you wanted?" Kelly had asked again. Her voice gave him the jitters, that little whine to it. As if she were surprised or something. He'd thought they were in on it together—all that winking and behind the back eye-rolling when Sandra got busy with her charts and deadlines and ultimatums.

"Who's to say I'm not doing it this very minute?" Daniel had asked.

"You really think your parents are going to let you grow weed in the retirement community?"

"Why not? I've got the doctor's order. They even have a medical marijuana association there. All those old coots are high as kites, floating above their cancer, stroke or ALS. I think they water the community garden from their golf carts and wheelchairs."

"So, you're finally going to start using one?" Kelly looked at him then, her mouth firming up. She put the suitcase down on the driveway. She'd looked him up and down, her eyes staying too long on his thickened legs.

"How the hell do you think your parents are going to be able to do what I do?" she asked. He'd steadily refused a wheelchair these two years. Kelly had never pushed him to use one. She had always ferried him where he needed to go, walked along with him chatting as if his pace was the most normal in the world for a fifty-seven-year-old man. He'd always assumed she was bored, eager for the distraction.

It took him back, the coolness in her look. Something sharp and more unfriendly there, less manageable than Sandra's fury. But Kelly didn't say anything more. She didn't even say good-bye when his parents arrived.

When he explained it all to his parents, they saw right away what a bitch Sandra had been, how she'd twisted everything. He showed them the prescription he'd stubbornly refused to mention to Sandra, letting her sweat a visit from DEA. (She should have trusted him.) But he also told them he wasn't going to plant any weed—even if there was a community medical garden, even if he had a doctor's say so. He was sober now. He was staying with prayer. And percocet.

They had all joined hands around the table, his father, Tom, having the last word as usual.

"Our Heavenly Father, we thank you that our son, Daniel, so long lost to us has returned to us and to you, Lord, his heavenly Father. We know you share our joy."

Daniel had opened his eyes and looked at his parents, their clasped hands resting on the plastic mat laid over the floral tablecloth, at the sentimental cross-stitched sampler above their heads. This was good, he'd thought. This was as it should be. And he'd felt something sweet and liquid rising from the soles of his swollen feet through all that cancerous sludge, something good and pure and simple and clean-hearted as the boy he had once been filling him, reversing this horrific, interminable process that could—all their prayers to the contrary—lead to nothing, absolutely nothing good.

"My dear boy, there's no need to hang on anymore," Daniel hears his mother say to him, her voice soft and kind, as if she is the Virgin of Guadalupe, ready to run interference. The darkness around him is sweet, thick and gold as syrup. Sound amplifies there.

"Don't trust her," Jésus says. "Whatever she says, remember she's just an instrument of your father. A puppet."

Jésus would lift his elbows and knees like a marionette, the smile on his face alluring as the Virgin's, and then Jésus would put on Daniel's father's voice and boom, "Daniel, leave Sodom. Put yourself in the good Lord's hands. He hates the sin, not the sinner. Come back to Him."

"And I," Jésus would tip back his head and his laugh would fall back in his throat as if he were gargling, and then he'd lean forward choking out the joke, "I, Jésus, am your original sin. Without me you would be their golden boy, still living with your sanctimonious dyke bitch of a wife. Both of you saved from your real, wicked natures. Both of you living the Holy lie."

Jésus was a beautiful man. The name was so common south of the border, it was like Mark or John, nothing that called attention to itself, or beyond itself. But here, in Jesus land, he played up the namesake with his long black hair, the beard, the gesture he had when he was real stoned, like he was quieting the sea so he could walk on it without wetting the hem of his garment.

Daniel had never seen a more beautiful face before or after. *I want to die with his eyes on me*, had been his first thought when he saw him, standing by the side of the road, hitchhiking bare-chested, his skin the same color as the dry September hills. He knew he shouldn't stop. Knew he couldn't stop himself. Thirty-five, he'd given that all up when he married—after the ceremony where they drove the devil out of him. He had everything to live for. His job, his marriage to someone fighting the same fight he was, his daughter, his baptism.

"I'm yours," Jésus said, when he'd pulled over. "Take your rod and follow me."

"I never dreamed you'd outlive me," Jésus said that last night. They'd been together eighteen crazy years by then. "I have the genes, man. And the *suerte*. And the *don*. You're just wonderbread."

"In a white man's world," Daniel had said, "you can't beat it." He wondered now why he'd said that.

"The next one won't be," Jésus said.

And he could see Jésus was itching to get there, to see if he was right—and if he wasn't, already itching to fight it out, *mano a mano*.

"*Te quiero*," Daniel had said and Jésus had rolled his eyes, grimaced. And that was it. Daniel had kept his arms around his lover's wasted body, heaving with equal parts terror and fury, until there was no heat left. There was nothing, ever, that would make up for what he'd just lost. In this life or whatever came after.

Tom

Tom Gordon was waiting outside the door, ready to take his wife's place, to send her back home with Janie. Cora was fragile. She didn't usually show it until it was too late. But he knew, after all these years, he knew the signs.

"A half hour," he'd told Janie, "and then take your mother home. I'll stay here. Your mother is getting a little run down."

Janie had looked up at him with those big eyes of hers. He never had to say much to his daughters, especially the younger two, who although too young to remember the post-partum hospitalizations, were in their teens when Cora had had the menopausal ones.

"It can't be much longer now," he'd said. "Daniela's coming—she's leaving the children with Sandra." His granddaughter was a surprise to him. He didn't understand how she'd found the strength in her own circumstances, the father who had abandoned her, that controlling perverted mother of hers. Those babies she was raising alone while going to school and working were doing fine. Still she had time for her father and her mother and her mother's woman friend, Kelly. And for Cora. And for him.

"It means so much to Daddy, Gramps," she had said to him. "Your taking him in. Visiting with him now. He never felt favored enough growing up."

So here his son was, in the nursing home six months already—all the women at his beck and call. Mother. Ex-wife. Daughter. Granddaughter. Sisters. Starving and bloated at the same time. Daniel wasn't an easy man. As a boy, he had been eager enough to please, but he always turned to his mother and his sisters when he wanted a favor. Something a little back-handed, cowardly about that Tom had always thought. But he didn't put a stop to it. He'd had enough to attend to, getting the factory going, taking care of the five of them alone when Cora went to the hospital after Jill and again, three years later, after Janie. Six months the first time. A year the second.

The doctor said something about a hysterectomy or tying Cora's tubes during the hospitalization that began less than a week after Janie's birth. Tom had told him no. "She lives for her children. They are part of God's blessing. Each one's proof to her that He hasn't stopped paying attention. Her mother left when she was young. She doesn't want to say no to life. Ever. Taking that affirmation away from her—I couldn't do that."

The doctor had shrugged. "Hysterectomy or electric shock. You know there's a good chance she's not going to come back this time. Even if she does, even if you have no more kids, you may lose her again at the change." The doctor thought estrogen was the cause of her delusions.

"We'll take our chances," Tom had told the doctor. What choice did he have really? He would have lost Cora for sure if he'd agreed.

But he'd done everything he could to see that Janie was their last. He'd kept better track of Cora's cycles than she had. Soon as it came out, he had her taking the pill. He'd made sure the children didn't hold those bad times against their mother. Except for Laura, the oldest, he didn't think they did. And during that messy time when the youngest were teenagers, when Cora was planning to run away, start a whole new life for herself in Hawaii with a man she'd seen once at the mall buying an aloha shirt, he'd stepped in. Took Cora back to the hospital. More than once.

"There are things I don't need to know," Tom had told the doctors and nurses each time he had signed Cora in. "Things better left unsaid."

Unsaid wasn't the same as forgotten. He wasn't a stupid man. Or a coward. But the war had taught him it didn't pay to remember what you had no hope of changing. The look on the face of the man who took your bullet, for example. The look on your best friend's face when he saw the blood rushing over your hand, too fast, too long for there to be any other outcome.

"Why didn't you stop it?" his oldest, Laura, had asked him. They were sitting by the pool, a summer day, twenty years ago. She had brought her sons over. They were about the same age she was when Cora went into the hospital the second time, when Tom thought they'd lost Cora for good. At first, that's what he thought Laura was referring to. The pregnancies.

"We did all right," he said. He was reading the paper. This was an old conversation. He didn't have to think about it. "You and me and Great-Aunt Dora, we did fine. We *all* made it through."

Laura didn't answer, the way she usually did, "That's true. It sure prepared me to be a mother." This time she just sat there in the lounge chair, her hands resting lightly on the arms of the chair, no tension there. So he didn't know what made him look up, follow her eyes, see Cora and her father in the kitchen.

Cora was sliding the screen door open and helping her father with the oxygen tank, ushering him out to the patio. It angered Tom, it always did, that Cora tended to her father as carefully as she would any patient at the hospital—and never a word of thanks, he just acted like it was his due. After all she'd been through. But he knew better than to try and interfere.

He looked at Laura who was still watching her mother and her grandfather. She was hardly breathing, like a possum playing dead. Just the tears falling from her lashes, drying, in the high California heat, as soon as they touched her cheeks.

Tom had taken his time to answer, but he hadn't pretended not to understand her.

"I was hoping you wouldn't remember."

"We all do," she said.

It was the quietness of her voice, how for a second it lost that girlish light and came close to sounding like Cora's during the breakdowns that got to him. He'd just sat there, his paper on his lap, watching Cora settle her old man on a chair on the far side of the pool, taking the time to make sure the tubes were running straight into his nostrils.

"It's like yesterday," Laura said. "It is always just like yesterday."

Tom reached over then, covered his daughter's hand, and said, "I'm so sorry."

"Me too," she said. Her voice shifted back to that practiced girlish lightness she had learned from her mother, taught to her sisters in her mother's long absences. "Me too, Daddy."

They watched her boys swatting the water, diving for the bottom, and beyond their happy flurry, that wicked old man, his face just skin over a skull now, his glasses flashing light, his small mouth tight.

"He can't die too soon for me," Tom had said as he picked up his paper, cutting off whatever she might have said in return.

"What did you expect?" Tom had asked Daniel when he came to him with the news of his firing. It was a bad word *turpitude*. But better than the alternatives.

"I told him as a friend," Daniel said, tears in his eyes. He wasn't feeling shame, just anger and fear. "He betrayed me." He was talking about the principal, who had just fired him because Daniel had told him pointblank he was homosexual. What had he expected?

"Your own actions betrayed you," Tom told his son. "And not just in this world."

"Love like this cannot be wrong, Dad," Daniel had said.

"Try that on your mother and your sisters," Tom had answered. "They're romantic."

"And you're shocked and playing God," Daniel had snapped back. "Don't tell me you didn't know."

"We don't betray our women or our children," he'd said. "For any reason. *Any* reason."

"We just look away, right?" Daniel said. "I want you to look me in the eyes, Dad, and tell me that isn't a betrayal."

"I want you to look me in the eye, Dad," Daniel repeated. "I want you to see me. Just once. I'm a good father. A good teacher. A good son. But that's not enough, is it? Never was."

"Why did you come here?" Tom had asked.

"To let you know before the paper does. To ask for a job. Just until I can get back on my feet."

"You'll never teach again," Tom had warned his son. "No parent will trust you with their children."

"It's not people like me children need to be protected from. I'm not a pederast, Dad." Daniel acted as if it was a better word than child-molester. "Jésus is my age. I'm a man who loves *men*—not boys." The look Daniel gave Tom was far from loving.

"We've got no openings," Tom answered. "I can give you $5,000, enough for a new start. Another city. Maybe another state."

"You're writing me off?" Daniel had asked, his voice dull. "Just like that. No questions, nothing. Nothing counts but this. Not a fucking thing. Nothing I've ever done for you—not all the summers working for no pay here, not all the studying, the degrees, the beautiful daughter I've fathered and helped raise. Do you have any idea what I've done to myself to try to be the person *you* wanted me to be?"

Tom was already writing the check. He made it bigger even though it would make it difficult to meet payroll that week.

"Don't go calling your mother. Don't disturb her. I'll tell her what she needs to know." Tom looked up, saw Daniel opening his mouth to protest, and shook his head. "Your mother and I will never stop praying for you, son. You come to Him with a contrite heart, our Heavenly Father forgives everything. He alone can keep you from temptation."

"How can I be contrite about the nature He gave me?" Daniel tapped his chest, suddenly looking stronger and more manly than his father had ever seen him before. "*This* is what I love out of, Dad. *This* is *His* temple. He's not the one rejecting me, it's you. Just you—"

"Don't go so far you can't come back," Tom had said, placing the check in Daniel's hand. "Word or deed, son. Word or deed."

Tom was looking at his watch when he heard the scream and saw Janie come running out of the room. She had her hands over her cheeks, her hair falling over the fingers, and her mouth was a big red hole through which this awful sound kept pouring. The floor was shaking as she pounded down the hall.

Tom moved forward about to ask, "Where's your mother?" But Cora was right behind her daughter, her face quieter than Janie's, her mouth pressed shut, but tears beginning to flood.

He pushed into his son's room and gasped. Daniel was standing stark naked on the bed, his hands stretched wide like he was welcoming someone, like he was waiting for nails. He was a horror to behold, standing on those

legs so full of pus and lymph they could have belonged to an elephant. It
was like he was two different beings—his lower parts, those discolored legs
and groin, and his engorged penis, balls big as melons now, waving back and
forth. Sickening. And all the rest of him corpse white, skeleton thin. Daniel
had this cruel little smile on his face like he knew exactly what effect he was
having, knew no one could stop him now.

"Get down," Tom yelled. "Cover your filthy self."

But Daniel just spread his arms wider and tossed his head back,
laughing. He shifted his feet back and forth on the mattress, making his
privates swing.

Tom slammed his hand down on the nurse's bell and then reached
over and slapped at his son's legs and thought he'd be sick at the feel of them.

"You crazy bastard," Tom said. "Get a hold of yourself. How dare
you expose yourself like that in front of my little girl."

Daniel didn't hear. He was weaving more now, like he was dancing.
One of those Indian dances he and Jésus had liked. Going back to their roots,
they called it.

He'd reached up again and grabbed for Daniel's hand, like a child
lurching for a ring on a merry-go-round. Two nurses and an orderly came in.

"Whoa, man, that's some kind of groove you've got going," the
attendant said with a smile. "Let's get you down now so you can teach it to
us."

"You can leave," the nurse told Tom, touching his hand gently. "We
can take over. You don't need to see this. Go find your wife and daughter.
Come back later."

Tom did what she said, but he couldn't find Cora or Janie. He waited
a good half hour outside the ladies room. He couldn't stop shaking.

The nurse came down after awhile. "We gave him something to
sedate him."

Why don't you just get it all over with Tom wanted to ask her. End
this misery once and for all? As soon as he thought it, he knew better than to
open his mouth. What God gave only God could take away.

"Can I help you?" she asked, putting her hand on his back. He
swallowed hard.

"He had no idea what he was doing, Mr. Gordon," the nurse said,
moving around to look up into Tom's face. "It's the HIV. It's in his brain.
And the dying process. This time, toward the end, is like a dream to them.

They're getting ready to go, they're greeting ghosts and lost relatives."

That's when he started to cry.

"He had no right," he said. "He had no damn right to expose himself that way to my little girl."

"You mean your daughter?" the nurse asked. For a second there, he saw Janie the way the nurse might, with the gray in her hair, her wagging gait.

"She wasn't prepared," Tom said. "No one prepared her for this."

"He had no idea what he was doing," the nurse said again. "He's not accountable. I think your daughter will recover." Tom didn't like the look on her face now, it had something a little hard in it, not hurtful so much as disdainful. "Surely it's worse for him," she said as if that put an end to things.

Tom closed his eyes then. It all flashed right back up. He felt sick.

"His groin. His legs. I had no idea."

"He didn't want you to see. When he was in his right mind, he was very clear about that. He didn't want us to see either, but we assured him we were professionals, that we'd seen worse."

"Is that the truth? You've seen worse?"

She nodded briskly. "Burn wards. Late stage gangrene. I'm not saying it is pretty. If you want to come back with me, you can see he is resting easy now."

"I'm going to take his mother and his sister home. Get them quieted down."

"It's another day at the most now, Mr. Gordon. Try to come back one more time. You don't want this to be your last memory."

A woman called out from one of the rooms as Tom walked away from the nurse. She asked him if he was looking for the woman who had been screaming as if she'd seen a ghost and the old woman who had run after her. He said yes and she directed him toward the courtyard, where Janie and Cora sat on a bench under a swag of red bougainvillea chatting as if nothing at all had happened. They were laughing in that soft purring way mothers and daughters sometimes have, like the rest of the world's left out of some charmed circle.

But as soon as they saw him, Janie was on her feet, crying out like a little girl, "Oh, Daddy, it was so horrible." She reached out her arms, her right one encased in that tight skin-toned elastic sleeve she'd been using since the breast surgery so her arm wouldn't start swelling. "I kept wondering, you know, if it were me, a couple of years from now, would I look like that, would my children be ashamed of me?"

"The nurse says it's the HIV in his mind. He doesn't know what he's doing."

"I thought he might be asking the Lord to come for him now, right now," Cora said. "That maybe, finally, he's ready to go."

They all knew where Daniel was going. They pretended different, but they knew. Maybe they wished different too. Certainly Tom did. Daniel was his own son after all. But today when Tom had looked up and had seen Daniel, those ears, those sunken cheeks, that wicked little smirk on his face like no one was ever going to dare stop him, call him to account, he'd realized that his forgiveness didn't mean a thing, it wasn't his test at all, it was Daniel's and the results had come in a long time ago. When Daniel got there, saw the company it was now his to keep, it would be like looking in a mirror.

Laura came by to drop some food off just after they'd finished dinner. "For the vigil," Laura had said before she saw their faces.

Cora and Janie told Laura about the scene at the hospital, but when Tom saw Cora getting upset, he said, "Let's change the subject," and gestured to Janie to take her mother into the other room. Laura stayed with him to help clean up.

He loaded the dishwasher, taking every rinsed dish Laura handed him and setting it in there the way it should be. "I wanted to kill him. I wanted to kill the son of a bitch," he muttered to Laura. "I wanted to shoot the son of a bitch for exposing himself that way to my daughter. The nurse explained it to me later, but I still wanted to shoot the son of a bitch."

"You still can," Laura said, patting him on the back with a laugh. "He's not dead yet." And then she just let her hand rest there on the middle of his back as he bent over the dishwasher. "It sure doesn't help that he looks so much like Grandpop, does it? Sharing a name was bad enough. How could you and mom do that to him?"

And then he began to shake and the words just came out, toppling on themselves. "He's my only son. This is not the way it is supposed to be. She explained it to me, the nurse did, how the disease went to his brain. It's a judgment, a terrible judgment."

"And soon his suffering will be done," Cora said, coming up and speaking in a voice that sounded as calm as the nurse's. "He'll go home. It will be a release for all of us."

"I think he's afraid of what's coming," Laura said quietly. "I think he thinks God can't see the difference between him and Grandpop."

"Not in front of your mother," Tom said curtly, standing up between his daughter and Cora.

"Or Janie," Laura said with a bitterness that stabbed him like a knife.

She waited until her mother had left the kitchen again and then looked directly at her father.

"Just in front of me. Just in front of Daniel. By all means, let's protect the little ones. Their mom's in the hospital having her memories erased. If we don't say anything, theirs might go away too. Right, Dad? Just say it isn't so. God Himself would turn a blind eye, if it kept the family together, right Dad?"

Laura was unfair to him. Once Tom knew, he'd never left them alone with the old man. But he'd never let them talk about it. If he let them talk about it, sometime they might say something in front of their mother. That's what always sent Cora to the hospital. Beginning to remember. Remembering was a living hell to her—and he was never going to be responsible for sending her there, or let his children be either, for something that poor little girl had no hand in. Whatever Laura and Daniel had seen, Cora had seen and felt worse—with no one like Tom there to step in and stop it. Cora needed to believe she lived in a world where things like that couldn't happen. She needed to treat her father like the man she wanted him to be. She needed that the way the rest of them needed air. Take it away and the remembering would begin, the way it did when she saw herself in her own helpless babies and understood what could happen to them too, what a world she'd brought them to. Take that away and Cora would never leave the hospital, she might as well be dead. And for Tom, a world without Cora, beautiful, trusting Cora, was inconceivable. He would do everything he could, in sickness and in health, to keep that from happening.

Laura arrived late to the funeral. Her sisters and Tom and Cora were all assembled on the green carpet. The sun was merciless. It was just the six of them and Daniela and her two sons. Daniel's sisters had left their spouses, children, and grandchildren at home. The priest Daniel had asked for, the one with the big smile and something fishy in his wrists, rushed them through the Catholic service as if he was afraid any minute they'd object. Daniela was talking about her father when Laura came up with a crate in either hand and set them on the grass just next to the plastic carpet. A fluttering and moaning came from them. A man in a drab suit came around the awning and set down a boom box next to the crates.

"I always thought dying was the worst thing that could happen," Daniela said. "But in this last month my experiences with my Nana and my father have taught me different. I told my dad there was no need to be afraid, that it was safe to let go."

Daniela looked radiant, her face the same shape as her father's when he was a young man, her features a softer version of her mother's. Her two boys looked up at her, rapt, as if she were a vision of this Virgin their grandfather, Deeda, they called him, kept painting for his friend Jésus. "The one who went first," Daniel had said to the boys, smiling when he saw the expression on Tom's face. "The one who is waiting for me. On the right hand of the Father. Right, Dad?"

Now Tom began to understand where Daniel had gotten all that crazy stuff from. The priest talked about how Daniel was now with the Father, how he'd lived out the cross theology, the vertical and the horizontal, waving his arms like he was writing, making sure to cross the "t" when he came to it. The priest talked like being baptized into the church of Rome was a good thing. Like it erased everything.

Laura stood up after the priest said his blessing. "Daniel and I talked about how to honor his last journey, the one where he is at last free of this heavy mortal body, and we decided that it would be a good idea to release some symbols of the spirit." She nodded to the man in the suit who leaned over and turned on some music and began to read from a brochure about how the dove was a symbol of grace, and then he gestured to Daniela to come up. She looked as surprised as Tom felt. The man gestured for Tom to come too.

The man placed a white dove in each of their hands. Tom felt the dove's heart beating against his fingers. It frightened him, like he had all the power in the world, just to squeeze and keep squeezing. Daniela lifted her arms over her head, the bird moaning between them, and then she opened her hands and just swept them out into the air, the bird's wings spreading out filling the widening space as it lurched then winged free. And Daniela just stood that way for a second—her arms outspread. "I love you, Daddy," she whispered. "Never forget."

Tom held his own bird close to his chest. He could feel his own heart, so old, slowed by the heart drugs, and he could feel the dove's heart fast as a startled baby's, and he raised it up, just like the priest said, in that vertical that went straight from the fires of hell to the Father.

His legs felt as huge and discolored as his son's. How could he ask God to love him? How could he not?

"It's safe to let go, Granddad," his granddaughter whispered, just as she had to her father.

"They know where they belong," Laura said, coming up behind Tom, lifting her arms to his and covering his hands with hers, slowly drawing them away from the bird which, with something between a moan and a cluck swept out over the dry September hillsides and, joined by the other birds, settled into formation.

Tom stood with his head back, his arms at his sides, watching. He could still feel the bird's heartbeat in the skin of his palms. He couldn't move. There didn't seem to be any point. There was nothing more to be done. The birds, winging toward the mountain, began to circle back over them.

"I did my best," he said, speaking uselessly into the empty autumn air. "There's nothing more to be done. There's no undoing any of it."

"We know that, Dad," Laura said, putting her arm around him.

"He did too," Daniela said. "My dad did too. There's never going to be any relief until you accept that, Granddad. My dad, truly, did the best he could."

The flash of rage Tom felt was immediate. The sorrow was even sharper, harder. *Where did that leave Daniela?*

Tom shuddered, pulled himself together. He smiled at his granddaughter and his daughter and opened his arms wide and pulled them both close. "Enough said. Let's go join the rest."

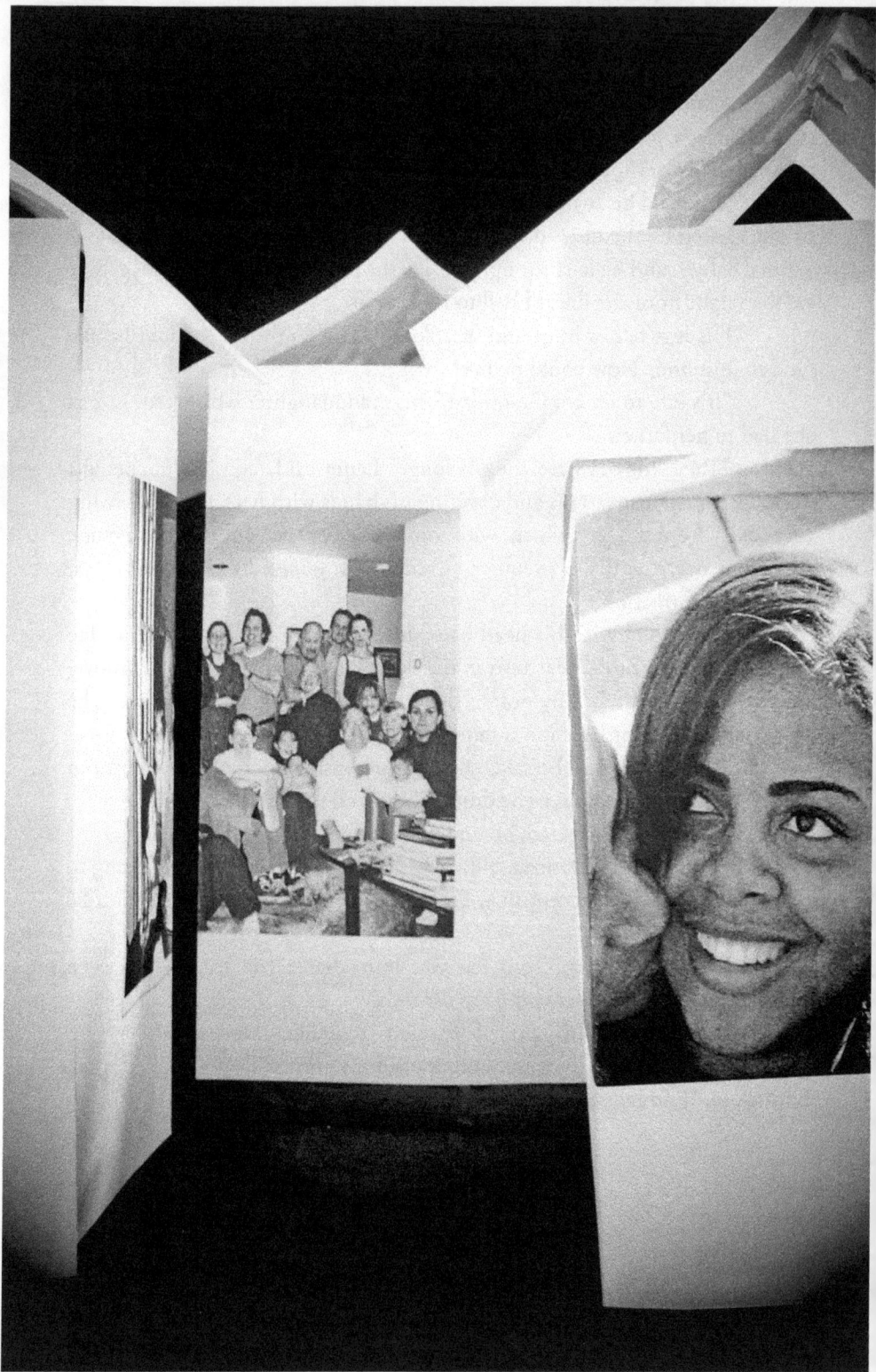

III
ROMANCE

CAITLIN BUCKLEY

IGNORANT BLISS

He's standing outside, just below my apartment window, shuffling his feet in anxious excitement. He bounces up and down on the balls of his feet, trying to pump himself up. I want to smile at the way he raises his hand to flick the doorbell then retracts just as quick.

My mouth quirks.

Bubbling, boiling bursts of dread rise in my stomach. I want to lash out. Fling open the window and yell at him to go away.

After all, this is all his fault.

He had to take the job. Across the country. Assures me we'll be fine. That we were strong. He'd be faithful. He promised. He flew away.

Two months ago, he told me on the phone in his soul-searching, soul-destroying tone that he couldn't come visit that weekend because of some extra project he had taken on because his boss asked him and he couldn't say no to his boss. I imagined him smiling and the brilliant gleam would almost be blinding enough to hide the fact that he just said the next time I would see him would be at Thanksgiving and it was so long, but he would look so good with his new haircut that I couldn't stay mad.

But after the frenzied excess of turkey day when we'd go from family to family dodging questions of when we'd get married and could it be in the summer or where will you move because you can't stay away from each other very long when you're married, we'd get a weekend. Our long weekend, he told me with a wink. I shrugged my shoulders and fell into bed hating myself, pretending that I was somewhere else with him.

The blaring ding of the doorbell shakes me from my thoughts. I turn away from the window and the bustling streets filled with people evading snowflakes who are so excited that there'll be snow for Thanksgiving because it just makes it that much more festive.

Waves of nausea roll over me.

I'd been practicing for weeks what I was going to say. I've often wondered what I would be thinking moments before someone told me life-shattering news. I hope that it's trivial bullshit, devoid of meaning and reason so that when I ruminate on it later I can say to myself, remember before *that* happened and I was just thinking about how much it sucks to be caught in the rain without an umbrella. And then I would realize that the bullshit wasn't bullshit, it had some strange metaphorical connection to the news I was about to be told.

He would be looking at me with a small smile on his face. Undressing me with his eyes, how I had never looked better because after four months he was going to be famished. And then I would tell him, and he'd never get those moments back. But at least he'd have the memory and the ability to laugh at the irony.

Before I know it, I'm at the door, pushing the button to let him in. Deep breath in. Deep breath out. Footsteps thunder up the stairs. Damn his long legs.

Closing my eyes, I take another deep breath and hold it. With a gasp, I throw the door open. He's standing at the top of the steps. Staring at me. He readies himself to speak, so I open my mouth to protest.

I need to be first or what I need to say won't be said at all. I want to tell him that I'm having his baby and I can picture his reaction as he stares at me in shock. Then a wide smile will break across his face and he'll take me in his arms and swing me around in cliché fashion.

It won't happen like that.

I look at him with darkened eyes and prepare for the breakdown.

But then I'm in his arms. And my hands grasp the dark curls at the back of his neck. He's kissing my hair, murmuring sweet nothings I can't decipher. My feet are off the ground and the door shuts. His mouth is on mine and I can no longer speak. I don't remember what it is I was supposed to say. Coherent thought does not exist. He's laid me down on the couch.

Hours later in my vague dream-filled state I feel him lift me up in his arms and carry me into the bedroom. He doesn't notice my hand resting on my stomach.

I don't tell him.

Because the snow has had a whole day's start over me and now it's covering the street. The plows have failed to keep up and if I told him now, he'd leave, but he'd have nowhere to go. We'd be stuck together and it's dark and we have all of tomorrow when we need to act together.

We're sitting at his grandmother's table and even though I know I'll be starving later, I can't seem to shovel the food into my mouth to match everyone else's enthusiasm. His grandfather, who's always been the bluntest because he's old and he can, asks us when we're having a baby. Pure panic rushes through me. This question is new and there's no way he can know because I can't be showing, but the paranoia seeps in and I feel like I'm drowning.

And he just smirks next to me and gives me a wink. We've talked about it before, but it's not something we want, at least not right now. He wants me, just me, and maybe he'll think about it later. He shrugs his grandfather off and when he squeezes my hand and notices how sweaty it is, he whispers with a laugh coating his voice, asking if I'm really that put off at the prospect of having his baby when he has too much fun practicing and you never know what might happen.

I pretend to laugh because if he knew, he wouldn't find it funny at all.

He's sitting so casual and calm, talking with my father about the next season of baseball even though this season has just ended. I can hear him from the kitchen as I'm helping my mother clean and she tells me I look like I could use a drink, but I tell her I'm too tired. And she looks at me in that way only a mother can, and I know she knows, but I can't tell her because it's too soon. There's too much that needs to happen before anyone can know.

But when we leave, she squeezes a little harder when she hugs me and I know at least I have her.

In bed, he's holding me close and whispering that he loves me, but we're both so tired because he's had too much turkey and I've had too much thinking. We pass out before anything more can be shared.

I'll tell him in the morning at breakfast, between bacon and eggs because it's the fair thing to do and he deserves to know. But when I wake up in the morning, I think he doesn't deserve anything, and what I wouldn't give to be in his position right now, snuggling against the pillow and dreaming of me without a care in the world.

His ignorance is bliss—for him.

I'm about to pick up the pillow and pummel him with it as I scream what he's done. All those frozen meals for one. Nights when I'm the third, fifth, seventh wheel because nowadays we never go out alone. We travel in mated packs, yet my *mate* is far away living in his dream world and leaving me alone for four months.

And I've never complained, but this was just one missed trip too far.

I'm clearing the dishes from breakfast, but he keeps taking them out of my hand and tossing them back onto the table. He pulls me to him and kisses me, and I get lost, but only a little. He looks out the window and tells me he loves to be trapped on long weekends by the snow.

I worry that the snow will keep him here longer.

We're on the couch and he's telling me about his life in San Diego. About his buddies and the sunshine, his work and how his boss knows his name and they play golf on the weekend. All of the celebrities he's seen because he knows that I love that type of thing and how he tries to keep track. He sighs in contentment when he says that they all loved me when I was there, I was so bubbly and bright and so right for him, but that was six months ago and I need to come back. It shouldn't always be him coming here.

He doesn't ask me to move with him, but I see it in the way his eyes squint and his nose scrunches, but I ignore it like he's ignored my signs.

When his friends call and ask him to meet them at the pub down the street, I try not to look relieved as I assure him I'll be fine here. He kisses my chin and threatens in a cute little promise that he'll wake me up later if I fall asleep. When he's out the door, I collapse onto the couch.

I'm looking out my window, watching stray snowflakes still falling from the sky. I must have fallen asleep because he's there, laughing at me for sleeping up straight against the wall as he kisses my head.

He's a little bit drunk, looking a little too happy, and he takes my hand in his and tells me how much he loves me. He can't live without me.

I'm mesmerized by how small my hand looks in his, and I wonder how small a baby's hand would look in mine. I ignore the impulse to pull back, tell him how many nights I spent hugging his pillow in the cold, empty bed. Let him flounder and drown in all the tears I've cried in place of sleeping.

Instead, I kiss him and allow him to lead me into the bedroom in the valiant way he adores.

When he finishes, he's curled around me, holding me so tight that I can't breathe. My breath is ragged, my pulse racing, but he thinks it's just from the heat of the moment and he pulls me closer.

He falls asleep in a smooth trance, and as I trace the lining of muscle on his back, I can't help but want to pinch, just a little, as hard as I can so he'll wake up and not leave me awake and alone, mind running rampant, taunting twisted thoughts that drive me insane.

We spend the entire Saturday watching movie after movie, but I watch his reactions to them instead. He seems so happy and care-free, I can't even bother to give him shit for making me watch one too many action movies.

The gory, crimson mess is a little too satisfying.

When a baby pops up on screen, he even has the nerve to laugh with an endearing chuckle, and the glint I see in the corner of his eye tells me he's thinking—*someday*—before storing it in the back of his mind and forgetting about it.

I let my eyes flicker towards my stomach for only a moment, but he catches me and thinks I'm hungry. So he runs down the street to get a pizza from his favorite place. When he comes back, he's so proud of himself for picking up on my little signals that I laugh in a genuine sort of way, but he doesn't know it's *at* him, not *with* him.

Before we go to bed, he kisses me, longer and deeper than he has before. He tells me he's going to miss me and he doesn't want to go back, but he loves it there. But he loves me here, and wouldn't it be great if there and here could be the same? The gleam in his eyes this time is challenging, but I'm too tired to argue like I would otherwise, so I tug at his head and pull him towards me. I guess it's both our faults.

In the morning, I'm lying in bed, staring at him as he continues to sleep. I'm not mad at this moment, just a little confused and a lot sad because I'll never again get to see him this way. So steady, happy, and calm. I brace myself for when he opens his eyes, and I take a mental picture to memorize the lines of his face, the blue of his eyes, the way his Adam's apple bobs against his throat when he whispers he loves me.

He's going to leave and I'm going to miss him, but I can't think about myself anymore. I made the decision and my hand is on my stomach, cradling the non-existent bump in a protective embrace, and I open my mouth to speak. I falter because he's looking at me like I'm the strangest, most wonderful person in the world.

He sighs as though he's the biggest disappointment, and I wish it was *him*.

Then he asks why I'm so quiet, so distant and far away and then he laughs because I've never been able to stop talking. He turns serious and clears his throat to inform me that it's been a long four months since we've seen each other and he doesn't want to leave me like this. He must know what it is he's done wrong and how he can fix it.

Four months, I repeat over and over in my mind. I could tell him four months.

My eyes narrow and I swallow the lump that has been sticking in my throat. My voice is unrecognizable when I tell him there's nothing *he* can do because I'm *two* months pregnant.

With a slam of the door, I know he is gone. But I've gotten used to sleeping alone.

SOPHIA J. NOLAN

NO RESERVATIONS

I apologize again, "Johnny, I'm sorry." I'm drunk on one shot, a cranberry and vodka, and lack of sleep. The light from his one-person kitchen spills into the living room that also serves as his bedroom where we lie on the bed. I'm on the bottom and he's holding himself up over top of me.

It's 2:37 a.m.

He puts his hand on my face, thumb on my lips, and uses words to make me hush. "Amanda, I've already told you, it's in the past." He nestles down closer to me and his bare chest is warm even through my T-shirt. He holds me close to himself, slides his fingers through those of my right hand and drunkenly begins to whisper.

I drive to the Whistle Stop Café in Narrowsburg, New York, just over the border from Beach Lake where I live. It's June. The sun is hot, the wind cool. It's been a rainy summer mostly, but we catch it on a good day. Johnny picks me up in his charcoal Mustang. He's late but now it's shiny and clean both inside and out. It's been years since I've actually *seen* him and I find myself surprised by the deep sound of his voice.

We race along the backroads of the boonies we've both spent good chunks of our lives in. He turns the music up loud and opens the windows. The wind sends my hair in every direction and I find myself inadvertently smiling at the ridiculousness of all of this. He grabs my hand between shifting from fourth to fifth gear, continuously speeding through the pined forests, and shakes it around in an attempt to get me to dance.

I'm too shy to tell him that I'm cold with the windows down. I'm enjoying it too much to put the window back up. I feel young and free.

He apologizes several times for the mess of work clothes in the back seat but I assure him over and over again that I don't mind at all. He hasn't seen the inside of *my* car.

He takes me to an early dinner at The Carriage House where he orders a beer and we both order sandwiches. I'm hardly interested in the food and mostly too nervous to eat, but happy to be reminded of the fact that he can carry a conversation.

I'm wishing I wasn't too nervous to talk.

The Mustang roars to life once again and soon we're racing off in no certain direction; we just know we don't want the night to be over yet.

A decision is reached eventually and we take a drive to his father's lake house. Ben, his father, and Kathleen, Johnny's stepmom, are there opening it up for the summer, airing it out and cleaning when we arrive, but assure us they'll be leaving soon. Kathleen gives me a huge hug; the last time I saw her was on our cruise to Canada three years earlier.

It feels like my family, which is close to his family, has been trying to get Johnny and me together for a while, always asking how Johnny is or if I'd seen him recently as though we went to neighboring schools, not schools four hours apart. Ben talks to Johnny like a friend rather than a son but it's nice to know they are so close in that way.

"How have you been, Kathleen?" I resort to starting our own separate conversation to avoid feeling as though I'm hovering.

Kathleen excitedly replies that she's been doing well; her smile is friendly, captivating, and unavoidably makes me smile too. I feel eyes on me and turn my head only to find Johnny taking a glance back at me.

Ben and Kathleen go inside. Nervous that he'll push me in, I follow Johnny to the end of the dock where we dip our feet into the dark, brisk water. He shows me the Celtic tattoos on the arches of his feet and tells me how they mean something about family. I tell him I don't have any tattoos yet.

His father and Kathleen yell goodbye from shore and they've only just pulled out by the time we're taking off our shirts and shorts. I applaud myself for having thought to wear a flattering bra and panties that cover my rear as I follow Johnny who jumps fearlessly into the water. I'm a better swimmer than he, but I'm deathly afraid of dark water. I beg Johnny to stay near me; he gives me that quirky, overly confident smile, his blonde beard glistening with water, and assures me he'll never let anything happen to me.

I blindly believe it, every word of it.

Eventually the sun begins to plunge below the mountains surrounding the lake and we're shivering. Kathleen left us towels on the picnic table and we grab our clothes before heading inside the cozy cottage. Johnny finds dance music on the radio and we change before exchanging massages in one of the bedrooms. There aren't sheets on the bed and Johnny's massage is rough and a little too hard for my stressed, overworked muscles, but I don't say anything. I'm just too shy to make a fuss.

It's November and I haven't talked to Johnny in too long a time.

I'm on the phone with my fiancé stuck on the only word that makes this conversation important.

"Gorgeous, what is it?" suddenly an inkling of concern strikes his tone and I picture the night he proposed, the way we danced under the moonlight to country music playing from his truck . . . the way we used to be happy, always *fucking* happy.

I think about changing my mind, backing out and not telling him, but the word finally escapes my mouth.

The line is silent for a few seconds before he utters something like concerned remarks and the only words I can't make myself brush off, "Why'd you have to tell me this now? I have so many tests this week."

I shouldn't, but I think about Johnny. Wonder what he's doing and wonder if he thinks about me just like I'm thinking of him now.

Winter break has come and I still haven't decided if it's come too late or far too soon. Going home means pretending I'm okay. Going home means not having a psychologist to keep me from falling off the edge.

"Aren't you excited to see your friends?" Katelyn asks tossing clothes into a plastic bin.

"No." I pack my things up, thinking how nice it will be to leave college behind for a while. My roommates are excited; I feel obligated to feel the same way. "But it'll be nice to go home and work, get my mind off things," I tell her.

This winter is cold but joyless. The ground is barren of color and barren of the blinding, wet, white substance that since childhood has been a happy arrival. I don't miss it. I don't miss being obligated to play in the snow.

Mid-December winds have subsided for tonight, but I still bury my hands into the pockets of my orange Northface coat just so they aren't floating aimlessly. I *want* to hold my fiancé's hand, but I *don't* want to keep pretending that his actions—or lack-there-of—haven't hurt me. We step into Sneaker King to get out of the cold and I start, "This isn't working anymore, is it?"

"I don't know." He puts his arm around me. I'm not sure if I'm appalled by this or if I wish his sudden ounce of concern had come sooner rather than too late.

"I think we should break up," I say crying, and he tells me we shouldn't do this in here.

The cold air freezes my damp cheeks. All I yearn for is warmth.

Geneseo, New York is three and a half hours from Beach Lake, Pennsylvania. Three hours from Bloomsburg, Pennsylvania.

I have to stop three times on what turns into a five-hour drive. Once to pee, twice for food, and this upsets me. My blood sugar deficiency upsets me. I text Johnny each time I have to stop so he won't think I died. I avoid turning the heat on so as to save gas and my check-engine light has been on since I left. I keep praying I won't break down. *Please, just let me get there in one piece.*

His apartment is literally a one-person apartment; there's a kitchen big enough for one, two if you stand back-touching-back, and the living room doubles as the bedroom. The closet is bigger than the bathroom. But it's quaint and warm and private. Atlas is jealous of having to share Johnny's attention and is constantly sitting between us or pawing at us when our hands aren't on him. Atlas barks when Johnny tries to kiss me or get close to me.

We let him sit on our laps while we watch a movie that neither one of us seems interested in. He holds my hand, and I feel as though no time has passed since the last time we saw each other.

Only minutes pass before Johnny offers a massage in exchange for the same. I agree—after a long, strenuous drive to see him, I need one. He goes first and I start at his shoulders, press my tiny thumbs into his muscles until I find a knot. My boney fingertips create ripples in his skin as I slide them slowly up and down his spine, searching for masses and hard spots. His skin is pale but harbors warmth, more warmth than my cold hands ever do. His dirty blonde hair curls around his cranium and I swim my fingers into it reaching for the tip of his spine. The base of his skull, the very top of his neck.

His muscles are large and strong and I remember all the talk about him working out and realize it wasn't just "talk" but action. I know I shouldn't compare people—that's just not fair—but my ex-fiancé never did anything he said he would.

I work my way down to his lower back, work on his thighs and calves and even his feet. The Celtic tattoos on the insides of both his feet remind me of the summer. They remind me of a happier time when we stripped down to our skivvies and jumped into the lake, no reservations. Nothing to hold us back.

I make my way back to his shoulders again. He reaches a hand behind and touches my leg gently. I take a deep, silent breath and reach my hand down to his. He moves to sit up and it's my turn apparently. His massages have always been a little too hard, but this time I embrace the pain. After a few seconds I take off my tee, tank top, and unclip my bra. He continues and before not too long I find a certain kind of calm in this despite my recent reservations about all human contact. His fingers feel soft against my sensitive skin despite having farmer hands. His massage has moved to the muscles just under my arms and close to my breasts. A moan escapes my lips and we're both caught off-guard by this.

Our relationship has never been sexual before this moment.

I turn over and he seems shocked—I'm shocked at myself—and he gently massages my chest and stomach. He slides down to kiss me and kissing turns into me without pants and his pants open. His fingers are magic and I realize I haven't been touched in so long, it seems. This is the moment we've been waiting for since we were fifteen years old, since we first met in my uncle's living room Christmas night. I was wearing a teal-green, long-sleeved shirt with a hood, and he was wearing a baseball cap, those curly locks falling out from beneath it.

I'm not wearing anything now.

Earlier in February I'd mentioned that I wished I could see him for Valentine's Day. I remind myself of this as I wait, crouched behind the kitchenette of the hotel suite near my college that Johnny booked for us for a few days. It wasn't hard bribing the guys at the counter to let me in despite Johnny not being with me. I sit there for some time texting him as though I'm stuck in class and I'll be just a bit late. When he opens the door I jump out from behind the counter into his arms. As he drops half the groceries, I kiss him. He wraps his arms around me still in shock. "I'm impressed," he says after we've released each other from lip lock. "It's not very easy to scare me and you have succeeded."

I smile and help him put down the rest of the groceries before disheveling the king-size bed and turning it into the stage for a sexy foreign film. He makes love to me and I work hard to hold back tears. I'm not sure if they're good or bad, but I know I don't want to be anywhere but here with him.

We go to Denny's at 2 a.m. to pick up food and then watch an old ghost movie on the television.

The bed suddenly feels like a family room.

He picks me up from class on Valentine's Day and takes me to the hotel where two dozen pink and red roses rest in vases on the marble counter top. He's cooking fish and homemade salsa. I'm so happy I feel tears.

I feel guiltier than I have ever in my life.

The woman in black appears in the rocking chair and a scream escapes my mouth. Everyone in the theater looks at me as I bury my face in Johnny's shoulder, embarrassed that I've screamed at a scary movie in public. He assures me that it's fine, even laughs and says it was cute.

I feel like a child. Scary movies are my thing.

We both wore flip-flops and opted out of warm coats. We shiver for several minutes before the car warms up on our way back to the hotel. The guilt eats away at me and I know it's because I'm falling for Johnny. I know I *should* tell him, but I also know I may lose him if I do.

I'm quiet on the car ride back and Johnny asks several times if I'm okay.

I hate that he can tell when there's something wrong. I hate that we have that in common.

We lie down on the bed and he asks for a back massage. I start to massage his shoulders before spilling my guts, "I know I should have told you sooner. I was engaged, and last semester I was raped."

Silence. I'm used to this.

"I had a feeling," he says before getting off the bed to grab a bottle of wine that I don't like. He grabs his laptop and starts playing country music off YouTube.

Several minutes pass before I lose it, begin to cry in waterfalls of passionate gasps for air and translation-worthy words or phrases, and scramble from the bed to the area where our things are strewn about. I drunkenly try to gather my things as he asks, "What are you doing?"

I want to tell him I'm going for a run, but I don't have my sneakers. I'd drive back to campus if I wasn't so drunk as to not feel my smaller limbs. And it'd be too easy to say, "I'm leaving," but I really have nowhere to go.

Nearly a month has gone by; it's March. Johnny says I have to gain his trust back. I remind him that I'm completely emotionally unstable since the assault in October, but admit that I understand why.

I'd told him I loved him the night of our fight. I meant it. He said it back.

But I'm growing to regret it.

Despite what progress we've made at fixing what was never made, I still find myself sitting against the door of my dorm so that neither of my roommates will walk in on me as I hold the razor to my leg. I'm not crying and I'm not sure why. I'd like to think it's because some part of me is stronger than I once was, but a greater suspicious part of me knows it's only because

I've reached a point of emotionless being.

I've just been here since October. A lifeless human body, breathing and lying to people, "Yeah, I'm fine."

I press the blade against my thigh and slide it down an inch or so. I press a bit harder and slide it down to match the other. I place the blade a third time and feel the metal inside me having pressed harder than I ever have before.

My leg bleeds profusely and suddenly I'm afraid because it just won't stop bleeding. One Band-Aid is not enough this time.

A week after cutting myself and then promising myself I won't do it again, I'm on a plane to Florida. I write the paper about a memoir I didn't care to read for a class I should be writing in and email it to my professor. I would normally look to a writing class as a relief, a way of expressing myself and disappearing the only way I know how to: through written word. But this class proves neglectful of my personal needs.

I call this trip to Florida my *mental health vacation* and disappear for a few days without telling nearly anyone. I assure my mother several times that I'll be fine, but she makes me call her every night anyway.

Pool side on the third day I'm not hesitant to don a bathing suit and hit the pool already aware that I bare marks most people are too nervous to question. The chlorine does them good and my cuts are healing.

While in Florida, Johnny tells me that he's in the hospital; his appendix has to be removed. It's 10:30 p.m. on the Sunday I get back from Florida when I decide to be crazier than usual.

I drive the three hours it takes to get to Johnny's apartment. I knock, let myself in. Atlas greets me, and Johnny struggles to get off the couch without hurting himself. He's got three incision sites, and I refrain from telling him that we match. Just like rape, cutting is a socially awkward subject.

Despite him having surgery the day before, it doesn't take us long before I'm on top of him being as gentle as possible.

We're careful not to get cum in his staples.

I find it ironic that I find so much pleasure in pain and rough sex after having been raped six months before.

It'd be cute if we could call it an April Fools' joke, but it's April 2nd, and I've asked Johnny to tie me to the shower and the bed. The zip ties leave rub burns on my wrists, and I like the way it feels when he applies slight pressure to my throat.

We leave the bar by 2 a.m. and I keep thinking about the drive back to Bloomsburg at 5:30 a.m. and the art critique I'm not completely prepared for. I say I want to go to bed when Johnny says he wants me to tie him up. He makes me eat a granola bar because my blood sugar has dropped. "You dying is bad," he says. It intrigues me that a granola bar can lead to him on top of me and then some.

The water for mac-n-cheese boils over by the time I'm on top of him and I run to turn it down before we continue.

I apologize again, "Johnny, I'm sorry." I'm drunk on one shot, a cranberry and vodka, and lack of sleep. The light from his one-person kitchen spills into the living room that also serves as his bedroom where we lay on the bed. I'm on the bottom, and he's holding himself up over top of me.

It's 2:37 a.m. I have to be up at 5:30.

He puts his hand on my face, thumb on my lips, and uses words to make me hush. "Amanda, I've already told you, it's in the past." He nestles down closer to me and his bare chest is warm even through my T-shirt. He holds me close to himself, slides his fingers through those of my right hand and drunkenly begins to whisper. "I've been thinking a lot about you and the future and it makes me happy."

I grab hold of his back and shoulders harder, whimpering something of a sigh.

MICHELE MARKARIAN

THE DREAM OF BOB

Last night I dreamed of Bob, now dead almost twenty years. Dream Bob was healthy and alive. What surprised me more than seeing him was the feeling that still existed between us, the feeling of two people who really knew and loved each other well.

In the dream, Bob and I are talking with each other, laughing. I am not my high school self—repressed, embarrassed by my looks and the power they seem to wield over boys, and looking for rejection. I am confident and sexual and knowing in a way that came much later. I realize in the dream that I don't need to be rejected to be alone; being alone is something I can choose myself. And dream Bob, just like the real Bob, likes me. Our connection is there, we are open to each other. He puts his arm around me several times. He is smiling, the big toothy Bob smile—he had nice, large, even square teeth—that was relaxed and happy.

"This is what was missing in high school," I note to myself in the dream. "This me is not one that Bob ever got a chance to meet. If I had been this me all along, Bob and I would not have had a relationship." We may have fooled around, but the glue that held us together—self-rejection—would have been missing.

In real life, I've made Bob into a funny story so many times that I'd forgotten what we'd meant to each other. In real life, Bob was gay and I was clueless. The first time I saw him, in the music room at Braintree High School, a wave of love and recognition and attraction came at me like nothing I'd ever experienced. He had a loose, awkwardly long-limbed body, a large head of brown curly hair, and round, deer-colored eyes. In a town of mostly Irish and Italian families, we were outsiders—he, Lebanese, me, Armenian. I knew he was destined to be my husband.

This was the 1970s. There was no GBLT Club at Braintree High School, or any other high school, for that matter. If Bob knew who he was, he kept it to himself and a few others who were like him. He wasn't lacking in female admirers, that's for sure.

Bob was a visual artist, and a good one. He also sang (bass) and acted. I drew, but not as well as he, sang (alto) and acted. I was obsessed with him. He was obsessed with whoever was his "best friend" for the moment— Walter, Joe, Mark—and with keeping me on the straight and narrow. He watched over me and protected me like a third parent, which was infuriating because I didn't want him to be my protector. I wanted him to ravage me. Then I would be ashamed of my desire. Bob was a nice boy. Most of my girlfriends in the Braintree High School Madrigal Singers were dating "nice" boys too.

Bob graduated the year before I did and enrolled at Mass Art. He talked me into going to Emmanuel College, which was right next door. This was the beginning of our end. The first week of college, all of my new friends were having a few drinks and talking about their boyfriends' penises. I was horrified—were they all sluts? Or was seeing your boyfriend's penis normal? I had never seen Bob's penis in the four tumultuous years we were together. Then I reasoned since most of these girls seemed pretty nice, they couldn't all be sluts. Maybe it was me, maybe I was ugly? But no, other guys wanted me.

"Michele," said my mother to me, "I am afraid that if you marry Bob, the marriage might not be consummated." WHAT? My uptight Armenian mother was actually afraid that I *wouldn't* have sex? This was not a good sign.

I would like to report that this propelled me to break up with him, but it didn't. What made me break up with him was that he took another girl to the movies, one from our hometown, who was even more sexually clueless than I was. My newfound friends and their sexual influence on me were beginning to make Bob nervous, and he had to go back to square one. I dumped him over the telephone from my dormitory, screaming, and then downed shots of Mogen David. I was devastated. My whole future, my beloved husband to be, disappeared in one phone call. We didn't speak for a long time. I hated him. Not only did he deceive me, but he left me, at nineteen, an inexperienced virgin. I couldn't even pretend it was a state I'd chosen for myself.

Before Bob died, he came out to me, over the telephone. "I already knew that," I said, not unkindly. "You were always two steps ahead of me," he said. But really, he taught me a big lesson. I didn't give much thought to gay people back then. After Bob and I broke up, because I didn't have the heart to tell him what I already suspected, I wrote a story about a girl whose beloved brother was gay and the injustices he faced because of it. I made friends with gay men and went dancing with them. I thought, if this is what Bob is, I want to understand it and accept it, even if he can't.

A few years ago, I found some letters that Bob had written to me while I was staying for a month on the Cape. What escaped me in the retelling of the gay boyfriend story was how much Bob and I shared—we were really good friends, despite the fact that we were always breaking up and never even came close to having sex, never mind making out. We had all the dynamics of an old sexless married couple, or a co-dependent brother and sister. Which wasn't what either of us ultimately expected from a first serious relationship, even if we couldn't say it.

The morning I awoke from the Bob dream, I was dismayed to think that I wasn't done with him yet. There had been lots of lovers, a husband and a child since I fell in and out of love with Bob so many years ago. Bob was the funny story, my gay first boyfriend.

A funny story would have been easier to let go of than somebody who, in his own way, loved me. Maybe not the love I expected, but love nonetheless. Remember this, said the dream Bob, and in doing so, I said goodbye.

CAROL TUFTS

CORRESPONDENTS

Those years I ached for you
like some torchy singer
in the records you never played,
like a dimestore gothic
maiden burning behind closed doors . . .
But we're correspondents now,
recast characters
out of an epistolary novel:
The Former Teacher and His Student.
The Former Lovers Who Never Were.

And I think how I couldn't touch
what it might have cost you then,
how I would have tossed it all
like a handful of dull coins
into the scattering air
and never cared how it fell,
how I would have made us
movie lovers at the fade out,
fireworks flaring in the background,
the ocean throbbing just beyond the terrace wall.

But we're correspondents now,
"soul mates," you write
in a language lifted from library shelves
and literary renunciations,
and I've moved on to middle age,
where you were then, and marriage,

where you are still, and I've learned
to turn a phrase as you taught me,
words chained to fence
your late confessions out.

Only they gather now to unfold you
like an easy lover lingering the afternoon,
till I come to feel what I felt once
some counterfeit constraint—
a shuttered window you might have shattered,
a one-way street you could have turned from
and sped away—a kind of wisdom
I never looked to have,
a grace so thoughtless
it keeps me before you still
the young woman I haven't been for years,
the hoarded passion you never spent
in a single squandering embrace,
the correspondent you hold now
your last dear friend
because you knew somehow
to walk away
and never let go.

MARTA TVEIT

THINGS I SAID TO ANNIE

Annie?
Yea?
Stay.
I can't.
Right.

Annie?
Yea?
Stay.
I can't.
Right.

Annie?
Yea?
Where did you put the small frying pan?
Cupboard next to the stove, on the right.
Up or down?
Down.
'Kay. Right. Eggs?
Sure.
   . . . Wait no we're out of eggs. Should I get some more?
No don't worry.
Sure?
Yeah forget it.
If you wanted some I really could get some. Did you want some?
No really I'm fine.

'Kay . . .
Yes.

Annie when does the truck get here?
Five, five-thirty.
Five or five-thirty?
The man didn't say.
Who says between five and five-thirty?

. . .

What if they show up at five and we had plans at five-thirty that we needlessly would have had to postpone because we were expecting the truck at five-thirty. Or we might have been engaged till five and needlessly rushed home to meet the truck. Separate engagements of course. Totally unnecessary.

. . .

I would even call it disrespectful. Towards us. Our schedules.
A company that deals in arranging times in which to move people's stuff. One could expect better.
Totally.
Disrespectful.

Annie?
Yea?
What does God say about spiders?
What?
What does God say about spiders?
Nothing much I think. I would have to look it up.
I think they're pretty evil-looking.

. . .

What does God say about sex?
It is right and can be beautiful when it is between a man and a woman who really love one another. That's at least what I think.
And what does God say about the thing you did to me that night in St. Augustine? Does he know about that?

. . .

Sorry. I'm sorry.

Annie?
Yea?
Will you get Christmas presents there?
I don't think so.
Why not?
Christmas is not supposed to be about the material aspects of life. Material wealth can corrupt us with false lure and distract us. I have already been blessed with the greatest gift—
Remember that year I gave you eternal rights to borrow my socks?
. . . Yea?
And you thought I was serious? Remember that?
Yea, and then you—
And then I pulled out that golden necklace from one of my dirty old socks. Remember?
. . . Yes.
Do you still have that necklace? Did you pack it?
I have it. But I'll have to give it up once I'm there.
And will you? Let them? Take it away?
. . . Yes.

Can I visit you?
No.
Ever?
No. I told you—
To forget you and date people and be happy. Got it.
Don't do this again.
You're right. Always right. Always, always, always right.

It's five o'clock Annie.
Yup.
The truck isn't here yet.
Nope.
. . .

I've been wanting to swear at you, Annie.

. . . Have you?

Yup. I've thought about it a lot. I've been wanting to swear at you pretty badly actually. Say really awful, mean things. And curse and say swear words.

Why don't you?

Well I think about that flinty-eyed matron lady we met. Sister Gail.

Yea, I imagine her scolding you there. If she knew that I'd said terrible things to you and then she'd be mad 'cause before you used to spend time with people like me and I would never want to . . . where are you going? Annie. Annie!

. . . Baby the truck's here.

. . .

. . . Annie. You need to get out of there. All your stuff is downstairs, you've got to go. It's time to—

So now you want me to go.

No! That is. I want you to be— . . . I've always— . . . That's just h—

Don't you even freaking say it—

Annie!

Jas?

Yea?

What if I'm wrong?

. . .

What if I misunderstood the— . . . What if . . . what if it's us? What if it was about us? What if our love, all love, is the highest . . .

highest . . . highest . . .

. . .

What if . . . God is . . . me? With you?

You'll have to find out.

Excuse me?

You'll just have to find out. You'll just have to wait and see.

. . . Nope.

Yup. You've thought this through, you've gone through the pros and cons, I mean, you know what you're doing here. Get out.

. . .

Get out or I'll break the door down.

Ha!

Annie . . . don't make this . . . you know what you're doing here . . . I mean the truck . . . the truck is waiting . . . you need to out-battle yourself right now.

. . . Can I cry in the truck?

Yes you can.

In front of all those mover-guys?

Sure.

Can I keep the gold necklace?

No you cannot.

Jas . . . oh Jas. Jas! What about you? Jas.

I'll make it.

Will you?

Yea. I will.

Will I?

. . . Annie I'll wait if you like.

Don't you dare.

I will?

If you wait I'll never ever—

Okay! Okay . . . Okay. Right.

Jacket.

Annie?

Yea?

Annie?

Yea?

Annie?

IV
MARRIAGE

MELANIE REITZEL

WHEN SAMBA POPS THE CORNERS
for Cpl. Paul Bang-Knudsen

I'm on a mission—is what Samba tries to communicate in the big box store to anyone who reaches down to pet her when she forms the body bubble of space she was taught to make between strangers and her master—the soldier, home now, who still wakes at night hearing gunfire when a door in a country he can't leave behind is kicked open, who can't handle surprises, not a tap on the shoulder, not a *Heya, Paul!* from across the lawn and never a burst, a shout from the dining room at birthday time, who needs to remind himself when a fork pings to the floor that he's still in the kitchen. *No need to take cover*—his black lab declares *I'm going to hit the end of every aisle, the edge of every corner before you do, where I will look to the left, to the right, and if it's a situation I will stop, I will turn and then, Corporal, I will look you right in the eye, the warning I was trained to give that says "People are just around the corner, just plain people" so come on Corporal, hold on. And I'll keep doing it so that one of these days the rattle we'll hear from over in canned goods, of a shopping cart maybe carrying peanut butter and paper towels, being pushed by a father on his way home to his family, will be nothing more than what it is; a loose wheel in need of a wrench and a couple of drops of oil.*

BIG GAME HUNTER

Looking down at his feet at breakfast they thought at first it might be fleas but he remembered that couldn't be because their dog Emmett was imaginary and they weren't animal people in any other way, so he thought it might have been the night he couldn't sleep and went down to the couch and turned on "Kill Bill" because some nights the roaring in his ears makes silence unbearable and "Kill Bill" keeps her awake, then he recalled that his foot had been sticking outside the blanket but how did the little critter, whatever it was, get in the house he wondered and she tactfully reminded him that he liked to keep the bathroom window open after his shower and that was the only window in the house that wasn't screened so maybe something got in that way and made its way downstairs to the couch—no way to know, really, but it's probably gone now, having had its fill. But later that night there was buzzing near her ears and she went *swat, swat, swat* in the dark, then there was quiet but when she woke with bites on her hands any false sense of security *looks like we got it* was gone and sure enough the night after that in bed there was more buzzing, more swatting, until he announced along about 4 a.m. *I think we're going to need a net over the bed* to which she replied *And let's order up some quinine, too* but the next morning she hears this giant *fwap!* and he says *I think I got the bugger, right between the eyes* and she thinks *How very male of him* but remembers he had been a marksman in the Marines, so she smiles instead and says *My Hero.*

GRACE

As she climbed the stairs she heard a little fluttering sound and when she got to the bedroom, she saw a small brown bird struggling against the window so she called downstairs *We have a bird up here* and he came up the stairs two at a time and closed the door to the hall and together they watched the bird flit and flap from bed to nightstand to window and realized the windows were screened so they had no way to let it out. They looked around—no basket with which to catch it, no net, so chasing it felt both foolish and necessary— then the bird landed on the thick shag area rug he liked to feel on his bare feet when he got up in the morning and they saw it was trapped in the long strands of the rug and because it was lying so still they worried it might be dead. But when they knelt down, she saw that the tiny creature's chest was rising and falling, so he picked up the rug and carried it and the bird down to the deck while she fetched the pair of scissors from her sewing kit with the thinnest blades. She worried a bit, remembering his haste when he tried to do the right thing—the chipped soup bowl after doing the dinner dishes, the coffee stains on the carpet stairs, but she watched as he knelt down and one at a time snipped at the white threads with more patience and care than she had ever seen, freeing the bird's feet, then gently pulling a strand of rug stuck between two feathers so the bird was able to flutter and fly away to the top of a nearby pine. What she decided she needed to remember after this was how he stood at the side of the bed, every single morning, the cup of hot coffee held out to her, his *Good morning.*

BARI BENJAMIN

THE IMPORTANCE OF FOLLOW-UP QUESTIONS

A few months ago, while working on a chapter in my memoir book, I suddenly recalled a memory from my early childhood. It surprised me because, though it had not been totally repressed, it was buried deep enough that I had not thought about it for many, many years. The memory was dark and scary. It came at me in a rush and settled painfully on my neck and shoulders. I couldn't shake it. So, after dinner, I decided to share it with my newlywed husband of one and a half years. We were a marriage made in late mid-life, a second chance for each of us.

"Honey," I said, "I want to tell you what happened today."

Honey stopped and looked at me.

"This childhood memory came back to me; I was only about five and I was scared for my life." I described how a family member had played a rather sadistic trick on me. I was playing outside when she jumped out from behind my white brick, ranch-style house and grabbed me around my neck, digging her fingers into my skin. My sister was ill at the time, skinny and scary looking. I screamed then, trying to shake her off, thinking she would surely kill me. I had nightmares after that and was scared to sleep by myself.

As I spoke, my eyes moistened and I looked at my husband expectantly. Nothing. I stared. *More nothing.* He just stood there, a blank look on his face for what seemed like several, long, silent minutes. Then he busied himself, removing dishes from the dishwasher. *What?* "What just happened here?" I asked myself. I just shared a terrifying bit of my intimate history and my husband had absolutely nothing to say. And what's worse, he offered no follow-up questions.

Now I adore follow-up questions. I always have. Follow-up questions make me happy. They make me feel cared for and valued. They show me that someone is interested in me. Follow-up questions make me feel connected and close.

I know I'm not the only woman who cherishes follow-up questions. My dear single girlfriends, who are out there navigating the dating world, consider this issue seriously. They listen carefully during coffee conversations, trying to determine if this guy could be an appropriate partner. Does he seem kind? Is he interesting and smart? Does he appear to be a relatively happy person? And the all important, does he ask follow-up questions when they share personal tidbits about their lives? Nothing turns my friends off more than guys who only talk about themselves, or who quickly change the subject when they attempt to share their stories.

I wonder, is this a gender issue? In my professional life as a psychotherapist, I have worked with many couples who have been dissatisfied and unhappy in their relationships. I frequently hear these complaints from my female patients: He just doesn't care what I think *or* he never listens to me when I talk *and* he has absolutely no idea who I am.

I remember one couple I worked with on and off for several years. In the beginning of treatment, they were clearly emotionally estranged from each other. They seemed more like distant roommates than caring partners. Each spouse oozed an angry, defensive veneer that turned their communication into sniping matches. Simple exchanges of information became opportunities to shame and degrade each other. I wanted to help them get to the root of their anger. After much probing, it became clear that each spouse felt devalued in different ways. The vicious cycle was that she couldn't express affection because he couldn't show that he heard her when she talked. So she just stopped . . . talking and loving.

I gave them an assignment to begin at home. They needed to find a time when they could devote just fifteen minutes of uninterrupted attention to each other. Then they would start with simply describing their day and each partner would ask for further details. Ah, the beauty of follow-up questions. They would divide the time as evenly as they could. At first they resisted the assignment. This was no surprise as ingrained patterns are hard to break. I continued to encourage them, and one day they walked into my office and I sensed a subtle change. I could see it in their body language, the way they turned toward each other, the way they looked at each other. The ice was broken.

I inquired about their fifteen minutes. They nodded and spoke hesitantly at first, then expressed how it made them feel. The gist was that she felt understood (something I think we all wish for from our partners) and he was able to respond to her positive feelings. Soon, they were touching each other when speaking, holding hands and kissing goodbye in the morning. I marveled at how something so simple could make such a difference.

Back at home, my relationship was not going so well. After several attempts to talk to my husband, I finally lost it, forgetting entirely the rules of fair fighting.

"What's wrong with you?" I exploded. "Is it that you don't want to hear about me or is it that you just don't know what to say?" (I had heard that men often feel flooded by our emotions. I was hoping that was the reason.) This time I didn't wait for a response. My weeks of frustration spilled over, and I stomped out of the room, slamming our bedroom door. We went to bed angry that night, something I swore I wouldn't do. The air was tense between us the next day *and the next.*

Then he came home with an idea. "Listen, I've been thinking about something." (Much later he confessed that his idea really came from his therapist.)

"Oh?"

"We should try having a special time to talk, say after dinner. You get fifteen minutes and I get fifteen minutes. We can say whatever is on our minds and the only rule is that we give each other our full attention. What do you think?"

What do I think? Should I tell him I use that strategy with couples all the time? Would I be raining on his parade, so to speak?

So I said, "I think it's a great idea. Can we start now?"

And so we began. Our half hour of talking, listening, and asking follow-up questions, usually after dinner, has continued for months. What a change in our relationship! I feel connected in a satisfying, kind of visceral way. I feel loved and because of that, feel more capable of loving. I don't care about the dishes left in the sink. I don't worry about the unmade bed. It's so much easier to keep the little things *little* in my mind now.

This morning, I had some free time, so instead of rushing out of Starbucks, precious coffee in hand, I was able to relax at a small table near the window. I glanced around me and diagonally to the right, sat an elderly couple, deep in conversation. They looked to be in their mid to late seventies. Her face was lined with wrinkles; her gray hair was haphazardly pulled back behind her ears, and clipped with a large barrette. He had little hair, and his large belly protruded outward. They stared intently at each other, shifting and moving their bodies seemingly to the flow of their conversation. I couldn't take my eyes off of them. I watched her long, wrinkled fingers graze his palm, back and forth, back and forth. I saw him rub her elbow, around and around the pointy bone. It was both sexy and sweet. And they never stopped talking, questioning, answering and laughing.

I thought, this is what I want. I want to be eighty years old, looking into my husband's warm, hazel eyes and feeling that spark, that knowing of each other that can only come with years of honesty and self-revelation. Years of continuing to love each other, despite our flaws and the parts of us that aren't so pretty. My heart felt full when I left the coffeehouse. I couldn't wait to share my feelings with my husband so I rushed home, knowing that he hadn't left for work yet.

"Hey," I called, "I want to tell you what just happened." I described the elderly couple, who appeared lost in each other. I stroked his hand as she had done. I rubbed his elbow as he had done. Tears glistened in my eyes, as I conveyed my wishes for our future. I stared into his warm, hazel eyes. My husband stared back, saying nothing. *Not a word.* But this time, I smiled patiently, knowing exactly what I would bring up in my next fifteen minutes.

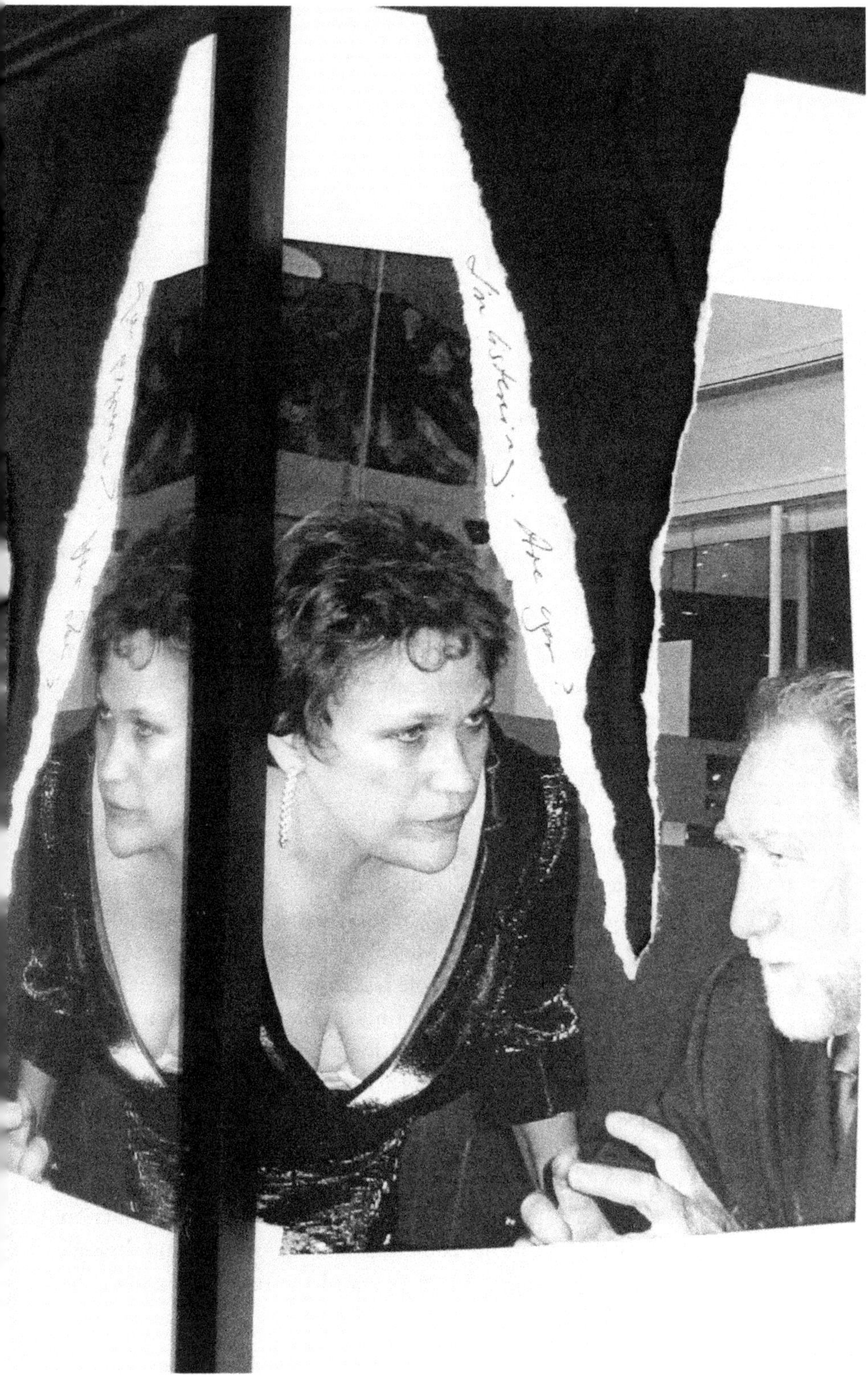
I'm listening. Are you?

PATRICIA BARONE

THE MOVING-DAY RESTAURANT

He was only nine and didn't even have a girlfriend yet, but he knew what his mom meant when she said, "Luke, sit at the table with your wife!"

His dad lowered his big head over the plate—the way his mom told him, his sisters and brothers not to do—and ate so fast that by the time she'd served everyone, he'd taken his second beer back to the shop, and Luke was glad.

Letting out a big breath, his mom sat down and closed her eyes before she ate. Luke knew she was as happy as he was that nothing happened. Once, when Luke helped himself to the last roll, his dad pushed his face into a plate of red beans and rice.

During college, graduate school, and his first job at a small paper in Minnesota, Luke had imagined returning to New Orleans with a wife and living in Uptown, four miles and a world away from Mid-City and the shotgun bungalow on Salcedo Street where he was born. On the first night, he would take Helen to a four-star Creole restaurant.

As he'd planned, they arrived in time for dinner, but Helen said she was too tired to rummage through boxes for her good clothes. So instead of taking the streetcar to Commander's Palace, they walked to a store-front eatery advertising Spanish and Chinese food.

It was so dim in the restaurant that it took some time to adjust their eyes. When no one showed them a table, they took one silhouetted against a sliding glass door leading to the courtyard garden. After eight hours on the road, it felt good to sit in the late afternoon sun, still shining through the catawba leaves as a torrent of rain bounced the rubbery leaves of the kalachoes.

Helen looked at him and laughed, a rainbow prism falling on her light hair. "I'm so tired I'm not hungry, but what's that appetizing smell? Tomatoes sautéed in butter?"

"Or garlic and caramelized onions?" Luke looked at his watch—they'd been waiting ten minutes.

"*Perdón!* I'm sorry to be slow. We make it up to you!" One of the waiter's small black eyes closed. "Menus, wine!" With a flourish, he poured a small amount of dark red malbec for Luke, who swirled the glass, sniffed, tasted, and smiled. The waiter filled their glass globes past the usual halfway mark—"On the house!"—then walked rapidly away.

"I bet he's the owner," Helen said, "despite his ruffled sleeves and embroidered black bolero. Just to be perverse, I'm going to order an egg roll appetizer."

No, they didn't have any Chinese dishes that day, the man said when he returned with bread, olives, cheese, and olive oil. No pincho, no cuttlefish tapas, no *pulpo a feira*. "But for an entrée, you will have seafood *paella*, and for your first course, *gazpacho!*" He turned. "Ah, here she is—I present my wife, Ramona Álvarez Delgado, well known in Spain and France for her Carmen! *For you*, she will give her last performance before we leave tomorrow for Barcelona."

"I'm surprised your restaurant is open tonight," Luke said. "You must be busy."

"Ah, we were packing and forgot to put the closed sign in the window!" The Señora adjusted the combs either side of her upsweep, laughing low in her throat. "*No importa!* Such a pleasure to serve young lovers!"

The Señor joined her on a dais with his guitar. As she sang, Luke's eyes brimmed. He made a quick swipe beneath them then took Helen's hand. Señora's voice soared over and over with longing then fell into stillness. Luke felt her last few notes fall inside himself; he came out of his trance with a start when Helen started clapping.

"That was *Cançó d'amor* by Enric Granados. I'll sing one more from his *Cançons Catalanas*, and then I will serve your soup."

As she sang, Luke noticed the way the lines in her face disappeared. When she finished, she was old again.

It struck Luke that his thick gray hair might make people think he was older than he was, but he sank deeper into the only chair, its padding bursting out in cotton dribbles. The others, even Sam, the shrink, slumped back on cushions strewn against the wall and over the mattress-like covering on the floor. The group bellowed a collective roar. One man kept shouting: "I won't let them! I'm strong!" Luke closed his eyes, opened his mouth, and said, "Ahhhhhh!"

Emotional release bullshit! He felt foolish.

At Holistic Therapeutics, it was Monday for Adult Children of Alcoholics, Tuesday for Hypnosis Therapy, Wednesday for Astrology Seminar. And every Thursday Luke entered the padded room, as the group called it, for Stress Therapy. It was sound-proofed.

The pretty one—Sally—sat on some cushions by his chair. Next to her was a large blonde, Mamie?; a short gal with muscular arms, who bared her teeth in a smile; a dentist named Wrench—or did he imagine that? A veterinarian sad as a bloodhound; a woman like his Aunt Doris in drag; then skinny Jim who had fetid breath when everyone exchanged a group hug to begin the session. Why in hell had he come? He wasn't that bad!

The room got hotter with the press of bodies, the push of emotions, and the stories—sexual abuse, infidelity, an estranged child, a career-ending accident—a litany of human misery. Souls crying out to the god of recovery. All that was missing was the response—a loud *Ora pro nobis!* or Pray for us poor schmucks.

"I'm trying to recover from anorexia," Sally told the group. "And my divorce."

Luke's turn, but how could he tell Sally, all of them—What an improbable coincidence, like a bad play! "My ex-wife was anorexic. We got divorced. Her idea."

Sally looked up at him. "I'm sorry, Luke."

All Luke could manage was, "Me too. Sorry, I mean, for your situation. Tough, huh?" Sweat beading along his hairline, he folded his arms across his chest to keep himself contained.

It was odd, meeting as if for the first time on a date. He knew so much more about her after seeing her crying over her ex-husband, head pillowed on Blondie's well-padded shoulder.

"Why did your former wife go to restaurants with you?" Sally asked.

Luke leaned toward her. "She stopped going. The two of us were an unhealthy pair, she said—both too interested in food. Dinner is a time for us to talk, I told her."

Up close Sally's eyes were green not gray—lovely, accusing. "People talk when they go to museums and the beach. Or on walks. Why did it have to be over food?"

"I had to eat out as part of my job. I'm a restaurant reviewer and travel writer for the Minneapolis Star Tribune. Helen used to be my photographer. She changed her job, to news photos."

"What did she mean—too interested in food? I mean, I understand where she was coming from, but you?"

"Exactly, Sally! How was *I* too interested in food? As my first work partner—at the Times Picayune in New Orleans—she should have understood. My work brought me steady raises and allowed her to travel all over the world. Early on, we won prizes together."

Sally frowned. The paper napkin frayed as she twisted it. Such slender hands. Luke felt an impulse to put his hand on hers, stop the constant fret of her fingers.

"Did you try to understand why eating out was hard for Helen?"

"I tried to help her. I told her it would do her good to relax, enjoy the different tastes."

Sally shook her head. "My ex told me something like that, and I said he hadn't listened to me—all the time I was talking he was thinking of a way to solve my problem!"

"What's wrong with wanting to help?"

"I asked him to just listen. Till I felt stronger, I didn't want to put on dinner parties for his clients and those politicians he had to impress. He was watching to see how much I ate. He cared more about how I functioned as his wife than about me."

"How do you mean?" Luke shifted. Helen had accused him of much the same thing.

"It wasn't a good sign, my ex said, if the hostess pushed her food around her dinner plate." She paused, then added in a low voice, looking at her hands, "I thought he understood me but refused to admit my viewpoint. Now I think he was unable to even imagine being me."

She stood. "He's no longer my problem. Back in a sec."

The swing of her skirt as she walked—she wasn't about to take on another problem. In her eyes, he was another clumsy clod, but it was better to have Sally think he was dense than a jerk. If only they were on a real date. Instead of coffee at Perkins, it could have been cabernet sauvignon and cordon bleu at the four-star La Nouvelle Cuisine. Goddamnit, the shrink was right—Sally was turning into Helen.

Their non-date was a sort of role-playing. Transference didn't just work between psychotherapist and client, said the shrink. Clients heal faster if they worked out their issues together. Do it over till you get a better outcome, like in *Groundhog Day*? What if it wasn't better? Wasn't that the definition of hell? Luke never thought he'd go into therapy, but maybe he'd want to get up in the morning if he spilled it out. Not just to a shrink, one man judging him. In a group, someone might understand him. Others would talk when he didn't feel like talking. Now he couldn't escape. Almighty Sam ordained it: Luke and Sally—a perfect therapy team. Recreate the tension you had with your former spouses, then change it!

"Yes, your ex is a clod, and I'm another." Luke stood up. "Let's go, Sally. Walk while we talk. I'm not going to take this sitting down!"

She looked at him, a worry line between her eyebrows, before she smiled. Holding the collar of her windbreaker up around her face, she shouldered the door open. Luke tried to hold it for them both, but it almost hit him on the backswing.

He steered her abruptly to the left where the trees in the park deflected the gusts pulling strands of curly brown hair from her low ponytail.

"Didn't you want your ex to show up for your events? What did you ask him to do?

Sally sat on a bench. "I told you. I asked him to listen to me."

"He should have, but that went for you too. He made a living by schmoozing, right? Did you expect him to hire another hostess? His administrative assistant? By the way, what's he do?"

"Owns a lobbying firm. So you think it was up to me to help him with his business!" Two red patches were forming below her cheekbones. Like he'd just slapped her.

"Married people help each other," Luke said without conviction, not able to meet her eyes. When had he ever been able to help a woman?

"I didn't want to help him *that* way, and I hated it when he tried to fix me so I could!"

Luke lengthened his stride to keep up with her rapid pace.

"How much I ate was my business. I had better things to do than be his hostess! I was—am—getting my master's in nutrition. I knew how to keep myself out of the hospital."

"Wow. Not sure what my role is here," Luke said. "I say the same things your ex said?"

She nodded, the red slowly fading from her cheeks.

"Sounds like you figured out where he went wrong with you. So shouldn't you be able to start a new life with someone different?"

"Eventually. I need to start over with myself—find out why I feel so sad. It's strange; when I was with him, I felt threatened."

Luke finally lowered himself to the floor and joined hands with the woman next to him and, after a moment's hesitation, the man on the other side of him. Sally was sitting across from him. After the ritual greeting, everyone reported on progress and setbacks. As usual, Luke passed.

"You remind me of my father," the wiry little nurse said. "He sat around with a sneer on his face, and my mother would say, 'Tell me what's wrong!'"

"Like my husband," Blondie said, "you don't know your own feelings! Luke, I'd like to bop you over the head!"

The bat was foam rubber, but Luke, trying to laugh, backed away.

Skinny Jim cleared his throat and said that when Luke was ready to talk, he'd talk.

Luke gave him a sheepish grin. Men had to stick together. The women didn't like him. So he tried, words forced out on exhausted breath—"Can't get over my divorce. Don't know what else to say." How much easier talking to Sally! If she didn't go away, he could work it out.

During the group hug, Luke noticed that Jim no longer had bad breath. Probably had a wife to clue him in.

Luke stopped rowing in the middle of the lake. "Our marriage started so well—we had fun. I'm so angry at her for spoiling it! At the same time I feel like a failure. When I met her she wasn't trying to starve herself."

Sally nodded. "I was fat when I was a teenager, overweight when I married."

"I still think about the day we moved to New Orleans. Helen and I were the only ones in a restaurant. Sun through the foliage outside made a soft green light inside, on our table, the walls. The food was superb, and Helen enjoyed every bite. The woman who sang for us recognized how much we loved each other. It was meant to be. *We* were."

"Doesn't it hurt to believe that now?" Sally looked at him. Though the sun had burned away the morning mist, she still wore a long-sleeved white shirt. "Want me to row?"

"No." Her wrists looked too fragile for oars. "I want to ask you something," Luke said. "I can't talk to the others the way I talk to you, and I don't see how I'll ever be able to—Would you continue to see me if I quit the group?"

"I'd be afraid to!" Her full lips set in a firm line, she leaned forward and took the oars from him, turning the boat so the prow cut into a speedboat's wake. "The waves almost caught us broadside!"

As she slipped into his seat, Luke said, "Sorry!" and moved in a crouch to her seat, conscious of the extra pounds he'd gained over winter. Their rowboat bobbed in the swell, and their words collided—"Are you afraid of me?" "Without Sam, we'd make each other worse!"—and she dipped the oars, pulling in a steady rhythm toward the shore.

"Maybe Sam is a bad therapist," Luke said. "He put us together!"

"Because we're bound to repeat our old patterns, so he wants us to do it consciously, try to change. Ever gone out with a fat woman?" She had beads of perspiration on her upper lip.

"No. But I love to see a woman enjoy her food. It's sexy. Did you ever see the movie *Tom Jones*? There's this scene where Tom and this woman have sex after staring at each other while they devour roasted meat. . . . Sorry— Guess that scene strikes you as repellant?"

The rowboat bumped against the dock, and Luke secured the rope.

"No," Sally said. "Freeing! As long as the woman didn't throw up afterwards."

Luke took her arm, meaning to help her out of the boat, but she said, "Got it, thank you!" and swung herself up by way of the pier strut. She would have looked cocky except for her tears.

At the next session, when it was Luke's turn, he said, "If you wouldn't be too bored, I'll tell you more about why I . . ."

"Why you're depressed," Sam said, and Luke was surprised. He'd never thought of himself as depressed. Just temporarily out of sorts.

Luke looked at Sally, who nodded. He took a deep breath. "My life hasn't turned out right. I told myself I'd give my wife a better life than my dad gave my mother. I was determined to be a better man than he was. My mom worked so hard that she died young.

"Once she visited me when I moved into a campus dorm. I treated her to a fancy restaurant for lunch, but she only picked at her food. She said she couldn't swallow a bite, worrying how I was going to pay for it. Even after I reminded her that I had a scholarship and worked, she ate less than half and had the waiter box up the rest for me.

"Over dessert, I got up the nerve to ask her why she was still married to my dad. She said her reasons wouldn't make sense to me because I didn't understand marriage. I still don't! My father treated her like his servant. I treated my wife like a queen, and my wife divorced me!"

"Good for you, Luke! You're here to get mad!" Sam said, shoving a mattress at him, the signal to start pounding.

"Let yourself go, Luke!" Blondie said and threw the bat at him.

He caught it in one hand, and whacked the wall. Too damn flimsy, so he flung himself down face forward. On his knees, he pummeled a pillow with both fists.

"Yell!" Sam shouted, "from the belly, cuss like this!" Sam put back his head and roared, "Fuuck! Fuuuck! Fuuuuuck!"

"Ahhhhh! Ahhhhhh!" Luke wanted to punch Sam not the mattress, but he pummeled away until he fell forward, exhausted.

"Good work, Luke," Sally said. Then all the others were around him with hugs and pats on the back.

"Welcome to the group," Sam said. "Welcome to the human race."

Was he really like everyone else? Luke felt drained but unreal. Like an actor in a movie.

His mom always took the seven of them to Saturday matinee, cartoons and Gene Autry. Once it was *Night of the Living Dead,* which gave Luke enjoyable goose bumps. When the ghoul kid began to eat his own mother, one of his sisters screamed, so his mom hauled them all up the aisle and each one got their 40 cents back. Then she took them across the street to see a soppy movie with kissing. The next Saturday Luke said he wanted to play baseball instead, but she said, *Oh Luke.* Saturday movies were their family tradition, and she needed him to help with the little ones. She looked so disappointed that he went along.

While Luke wrote Sam's check, Sally was buttoning her raincoat. Was she lingering on purpose?

"Coming along with us for coffee?" she asked.

"Where? No one said."

They started up the stairs at the same time, bumping into each other. She chuckled, and Luke hung back to let her go ahead of him. Her scent was fresh, like Ivory Soap.

"Just Perkins." She put up her hood. "Have to get going?"

He opened the door for her and a blast of rain smacked them.

"No." Luke said. "Hope you understand, but I don't want to be with a crowd just now. Especially after I—"

Sally nodded and, with a wave, started to go down the walk.

"Wait!" Luke hurried after her, almost losing his balance in a puddle. He grabbed her arm to keep from falling and almost brought them both down. "Sorry! How about just the two of us?"

Sweet and Savory Cafe specialized in appetizers, wine and craft beer. Awarding three and a half stars in his review, Luke had put it on the local gourmet food map.

She ordered tea, and he asked if she wanted to look at the menu. When she declined, he was about to insist when he remembered what she'd said about being watched while she ate.

Before taking a second sip of his merlot, he said, "I'd like to tell you more of my story."

"You're not going to tell the group?"

"I don't know—maybe I'll want to tell them too, maybe not. Do you mind?"

"Yes." She held her steaming cup of mint tea under her nose. "But go ahead."

"Well, everything was great for us at first. Our expense accounts took us to the best restaurants—Antoine's, Gallatoire's, Corrine Dunbar's, Masson's Beach House. And La Ruth's—you haven't lived if you've never tasted Warren La Ruth's roasted rack of lamb, marinated overnight in rosemary, olive oil, and lemon!" Luke looked down at his menu—what a stupid ass he was. Going on and on about food to an anorexic!

"Makes me wish I was there right now," Sally said. "That lamb sounds so good."

"You look so surprised—Your ex must have explained that she didn't lose her appetite? I love the taste of food. The problem is, when it's in front of me, I feel out of control and that's awful. I'm working on that."

"Would you like to work on it right now? These portions are very small." Luke's stomach rumbled loudly, and he felt his ears get hot.

Sally's laugh was deep, continuing even when the waiter came to take their orders. Finally she subsided into hiccups. "Sorry. I didn't mean to . . ."

Luke ordered sourdough rolls and artichoke dip. Taking a deep breath, she ordered the roasted vegetables. "I used to just eat lettuce." As the waiter turned away, she asked for wine." I've never been to New Orleans. Did you and Helen like living in Louisiana, Luke?"

"I'm from New Orleans. Didn't like it much growing up. Especially after my mom died. My brothers and sisters moved away like I did. After my dad died, I moved back and it was a great city to explore with Helen. At first, she loved the way people celebrated life—let the good times roll, all that. Then she got uptight."

"Uptight—that was the worst thing you could say to someone in our generation. My ex called me a tight ass." Sally broke off the tip of a roll and swiped it with a thin smear of dip.

Luke looked away from her. "Talking to you is an emotional mine field. I'm sorry."

"*You* didn't hurt me. When did Helen start limiting how much she ate?"

"After we lost the baby. She loved being pregnant, said she felt like an earth mother when she got bigger. Then she developed gestational diabetes. The baby was stillborn."

"Oh, that's so sad! For both of you."

"It was much worse for her."

"And afterward she starved herself?"

"She lost 70 pounds, forty more than she'd gained. Tall and only 90 pounds, she looked cadaverous. I brought her milk shakes, begged her to eat, but all she could see in the mirror was her neck. She still had a soft diagonal crease when she turned or bent her head. It was her bone structure, the way her chin was, a family trait. It didn't matter—she was beautiful."

"Did you tell her she was beautiful when she was pregnant? Were you as happy about her pregnancy as she was?"

"In my ideal of marriage, neither my wife nor I would be tied to home because of children! My mother hated housework. When I was older, I took over some of the cooking."

"You were a good son," Sally said.

"Had an ulterior motive—wanted to get out of watching my brothers and sisters. What was your family like, Sally?"

"Only child, so I wanted a big family. We have one child, who lives with me, a sixth grader. My ex loves her but didn't plan on children. I forgot my birth control pills."

"On purpose?"

"Mostly. I'd taken a few then accidentally left them home when we went on a weekend trip. I deliberately didn't take the rest when we got home. I was angry at him."

"Was it fair to go ahead without his buy-in?"

"What sort of question is that!"

"I'm—No, I'm not going to apologize. Think about your question— Did I tell Helen she was beautiful when she was pregnant! What did you expect? That I said she was fat?"

"Guess I did. You're my ex—remember? That's how he made me feel, and all the while he craved another woman with big breasts. I'm sorry I judged you."

"I was out of line. I'm sorry too." He was very sorry he didn't have the guts to be as honest as Sally was. "No one makes someone else feel something, do they?" The words out of his mouth, Luke groaned. He didn't mean to challenge her. He really wanted to know.

"Makes—no. I was, am, responsible for myself, but he knew my weaknesses."

Now Sally's eyes were gray, not green.

Luke winced. What he'd said to Helen when she gained enough weight, but not too much, was just as manipulative as telling her she was fat. He told her she looked like a model.

"Think I'll take some vacation time next week." He hadn't planned to say that, hadn't even asked his editor for the time off. "You've given me a lot to think about."

"Works both ways. Look! I cleaned my plate."

She looked so absurdly proud of herself that he wanted to hug her. Her face was soft, pink. He imagined putting his lips on the slight line encircling her neck just below the curve of her jaw. As if she were his own familiar love.

Two months after Mardi Gras, beads and crumpled confetti still littered the creases of the streets. The city didn't feel unfamiliar, just off kilter; the streets radiating from Lee Circle seemed random. Like a pack of cards, shuffled, fanned, and dropped—thumbed and dirty.

"Look—a Civil War relic!" Sally said, pointing to an antebellum mansion between two shops on lower St. Charles Avenue.

"Just a broken-down set for Streetcar Named Desire," Luke said. "Rooms by the night or week." The taxi stopped a few blocks away at the Old Oaks Hotel, the same chipped stucco building where he and Helen first lived till they bought a home. "We don't have to stay here," Luke said. "Six blocks uptown, and it's the elegant Garden District and university section."

"Do what you need to do, Luke." Sally got out of the cab.

"Thank you," Luke said and meant it.

Sally's resistance to his impulsive travel invitation had only given way after she talked to Sam, who advised her not to foreclose a chance to break old habits. Luke, who thought deferring to a shrink was as bad as getting a priest's blessing, made the sour observation that Sam could hardly advise against their trip after marrying one of his own clients.

Before they'd left, Sally said she'd pay for her own room, as well as her plane ticket. Separate rooms seemed best before they left, but when they parted to wash up, and he heard her door lock click in place, Luke felt deflated.

Except that once, they'd never even held hands outside of sessions. Nonetheless, he'd been hoping that sensuous New Orleans might prompt Sally to remove her clothes for him.

No, Sally was right. There was also the problem of Helen. Three people in a room was one too many. What if both his and Sally's rooms were once a part of the apartment he and Helen had? Same floor—he could almost detect the fragrance of Delmonico's take-out.

He didn't want to ask the desk clerk if the restaurants he remembered still existed. Or the movie theaters where he began to imagine his future.

Before Luke got his driver's license, he and his current girl had to catch a ride with his mom to the matinee at the Coliseum or Saenger theaters. Girls liked the same kind of movies his mom did, and they said his little brothers and sisters were cute. "Only from a distance," Luke said.

So he and his girlfriend sat in the second row, not in the back with his family. During *North by Northwest*, when Cary Grant kissed Eva Marie Saint, Luke kissed his girl. During the crop-dusting scene, she clutched his arm, which made him feel strong, but the part that made Luke think he could have a better life when he grew up was when they watched Cary and Eva safe together while the police searched the train for him. Luke's girl whispered, her breath tickling his cheek, "When we're older, we'll go on a long train trip and have romantic dinners. I'll wear a low-cut cocktail dress."

"The Caribbean room in the Pontchartrain Hotel is just a few blocks away," Luke said, so they walked, which helped him get his bearings in a city that seemed smaller than he remembered.

Ordering only small amounts of food seemed to put Sally at ease, so Luke got the oysters Roffignac. Sally ordered chardonnay and another appetizer, oysters Bienville.

"Sally, after I first told you about the moving-day restaurant, you asked why I was so sure that Helen and I were meant to be there together. Because it was serendipity, karma! The owners left their door open by accident. I think they served us their own dinner."

Sally nodded, but her eyes looked sad. When Luke got to the part about Señora's concert tour, Sally put down her tiny seafood fork and interrupted him. "Did you believe her?"

"Why, yes! Her voice was velvety, unforgettable! They showed us a photo album with pictures of them on concert tours—their whole life together. I thought it was remarkable the way they shared it with us, two strangers."

"Why not? With the two of you, they had a captive audience."

"It makes me shudder—revealing my private life to anyone I don't know."

"I know. During the last group, you were very brave."

"Thank you. Well, our difficult times came years later. We were busy going to places like Arnaud's. Even Billie's Sandwich Shop—sounds mundane?—seafood gumbo, *coq au vin*, and Peking Duck. But when Helen stopped going out with me, I redoubled my efforts to find the moving-day restaurant. I thought I'd located the storefront where it used to be, but that block was being gentrified. Helen suggested that maybe the Señor and Señora had meant they were closing the restaurant for good, not just for the time they went on tour. So I sort of gave up.

"Then, on an assignment to review Dooky Chase, a soul food restaurant, I went to the Treme neighborhood in back of the Quarter. Next door was a small Creole bungalow advertising Spanish food, so I asked the Dooky Chase hostess about it. She said César Delgado owned it. I went home and told Helen, and she said she couldn't bear to hear Señora Álvarez-Delgado sing again! I begged her and, finally, she agreed to meet me there after work. It was summer thunderstorm season. Afternoons the clouds dumped rain, but that day it held off till I got to the restaurant around 6 p.m., just like the first time. I moved to a table at the back next to a picture window. Señor Delgado didn't recognize me. Well, why would he? But I felt disappointed. After I ordered a bottle of malbec, I waited almost an hour for Helen. Then the Señor asked me, was I expecting a blonde lady? Helen had come before I arrived. She'd asked about his former wife, he said, then left."

"Oh, Luke . . . Helen didn't even call you. Did she say why she stood you up?"

"The charade was over, she said. She was going into treatment because she wanted to gain enough weight to get pregnant again. She'd rather go to a sperm donor than stay with a man who didn't want children."

Sally clutched the sides of the table. "What did you say to her?"

Luke hesitated. He had to keep Sally on his side. "I told her I would change."

"I longed to hear those words from my husband! I should have done what Helen did, but I was too much of a coward." Sally stared at him, her lips parted. "Luke, that was so clumsy of me! I didn't mean that Helen did the right thing in regards to you. The opposite!"

"I know you didn't mean that." He reached for her hand, and she didn't withdraw it. It made him feel worse, how much she trusted him.

"God, if I hadn't been such a coward, maybe he would have respected me more." She lowered her head and dabbed at her eyes.

Luke reclaimed her damp fingers. "I respect you so much—your ex was a fool! You were trying to be true to yourself. That's not cowardly."

The waiter was about to approach, but Luke caught his eye and shook his head. "Sally, don't you think we should stop beating ourselves up for what we should or shouldn't have done in the past? Just for tonight, at least?"

After that, everything happened the way he'd dreamed. He fed her one of his oysters Roffignac in exchange for one of her parmesan-crisped Bienvilles. He smiled, thinking that oysters were said to be an aphrodisiac. They ate them all, then, hand in hand, they left.

The next day, they checked into the Cornstalk Hotel on Royal Street. "Aren't you an Iowa native, Sally? The original 19th century owner had the wrought iron fence made to console his homesick wife."

"Sweet," Sally said. "Look at the pumpkins below the corn! Peter, Peter, pumpkin eater . . ." She looked at him. "Ooops—Sorry."

"Don't be. Had a wife. Couldn't keep her."

"Anything else you need to do, Luke?"

"I was thinking of Delgado's restaurant. You could take the curse off."

He couldn't bear to see anyone's face. Sitting against the wall, Luke bent over, his forehead almost touching his raised knees. "No one came to greet us when we arrived. No one else was in the restaurant the whole time, even though it wasn't raining. We sat by the window until the Señor served us gazpacho and paella. It was even more delicious than before, so much . . . fun." He heard his own voice as if it were a robot's. "We were toasting each other's progress, when my cell phone rang. I excused myself, telling Sally it was work, but, by accident, I selected the speakerphone. Sally heard: 'Luke, it's Helen. I don't want you to come over!' I told Sally I'd explain, went to the men's room and promised Helen I'd stop calling her.

"I came back to an empty table—Sally'd left.

"At the hotel, she asked me what sort of game I was playing—why didn't I say that my ex-wife moved back to New Orleans? Then she left for the airport."

Luke raised his head. "Have any of you seen her? Sam, has she called? I don't deserve to be happy . . . she does! . . . I *hurt* her . . ." His words jerked out between each sobbing breath. "I *lied* to her!"

He put back his head and howled, and they surrounded him. A hum of voices, a warm pressure of hands.

TIM MYERS

HUSBAND AND WIFE: HARD TIMES

How easily it changes,
as leaves do in the darkening of the year—
how root-like it remains, though altered.
He's loved her for so many years,
anniversaries keeping pace with the solstices,
and now watches quietly as his own heart
learns a new form of desire for her. Underground,
all goes underground, waiting,
there is certainty in love
but passions shrink into themselves,
a quiet of deep ground settles over their lives
as these hard years unfold. One night
he hears wild honking from somewhere above the house,
geese crying ghost-like—runs out to see
the shifting lines of white bellies high overhead
as the flock sings its way back home through darkness.
Someday, he tells himself, standing in the empty street,
Someday,
weakened by having witnessed such ecstasy
but understanding the earth more
as love becomes a darker thing.

AT A CERTAIN POINT IN A MARRIAGE

He longs for her and watches how she moves,
dreams of laying his head against her breasts,
listening to her heartbeat. He wants
a secret quiet place where they can be alone,
he wants to tell her every thought, speakable
or unspeakable, that lives in him, would give
all he has to listen to her own. But so much
comes between them; for a while he must be
content to watch her as she moves.
So much comes between them—necessities
of living, and of this life they've made
together—even the breakfast table, here, now,
as they sit on either side of it.

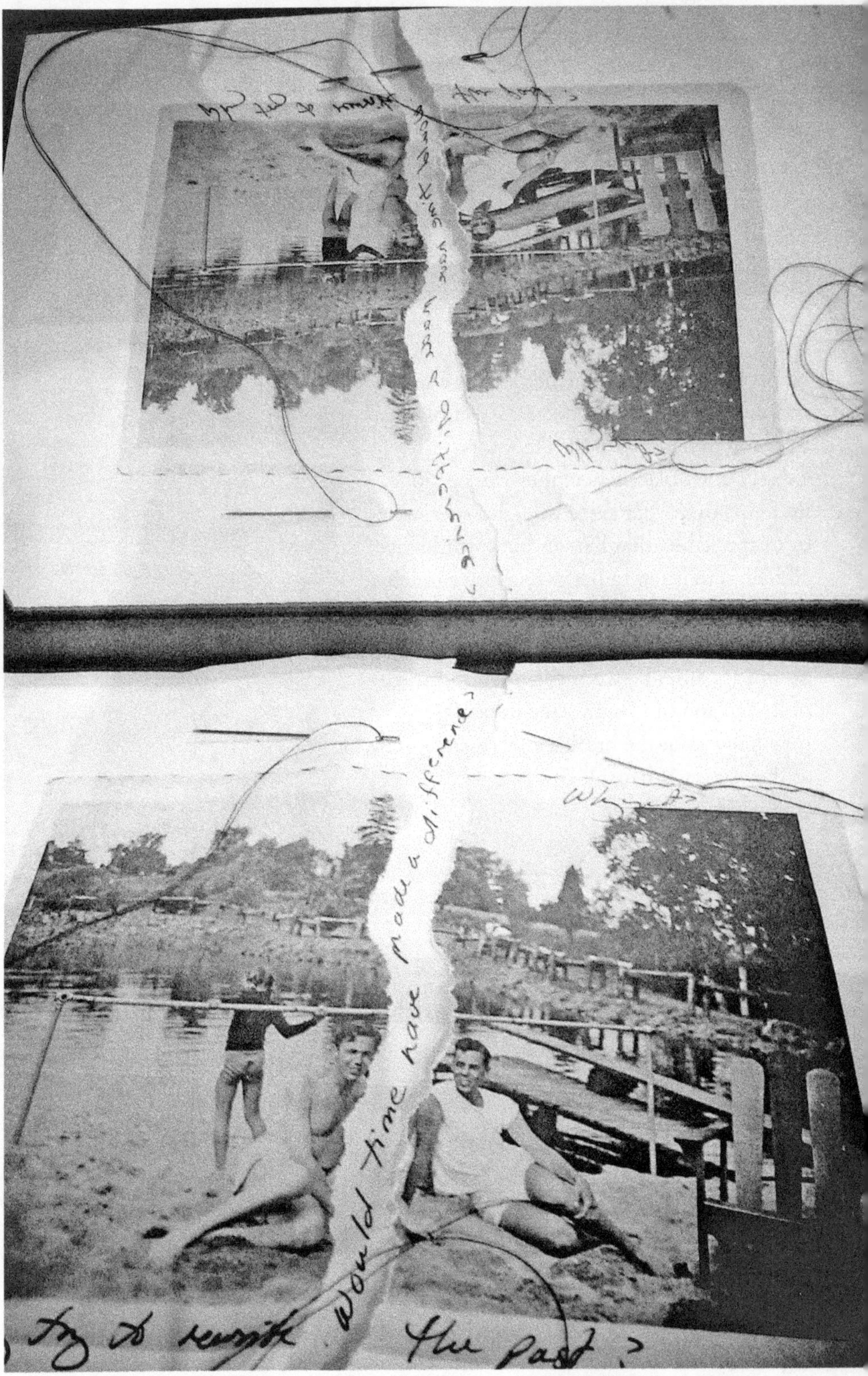
Would time have made a difference?
the past?

WILLIAM HENDERSON

SCAR TISSUE

I sought D out intentionally, or someone like him. I logged into a Web site that boasts it has more than 60,000 men online at any moment. D lived nearby. We listened to the same musicians; we read the same books. He asked me to bring wine and chocolate.

His pictures did not do him justice. He had a British accent. He was interested in me, which surprised me. While he and I were together, I waited for him to realize he could do better. Which I guess he did, in the end.

But before that, he asked me to date it out and see where a relationship could go. My wife and two-year-old son were putting puzzles together a few feet away from me when I told D I would be his boyfriend. She did not know about him; he did not know about her.

Holly and I met in college, and I asked her to marry me six months after our first date. I married Holly because I loved her, but also because I was afraid of what not wanting to marry her meant. I've always known I am gay, and so did the kids with whom I went to school. I was the faggot. In fifth-grade sex education, when I asked if two men could have a baby, the guidance counselor made it clear that two men could not have babies together. I was convinced he knew I had asked the question, even though we had been allowed to ask questions anonymously.

After Holly and I stopped having sex, we decided to have a baby. We used in-vitro.

Holly and I were strangers who shared a bed and bathroom, and then we shared a son, Avery. She focused on our son, which meant she wasn't focusing on herself, or on me, or on herself with me. She stopped seeing me, or maybe we stopped seeing each other.

Marriages, and the people inside of them, fade. You wake up one morning and you wonder how the person next to you got there. You don't want to be there beside that person. You think there must be someone better suited for you out there. You think you got married too young, or maybe that you don't have to be afraid anymore.

D told me one night that his mother had cancer. She had beaten it before, and she was planning to fight again. He told me he understood if his mother's cancer was too much for me.

"As is," I told him. "I promised to take you as is."

He had promised me the same thing. Repeatedly, he promised me the same thing.

Years before he and I met, on a night like most other nights, D cut both of his forearms. One cut was too shallow; the other was too deep. His scars were thick and uneven. I always saw his scars when I looked at him. I always kissed his scars when I was with him. He said he wasn't suicidal, that he just wanted to feel what bleeding out feels like.

"Why do my scars fascinate you?" he'd ask me.

"Because they tell me who you were before me," I'd always say.

"Scar tissue," he'd say, "is stronger than skin."

He and I didn't reveal ourselves to each other all at once, but by volleying these kind of stories (this story was brutal; other stories were not) back and forth, we discovered that we each had shattered pasts, and these similarly shattered pasts probably made each other more attractive than we would have otherwise been.

D and I started talking about marriage, despite my unwillingness to move in with him and how our disagreements were becoming arguments, were becoming door-slamming fights.

Always, we'd make up.

"It's taken me this long, and I've gone through so much to get here to be with you," he'd say. "Why would I ever want to throw it all away and never find happiness?"

"You could find happiness," I'd say.

"Could I?" he'd ask. "You think you could find something equal to or better than me?"

"I think I could find something different," I'd say.

"Usually, when you leave something good, you should have an upgrade in mind."

I couldn't see a life where I have to constantly come out. Me with D meant constantly coming out, and then explaining who Avery was. He is my son, but D wanted a legal tie to Avery. I thought Holly would move away once I told her I wanted a divorce. I couldn't lose my son, even if keeping him meant staying in an unhappy marriage.

Holly asked me one night if I was willing to try to conceive another child. We'd have to go through the in-vitro process again. Our first try had resulted in our son. She miscarried our second and third tries. I thought that a second child would be a good parting gift. No, that's not the right way to put it, but that's kind of how I felt.

When I told D that Holly was pregnant, he was understandably upset. A decision to have a second child with a woman he still hadn't met should have involved him, D told me. Wasn't he my partner?

I apologized. Of course I apologized. But I told him I wouldn't apologize for wanting to have another child.

Yes, months into my affair, and he still didn't know about her, and she didn't know about him. Or, they knew the other existed, but didn't know the extent of my separate relationships with them.

D accepted the baby. Of course he accepted it. As is and all.

But something had shifted. One morning I woke up and no longer recognized the shape of my relationship with D. Our arguments felt seismic. He started getting high several times a day. One night, he snorted pills.

"I wish you wouldn't do drugs," I told him.

He told me he would stop getting high once he and I lived together.

After I knew I would never see him again, I made sure he knew I had been married the entire time, not to hurt him, but to let him know how much I had been willing to give up for him. I wanted him to know how disappointed I was that he had been unwilling to make similar accommodations.

I told Holly the story of me and D in the middle of the afternoon on a Wednesday. We sat on opposite ends of a couch she and I had bought more than a decade ago—the first real furniture we had bought together—and we interacted as though we had not sat on this couch together most nights since the Saturday it had fit through a front door that was smaller than the couch is wide.

She took off her wedding and engagement rings later that day. I took off my wedding ring. Each time I had seen D, I had taken off my wedding ring, but I felt its absence for the first time the afternoon I sat with Holly, ringless.

I moved out one month later. I live less than two miles away from her. We passed our son back and forth, and after our daughter was born, we began passing her back and forth, too. Holly's family urged her to move away and take our children with her.

"He's their dad," Holly told her parents. "They need a father."

For a while, I think she and I were in shock. We interacted with each other as if we had survived something horrible. We did survive something horrible. All Holly asked was that I try not to talk about how badly I felt about my relationship with D ending. I would cry, and she would ask me if I was crying for her or for him.

She didn't really have to ask; she knew the answer.

One afternoon when Avery, who was three, and I were watching *Toy Story 3*, I cried at the scene when Andy drives away from his toys, from his best friends, and Woody sits up and watches Andy's car disappear in the distance and says, "So long, partner."

Avery noticed, patted my back, and told me it was going to be OK. I picked him up. He laughed, and I wanted to laugh with him, but I couldn't laugh. He kissed my nose, and then he rubbed his cheeks against my beard.

"Scratchy daddy," he said.

"I love you, baby," I said.

"I love you, daddy."

In time, the aftershocks of my affair with D stilled. Holly and I brokered an uneasy peace that has evolved into a stronger relationship than our marriage had been.

"I'm grateful for our rediscovered friendship," Holly told me that first Thanksgiving after I had blown a hole in our lives. "I think prior to everything, you had misery and unhappiness disorder."

"That's not a real disorder," I said.

"Doesn't mean you didn't have it."

"I'm sorry," I said.

"Don't apologize. Look at how far you've come."

"I know," I said.

After my affair with D ended, I lost sixty pounds, started running five miles a day, and developed a six-day-a-week yoga practice. Find balance in yoga; find balance in life.

"You're finally who you're meant to be," Holly said.

"I'm sorry I made life miserable for you," I said.

"I'm sorry I couldn't see you."

"You were not why I was miserable and unhappy," I said. "You were neither the problem nor the solution. I love you, and I always will. I am glad we're raising children together. You're my best friend."

"Thank you," she said.

Our daughter, Aurora, was born in December, thirty-three days before the one-year anniversary of my meeting D. I knew, then, that I shouldn't count days in terms of D, but I couldn't help but count days like this. And I tried to remember everything, convinced, as I was, that D and I would find each other again, and still feel like puzzle pieces clicking into place.

But I was wrong. Eight days before Aurora's first birthday, after moving to the small town in Kansas where his sister lived, D committed suicide. The police investigator assigned to D's case could only tell me that his death was ruled a suicide; he couldn't tell me if drugs were involved, or if D intended to die.

I called Holly, who was at her apartment with our children. She cried, for me, I think, but also for D, and for the love I felt—feel—for him.

"I'm sorry for your loss," she said to me.

"I'm sorry that he didn't know what else to do," I said.

He's gone, and I'm not, and I spend most of my days with my children, and some of my days with Holly, because she and I remain a family, albeit one legally dissolved. Or, at least, our marriage has been legally dissolved.

Dissolved. An interesting way to describe a relationship.

Sugar cubes dissolve, as does ice. Coffee grounds dissolve, as do salt and Aspirin and bath salts. Water, a required ingredient for dissolution.

However submerged and waterlogged, families do not break; they simply untangle and rearrange, because scar tissue is stronger than skin.

Sean said, The question is will I ever answer it?

WENDY JONES NAKANISHI

A STITCH IN TIME

I once believed that what had been broken could never be repaired. I felt that when something had gone wrong, it could never be made right. I had seen lives wrecked by acts of selfishness and brutality. It seemed that the survivors of tragedy could never recover, that they were doomed to wander the earth, visibly marked by misfortune, shunned by the happy and the secure.

It was my parents' marriage that inspired such reflections. They had married in their early twenties. Children themselves, spoiled by doting parents, they had no business getting married, let alone having children of their own.

Their wedding is immortalized in large, matte photographs. My mother is beautiful, wearing a white silky gown and pearls, her long brown hair falling around her neck in curls, her face radiant. My father is impossibly boyish and thin, a lank of hair charmingly awry, falling down his forehead. They look like blushing teenagers, stunned at their good luck, expecting a grown-up to intervene, to put a halt to the charade of such innocents entering into relations requiring gravity and maturity.

The ceremony was performed in the little white church of the tiny central Indiana town of Mount Summit. The reception was held at my grandfather's house, known as "The Maples" for the avenue of maple trees leading up a long lane to an old white two-storey farmhouse that is encircled by a large porch, its yard full of trees and flowering bushes.

The photographs depict a long-ago world. All the men are slender but muscular, individuals used to physical labor wearing suits and ties; the women are buxom and assured, dressed in their best finery, corsages pinned at the shoulder, contented, well-fed faces shaded by hats. They are pictured in rooms decorated with sprigged wallpaper and antique furniture and mantled fireplaces. Or the guests wander outside, around the front garden of a house that is isolated in the depths of the rural Midwest, surrounded by fields of corn and tomatoes, with the nearest neighbors over a mile away, housed in another farmhouse reached by a narrow dirt road. The friends and family of the bride and groom carry plates of cake or sip tea from delicate china. My mother's grinning nephews, aged eleven and thirteen, are caught out in acts of mischief—soaping the windows of the car that will whirl my parents off on their honeymoon, for example—and are pictured being admonished by their elders.

Even in these early photographs there is a hint of the troubles that will follow. In one, my mother's smile is marred by a smudge of lipstick on her upper front teeth; in another, she looks disheveled, exhausted by the demands of what is supposedly the happiest day of her life. My father seems to be gripping her hand with unnecessary force as they cut a three-tiered wedding cake with a single knife. My paternal grandmother is pictured clutching her eldest adored son in a possessive embrace. My father's younger brother fails to merit a single snapshot; my mother's elder sister glowers in a corner, looking indignant at being up-staged by the girl whose birth she so fiercely resented as a sixteen-year-old only child.

It is a remote world I can only glimpse in these faded old photographs that must have cost a pretty penny when they were taken. My optimistic maternal grandparents had splashed out on a professional photographer, blissfully unaware that the couple whose wedding they were celebrating was to divorce acrimoniously fifteen years later, after having four children within the space of the first five years of their married life.

I am not one of those individuals blessed—or, perhaps it is a curse—with total recall of my existence, from intra-utero through to the present day. My earliest memory is of being held on my father's shoulders as a toddler, watching a fireworks display. But old photographs confirm my parents' recollections that I was an unusually unhappy infant. I have been told I rarely slept and that I was always crying no matter whose arms were cradling me. I see fading pictures of a baby with a halo of dark hair framing a scrawny face positioned around the large O of a wailing mouth. My older brother and two older sisters sit around me, supporting me with bemusement as I look into the camera with an expression of what seems to be a sorrow beyond the power of assuagement.

In retrospect, it seems as though I was prescient, sensing I was an unplanned-for child born into an unhappy household. The infatuated couple that had wed with such fanfare soon discovered each other's inadequacies.

My father was very attached to his mother, a spare, stern woman who was fanatically tidy. My mother had been used to being waited on by her own doting mother and felt little inclination or disposition for housewifely chores. As the babies arrived in quick succession and the mounds of dirty laundry grew higher and the house more and more untidy, the mess and the noise increasingly infuriated my father while my mother, expecting assistance, love and sympathy, grew equally incensed. They blamed each other for failing to live up to the standards of their fairy tale wedding.

By the time I arrived, many things had been or were being broken. My brother has often told me the tale of how he returned home from elementary school one fine spring day to find my mother standing in the road outside our little house, methodically smashing my father's prized record collection. My mother felt her own childhood had ended when a naughty little boy, a cousin, broke the treasured collection of salt and peppershakers she had kept in an elaborate cabinet in her bedroom at "The Maples." I recall a chair being broken as my parents tussled in the kitchen of our own home. One of my sisters broke an arm roller-skating outside the small-town bank where my father worked as a manager; he refused to take her expressions of pain seriously and it was another day before she was taken to a doctor and had her arm set and put into a cast.

Any peace that might have reigned in our house was daily shattered by arguments between my parents. Even our car was destroyed when my mother managed to stall it on a railroad tracks outside the tiny town we inhabited; naturally, it got hit by a train before the vehicle could be pushed to safety.

My mother was a vain, affectionate woman who happened to be physically rather clumsy and, in temperament, inclined to laziness and self-indulgence. In these respects, she was quite unlike her own mother, who was one of those individuals gifted at everything and anything: a reasonably skilled pianist, a famed Scrabble player, a sweet, unassuming woman who managed a large household with unobtrusive skill, who could kill and pluck chickens and whip up a huge feast with seemingly little effort at all.

Similarly, my father was strikingly unlike his father. Although my father was the first in his family to go to college and eventually to get a doctorate, to become sufficiently wealthy to build his own home and to indulge in foreign travel, I think he may always have harbored a lingering suspicion that in some way he was inferior to his father, who was a skilled craftsman employed at a furniture shop. Dad lacked any mechanical aptitude at all, needing to ask my stepmother to perform such routine household tasks as mending plugs or even changing the proverbial light bulb. It was a matter both of chagrin and pride that his father had chosen to bequeath his tool box to my father rather than to Dad's younger brother, my uncle Jim. The tool box lay untouched for many years in an ornamental utility shed sited near my father's expensive lakeside dwelling, with Dad periodically dusting it off and remarking to us on the irony that it had been left to him, a man with absolutely no use for it.

It seemed, when I was a child, living in the sprawling old house that my father had abandoned when I was seven, to pursue his career and to find love with a new woman, that life would never change. My mother would continue to lie in her bedroom upstairs, eating chocolates, reading magazines and nursing a broken heart; our home would become ever more dilapidated and uncared-for; my brother and sisters and I would lead a nearly feral existence, quarreling among ourselves, dressed badly, an atmosphere of depression palpable in our lives.

For me, at least, "The Maples" represented an oasis of calm and even blissfulness in this otherwise gloomy period. My parents used to leave us there when they went off on holiday; after the divorce, mother was encouraged to drop us off to spend most of our long summer holidays there. I would arise with a feeling of happy expectancy, delighting to hear my grandmother's light footsteps in the kitchen below as she hurried from her wood-burning stove to the table and then to the shed to fetch more kindling. I had many favored destinations: a silo filled with corn cobs; the barn, with its loft of slippery hay; a corn crib in a field far from the main house that I thought of as my own private place; a neighbor's house two miles down the road, where there were children nearly my own age.

But I soon learned that it is all change. My grandmother died of congestive heart failure on my tenth birthday. My grandfather died a year and a half later. The doctors returned a verdict of pneumonia, but I knew that he had died of a broken heart, unwilling or unable to carry on without his beloved wife.

Both my sets of grandparents celebrated their fiftieth wedding anniversaries. My parents could barely force themselves to stay together for fifteen years.

Both my grandfathers were skilled with their hands. Grandpa Jones, as I have mentioned, was a carpenter and craftsman. My mother's father, Grandpa O'Harra had a wonderful little shed situated between the windmill beside the kitchen door and the road leading to the barn. This shed, usually kept locked, smelt of motor oil and housed all manner of wonderful machines, including a mechanical grindstone.

Are people who can make things happier than those who cannot?

When I was a little girl, I had three dreams: to have long hair, to have a horse, and to marry a farmer. Only the last has come true. Through an odd turn of events I never could have foreseen, I have ended up in Japan, married to a Japanese farmer. But would Grandpa O'Harra even consider my husband a farmer? Perhaps he would have called Takehito, who grows flowers, grapes and oranges, a market gardener.

But although my husband fails to own acres of land stretching to the horizon or to have any farm animals apart from the chickens we get our eggs from, I feel quite certain my dear grandpa would have taken to and heartily approved of my dear husband.

It is shaming to admit but, when we first married, I almost felt as though I had married beneath me. I was a university professor in Japan, a highly respected profession here but my new husband was a struggling farmer and certainly not considered a desirable "catch." Luckily, appearances are deceptive or, even more importantly, they are unimportant. It is what lies beneath the veneer that is of value. Before our marriage, a dear English friend described my fiancé as a "gem" and, in the twenty years we have been married, I have come increasingly to appreciate the accuracy of her appraisal.

I had hopes of becoming a writer. I had flattered myself that I was "creative." To my chagrin, it is Takehito who is the truly gifted and creative individual of the two of us. He can turn his hand to anything. He is a skilled carpenter who has built not only bookshelves, toy chests, tables and chairs in our home but also a considerable portion of the house itself. Five years after our marriage, after coming up with a design to his specifications, he arranged for the requisite materials for a log home to be shipped to our city in Japan, along with a crew of six American carpenters. The basic structure was put up within a month, the Americans departed, and my husband devoted all his spare time in the year following to mastering all types of new skills: laying a tile surround above the kitchen stove, putting in flooring and doors, painting and papering walls.

When our three boys were of an age to be interested in building things themselves, he helped them make kites and origami creations, to put together elaborate Lego creations and to assemble the complicated robots the boys were fond of. Now that our sons are older and largely independent, my husband continues to indulge his passion for "making" and "doing." He has single-handedly constructed two small log cabins in our large garden, one serving as his workshop and painting studio and the other as a special room, complete with a sofa and a piano and a desk, curtains and carpeting, for our youngest son who had clamored for a place of his own. On Monday nights he takes African drum lessons; Tuesday afternoons are given over to watercolor painting classes; Thursday evenings he studies French; Friday nights, he ventures to a city five kilometers away to practice harmonica. He spends many nights at the kitchen table, sketching flowers and fruit. I no longer need to worry about presents I can take back to relatives in the States; I simply beg Takehito for a few of his wonderful drawings to give away. But my husband's greatest love, his favorite hobby, is gardening, and he has transformed the area to the west of our house, once a small orange grove, into a magical green place of trellises draped with rose vines, of flowers and ornamental trees, of large stone basins filled with water, algae and tiny fish.

Whenever something is broken—a plate that has cracked, a video player that refuses to work, a clock that has inexplicably stopped—my children and I simply put it on Takehito's desk at night and find it miraculously repaired the next morning. Similarly, he is our family tailor: he needed to sew labels on all the children's school uniforms and nowadays, usefully, he can be counted on to sew on buttons or to hem and make alterations to our clothes. He has even re-covered the seats of our set of matching kitchen chairs.

I like to think that my husband's gift for mending what is broken or ripped has a metaphorical dimension. Certainly, it has a pedagogical value. When we first were married, I was prone to tantrums and sulks, unconsciously mimicking what I had seen my own parents doing. From the start, Takehito refused to engage in such behavior. He would not respond; he would sit quietly, as though my words were blows he was silently absorbing. At first, this infuriated me even more; eventually I found his even-temperedness soothing and even inspirational.

Too, I used to be famous for breaking things when I was in a rage. I would slam doors, I broke two windows in the family home as a child, and I once threw my sister's glasses and smashed them. I feel so relieved, as an adult, to have foresworn (mostly!) such childish ways, coming to the realization that any act of destructiveness harms the perpetrator as well as the ostensible target.

This was a lesson I felt I had learned from the negative example set by my parents. After my father left, my mother ended up drifting in and out of relationships with unsatisfactory men, alienating her children in the process and, in the final years of her life, she had to be consigned to an assisted living residence facility because she had never really learned to take control of her own affairs. My father had happily remarried a much younger woman whom, he supposed, could care for him in his old age, but she developed a genetic disorder that made her a wheelchair-bound invalid dependent on his care. He remained a querulous individual, stingy emotionally and financially with his children, always wanting to be the center of attention at any gathering, selfishly ignoring any pain he might occasion others. I still find it difficult to mourn his passing.

What is the basis for a loving, lasting relationship? My two sets of grandparents not only adored but also respected one another. They managed their marriages in quite different ways. Of my father's parents, my grandpa seemed quiet, even shy while my grandma was the loud and domineering one, a perception contradicted by my father's reminiscence that as a child it was his father he was most afraid of. My Grandpa O'Harra was fabled for his teasing, and his wife was his principal target. But I remember it as a very affectionate teasing that was generated by love, never by malice, and after Grandma O'Harra had passed away, we all were stunned to see our magisterial, powerful, wonderful grandfather reduced, at times, to whimpering misery, remembering her, thinking of his great loss.

My own parents, on the other hand, not only engaged in physical violence but, perhaps even worse, in belittling each other, the latter a dangerous habit I nearly fell into myself, after marrying my Japanese farmer. Dad also was unable to abandon his mother's family's predilection for arguing about anything and everything, almost as a form of entertainment.

There is a saying in Japanese to the effect that we cannot be friends with everyone. I quite agree but, equally, I have come to adopt, to the best of my ability, the Biblical injunction that I try to be on good terms with all whom I encounter. I feel it was quite fortuitous that I happened to end up in Japan, where displays of temper are interpreted as a sign of reprehensible weakness, as a humiliating loss of self-discipline.

The Japanese have been mocked as a people who lack the ability to be individuals, who always need to do things in groups. It was a stereotypical image that I once shared, but prolonged residence in this country has taught me otherwise. Now, I marvel at their inner resources and ability to control themselves, their friendliness and helpfulness, their stoicism and courage in the most difficult of circumstances. As Marcus Aurelius once remarked, the truly great man is he who has mastery over himself, not mastery over legions of armies. The former is much the more difficult achievement.

At one point in my life, when I was smarting from the pain of the breakdown of a long-term relationship, when life in Japan seemed too stressful to cope with, when I was troubled by obscure desires and longings, I felt control of my destiny slipping from my fingers, that my life might drift into directions I dreaded but was unable to avoid. I could imagine adopting self-destructive ways. I wondered if my future might turn out to be a bleak one despite all my hopes and dreams and efforts to succeed. At this critical juncture, I happened to meet a solemn-faced young Japanese farmer. Takehito stepped in and, with his quiet resolve and cheerfulness, proved an example that represented a kind of "stitch in time" that prevented any further unraveling. Although he is a practical, reserved man, not given to any expression of romance, somehow he managed to repair not only my broken heart but to mend the whole of me, allowing me the freedom to choose to resume to try to forge the future I wanted for myself.

It is said that we are the choices we make.

JANET LUNDER HANAFIN

AT LAST

"I'm sorry, Kathy."

That was the last thing he said, two hours before he died. His eyes were closed, and he was cold, so the hospice blanket, a hideous polar fleece affair with ducks and cattails and big black dogs, was pulled up to his chin, covering his arms and hands. We weren't touching. I wasn't holding his hand, and that's what I regret most now. I sat close to the bed, looking at his face, shrunken and yellowed, through aluminum bed rails.

For what?

I didn't say it, but I wondered. In fifty-eight years of marriage he had never before said he was sorry. So now, for what?

He didn't say it when he broke my grandmother's teapot, the one with the daisies. It was the first year we were married. He tossed his barn jacket at a chair in the kitchen, but aimed too high, and it hit my precious teapot, the one of which she had always said, "For you, dear, for when you marry your true love." It crashed to the floor and shattered. Only the little round top was whole. I have kept it ever since in my top dresser drawer, wrapped in tissue.

He didn't say it when he backed over the little mama cat, my favorite, when she was sunning herself in the driveway and he was in a hurry to get to town. I had her buried in the orchard before he got home with the part for the separator, and we never said a word about it.

He didn't say he was sorry when the pigs got out and rooted up my dahlias, the ones that were the most beautiful ever, the ones I was going to take to the state fair. I helped chase those nasty critters all over the section, all the way to the Eckles place, and when they were finally back in their pen I went in and made supper—pork chops—and then I went out and dug up the dahlia bulbs and threw them into the pig trough for their breakfast.

Was he sorry when we had to sell my engagement ring to make the mortgage payment the winter after the hail wiped out the corn? It was all we had. There was no crop, nothing to buy food for the cows, so he had already sold them. My ring. It was a beauty, not big, but a perfect diamond. When he gave it to me, when he asked me to marry him, he said he wanted me always to have the best. It brought enough to get the bank off our backs, and the next year the crops were good, but not good enough to get another ring. He never asked if I wanted one.

He stayed in town on Saturday nights drinking at the saloon with his pheasant hunting buddies. I took the kids home and got them to bed, and then he drove himself home in the old car. One night he finally wrecked it and Bud Jones, the town cop, brought him home and told me, with a wink, that I had to get him home earlier. Maybe he didn't remember Muriel Sands sitting on his lap in the back booth. Bud didn't tell me, but Doris Osvaag did, and Tilda Gresham, and Minnie Belz, who didn't even see it but heard about it from her brother-in-law. He never said he was sorry.

When my sister died, he helped carry the casket, and he sang at the funeral as she had asked, but he never took me in his arms and said, "I'm so sorry, Kathy. I'm so sorry."

He was strong, and he worked hard, and we were able to send the kids, all four of them, to college. When John, who was our only son, didn't want to farm, it broke his heart, I know, but he found good renters and we built a house in town. There were no pigs to root up my garden, and my big orange cat stayed safely in the house. And then his back began to ache. The pain got worse day by day, and finally he went to the doctor, who sent him to the hospital for tests.

Pancreatic cancer. How long? We don't know, Dr. Drager said. Maybe a few weeks, maybe longer. With pancreatic cancer we can't make a reasonable guess. We can control the pain. We can make you comfortable.

And it wasn't long. Only six and a half weeks until it was time to go to the hospice. They gave him morphine, so he was dopey and sleepy, not even restless. The girls came and went, talking softly, saying nothing.

John called from Kuwait. "I'm on the first flight out in the morning, Mom. They gave me a compassionate leave. I'll fly commercial from Germany. I'll be there in less than two days."

"Talk to him now, John," I said. "He will hear you. The nurse said hearing is the last thing to go."

So I held the phone to his ear, and I could see his lips moving as I heard John sobbing, telling his dad to hang on, that he was coming.

Susan fell asleep in the recliner, and Linda and Darcy went to the lobby to lie down on the couches. That's when he said it, so softly I think I wouldn't have heard if I hadn't been looking at his face, if I hadn't seen his lips move.

"I'm sorry, Kathy."

I couldn't ask, for what. So I said what I always did when, every morning, he told me he loved me.

"Me, too, Dave. Me, too."

V
BEREAVEMENT

JUDITH GOEDEKE

DAD

your rich dark chocolate voice stopped singing
musical compositions were torn up and thrown away
a box of playful drawings and tender poems was exiled to the cellar
as your radiant lyrical soul suffocated under a desk job
figuring profit and loss
for men with delis and taverns and sheet metal plants
writing numbers into orderly columns
your handwriting barely controllable
you went days without speaking to us
prayed the rosary on your knees, arms stretched out
a daily crucifixion
drank yourself soft in the night
you gave it all away, lived someone else's life
all for us
and it was not enough

it felt like sparklers inside
a hissing barrage of haywire electricity
at ten my room was impeccable
I cooked, set the table, cut the grass
kept my little sister out of your reach
we went hungry and wore orphan clothes
in a neighborhood with lawns and azaleas
you smiled at strangers, nothing was too much trouble
that was the scariest, you could turn it on, turn it off
I threw myself into schoolwork
a haven, ridiculously predictable
I was a shape shifter, invisible and silent

feeling your feelings while mine went underground
I did it all for you
but it was not enough

there were moments, though
when grace just wafted in the window
I pitched, you caught, gave me pointers
you took us to the Smithsonian
hugged me hard when I won the spelling bee
these were dreams wrapped in silk sheets
but bizarre, out of character, not to be trusted

I couldn't wait to get away from you
lived with a man who was no good
because I had no dreams
never expected a normal life
but I wanted to try to live better
so I came back with questions that might loosen the knots
but instead of answers you shrieked at me
and I said NO, not like this, with respect
the thunder rolled and rolled again
so I walked to the door, for good this time
my trembling hand touched the doorknob and you shut up
for the first time in our lives
we looked into one another's eyes
both of us frightened
and opened to something we never had, we talked

I heard what terrifying, needy strangers your little girls were
how you loved and resented us
how unbearable my mother's death was
how rage threatened to eat you alive
how you never meant to hurt us
I told you about living in constant fear
about stifling everything real and true
about learning to abandon and hate myself

about living as if I were worthless
and not deserving anything good

life is impossibly tangled
we became the kind of friends
who told each other the truth
and discovered we loved the same things

you are always there, floating in the background
especially when the old panic and desperation devour me
and inside I am screaming to be anesthetized
that is when you whisper to me
from beyond all the suffering
when trouble comes, follow what opens you
and hold on tight
sweetness is always there
softening the sadness

you old bastard
I love you

YOU CAME BACK FOR US

your face is gone
I know who you are in the pictures
but your face is gone in me
like a chalk drawing erased
leaving only faint lines
except your eyes
they look back at me in the mirror

you hung laundry in the sun in the cement yard
and sat in the shade snapping green beans
dropping them plunk into a pot
wore elegant hats to church on Sundays
then suddenly your plain house dresses hung lifeless
in the dark closet
l learned how to crack ice
slide it onto your tongue with a spoon
sit with you in case you needed anything
thinking that would stretch things out
I was quiet, so nothing could slip out
because the doctor said it would be too hard on you
to hear what you must have known
he didn't know there are different kinds of death

I watched you turn all yellow
you smelled rotten, putrid
then lay so still, so still, breathing hard
and he held on to you in bed at night and wept
I knew it was time
your nine-year-old girl began to drown

knowing the next wave and the next and the next
would come and I would be adrift
and never breathe again

but you came back for us
you came back from wherever you were
you opened your eyes and called to us
you wobbled up onto your elbow
and opened your arms
but Kathleen was only two
and probably didn't recognize her own mama
she stood in the doorway wide eyed, frozen
I promised to hold her hand, stay with her
but you couldn't wait
it was then that I began loving my little sister
as much as you did
as if a promise had passed between us

I never thanked you for trying to comfort us
for inviting us into the safest place in the whole world
in that endless moment of free fall
when everything was lost

a blurry fragment of a smile
and your titanic heart
have been enough

BETH LEFEBVRE

THE WIDOWER

As his Harley-Davidson cruises up Route 1 around fifty miles per hour, blacktop zooming under his leather-booted feet, John Najera holds his left arm outstretched. He waves to his wife, buried in Meadow Ridge Memorial Park Cemetery.

The motorcycle riders behind him have seen Najera salute each time he passes the grave. The riders ease back their throttles. The engines' hum softens, the wind eases against the riders' faces, and each person silently pays respect to a woman many of them never knew.

Najera always leads the riding groups to Daniels Restaurant in Elkridge, Maryland. It is part diner, part motorcycle show, open 365 days a year since 1975, only four miles north of the cemetery. He is one of the restaurant's mainstays, more legend than person, someone all the patrons recognize.

Riders easily spot him at the outdoor bar, even as they whizz past on Route 1. Najera adamantly says he's only six-foot-one, but so do the men who come up to his chin. Add a few inches from his boot heels, and his bandana-wrapped head easily pops above all the others. He's also the only Irish-Cherokee-Spanish-Filipino customer, his tanned skin standing out among the pasty white and sunburned faces.

Today, Najera swings into the restaurant, his large frame making the Harley look like a 50-cent mechanical kiddie ride. He parks and heads toward the back deck, away from the crowd gathered around the bar's tattered red leather stools. His childhood friend Cliff Capobianco grabs two beers and follows him.

"John, here." Capobianco hands him a Michelob Lager.

Najera turns, takes the bottle, and lets out a sputter.

"Damn doctors."

Capobianco puts his beer-free hand on Najera's shoulder.

"She didn't have to die," Najera says, his eyes reddening, his voice barely audible above the deafening tailpipe pops and engine throttles from the front parking lot.

Capobianco squeezes Najera's shoulder a few times, unsure what to say. He's listened to Najera cry for his wife, Lori, for four years. He wishes Najera would move on. Or not move on. At least accept that Lori is dead.

Widower. It's a weird sounding word, Najera says. "Widower. That's my identity," he says. "That's who I am."

And to friends like Capobianco, that's exactly Najera's problem.

Such visibly vulnerable moments are rare. Some of Najera's friends are unaware that his pain runs so deep. They just know Najera lost his wife.

"People can see the sadness, the distance from reality," Najera says. "People look at you differently. They don't know whether to talk to you or how to talk to you."

"John is always helping everyone else," Capobianco says.

Najera keeps their social network strong, coordinating barbecue get-togethers at his townhouse for summer holidays or Baltimore Ravens football games, serving up pre-fab burger patties, store-bought vegetable trays, bags of chips, and coolers full of beer. He schedules motorcycle rides, always the one deciding the destination, the ride route. Always leading the pack. He tells people to go home when they've had too much to drink, and they listen. He gathers friends to attend biker events, including the annual Blessing of the Bikes celebration at Daniels. The yearly event offers live music, beer, and a tattoo tent, where in 2008 Najera was inked with a Native American dreamcatcher in memory of his wife, listing her name, death date of 3-6-07, and a vow that the two will meet again.

Najera raced up the stairs. *I have to tell Lori*, he thought about the crazy dream he just woke from. Memory navigated his steps through the dark house, up the basement stairs, through the dining and living rooms, up the stairs to the master bedroom. It wasn't until his hand touched the gold-foil doorknob that it hit him.

Lori had been dead for two years.

It's in those flashing moments that Najera says he recedes into self pity. *He's* been left alone. Sometimes, he's angry that the doctors didn't figure out what was wrong with her sooner. Sometimes, he's angry at Lori for leaving him.

But what hurts the most are the questions.

When he met Lori through a mutual friend in 1990, all questions about Najera's rudderless life were erased. Within six months, they were planning their wedding. Najera had met Lori's youngest daughter, Kelly, but it took three or four dates before he learned she had two older daughters, Kristen and Jaime.

Najera loved children, and when he learned Lori was pregnant with their child, Jenna, before they married, he was thrilled. They shared the same values about family and children, he says, and that's what held them together, even through a year-long separation. The parting was spurred in part by the vicious cycle of Najera's long hours at construction jobs, Lori's coping with loneliness by shopping, and him working extra Sundays to pay the mounting bills.

In the few months before her death, Lori's health wasn't the greatest, he says, but nothing that set off alarms.

"We were running back and forth to the doctors to get this test, that test," he says. "It was nothing urgent, tests you could wait two weeks for."

So Najera felt comfortable leaving home for a several-week job in Ocean City, Maryland, at least a two-hour drive away from their house in Relay. During the project, Najera broke his arm and wasn't as useful on the job site. So he volunteered to drive to Baltimore when they needed more supplies. It was two weeks before he planned to be back in the area, and he wanted to surprise Lori before heading back to the job site.

He left for Baltimore on a Wednesday. That was when his cell phone rang.

Jenna, thirteen years old at the time, couldn't get in the house. She had been with a friend, and when she came home, the front door was locked. Her mother wouldn't answer the phone. Najera told her to go to the neighbors, who he didn't know well. He called Lori. No answer. Then he called the next eldest, Kelly, and asked her to check on the house.

When Kelly called him back, she was hysterical.

"Then I knew," he says. "Those two hours driving home were the worst in my life. I was absolutely losing it."

Najera was maxing out his white work pickup at 120 miles per hour and blowing red lights, half the time driving on the sidewalks and curbs of Route 50.

"Then I thought, I can't kill myself. Where would the girls be?"

He stopped, had a cigarette, and drove home in a slow blur.

Lori died the night before the medical test that would have helped the most—a heart and lung function test. In hindsight, Najera knew her heart was failing. He blames himself for not noticing she was out of breath crossing the room, or that she left the house on fewer and fewer occasions. The high level of pain medicine she was taking only made it worse, slowly intoxicating and destroying her heart. She died with the phone in her hand.

When Najera arrived home, the police were already there.

"It must've been a really busy day or something, because the coroner couldn't get there right away," he says. Najera arrived home around 5:30 p.m. and sat in the bedroom, next to Lori's body, until the coroner came six hours later. He never let go of her hand.

He shuttled the girls to the neighbor's house, shielding them from seeing their mother wheeled out on a stretcher, zipped in a body bag.

In the coming days, he made the calls he didn't want to make: her father, stepmother, sisters, brother, and Lori's first two husbands, Michael and Steven. Michael drove from Detroit, Steven from Virginia, and both stayed for a week to help Najera with the funeral arrangements. It helped that he had a good relationship with her former husbands, often golfing with the men who he says are "very different" from him. His favorite joke, and Lori's least favorite, was when Najera would tell her, "Go ahead, divorce me. Then we can have a foursome," he says.

Najera and the girls took two weeks off of school and work to grieve as a family. Three of the daughters were kicked out of their schools because they missed too many days. They lost their part-time jobs. And then, Najera lost his job.

"You can't feel the ground," Najera says. "You're just going through the motions. I never had the responsibility like that before in my life—getting a plot, making the phone calls. Without Steve and Mike, I couldn't have done it."

But the real problems hit later.

He distanced himself from the girls. He visited the cemetery every day, every night. Sometimes, he slept on top of the gray marbled tombstone, since he took all the bedroom furniture they shared—the dresser, the bed—to the dump. "I built them for us. Not me," he says.

Other times, he slept on the basement floor, no blanket, no pillow, not noticing the discomfort after downing bottles of booze. At some point, he moved into the basement, where the girls set him up with a twin-size mattress topper. They must have, he says, because he doesn't remember buying it.

He tried to fill parts of Lori's role in the house, such as her "OCD cleaning," he says. Especially when he was drunk. One night, buzzed on whiskey and beer, he cleaned the bathroom for six hours, wiping down the ceiling, dismantling the light fixtures and cleaning the insides. The next day, he picked another room. And then, he set himself on repeat.

His frenzied actions were fueled by lingering questions.

"The hardest thing to deal with losing my wife, who I still love, is the questions. All of a sudden, I have questions," he says. "I lost my identity when she died. I didn't know who I was anymore. I was a husband for fourteen years. My life was set, settled, and done. I was going to live out my days with her and spoil grandbabies. She looked forward to the girls getting married and the first grandchild, and she missed all of it. I had it all figured out. Now I have to rediscover who I am, and answer questions. Am I going to be alone forever? I'm back to square one. Well, negative three."

He doesn't recall when, but the numbness eventually subsided, replaced by overwhelming guilt.

"I hate myself now," he says. "I should've spent more time with the girls. They lost their mother. But I rationalized that I was hurting more. You don't get to pick your mother. But I chose her. Out of everyone, I chose her. She was the one. But then I remembered, I didn't have much of a childhood, and I want them to have as much as they can. They can be kids until they're sixty. Daddy can protect them."

His friends say no one could have provided better for the girls. He's constantly opening his wallet and his arms for them, and the girls—whether biologically his or not—lavish him with phone calls, "I love yous," and Facebook photos.

But he still felt he could do better.

So he cut back on the booze. He had one shot of whiskey last summer, a toast to the father he hadn't seen in thirty years. He bought the girls everything they needed. He stayed home more. He cooked more. He learned more about feminine hygiene products than he wanted to, he says. And he decided he needed to find a woman for the girls.

Najera admits he self-sabotages any relationship he gets into, because he bounces back and forth about whether he wants to find someone.

"That first flush of romance, where it's new and wonderful, goes away," he says. "Because they're not her."

There was the bleach-blonde Heather, whose drunken rambling insults at a couple playing pool at the Moontimes bar almost caused a fight. He pulled her out of the bar, stuck her on his motorcycle's back seat, where she barely hung on as she bobbled from side to side, and he dropped her off at home for the last time.

There was the petite, loud-mouthed Arlene, whose stinging insults about Najera's friends during his birthday dinner with the girls ended their short-lived relationship. "I gave myself a birthday present," he told friends about their break-up.

Then, Tracey Lane seemed to capture his heart. She was all the things he thought he wanted: She was blonde like Lori, independent, she drove her own motorcycle, she had her own money, and she had lost her spouse, too. Their mutual loss would be their strongest connection and their largest hurdle.

On the weekend of the third anniversary of Lori's death, Lane invited Najera to join her at a posh hotel for a realtor's convention she was attending in Georgia. He decided to stay home with the girls for a graveside gathering.

The evening after visiting the cemetery, and after sharing a few Michelobs with Capobianco at GL Shacks in Catonsville, he hopped in his truck and drove to Georgia. After hours on the road, he knocked on Lane's hotel door. She answered, frowning and curt with him. He wasn't sure whether anyone else was in the room, but he got the message. He went back to his truck and drove eleven hours home, crawled under his Baltimore Ravens blanket in his basement bedroom, and went to sleep.

"That was a mistake," he said of their relationship.

Not long after, he took the back passenger seat off the motorcycle. And he repeats the same phrase over and over when it comes to women.

"I'm retired."

Najera's house looks as if Lori's funeral was yesterday, not four years ago. On the white fireplace mantel sit several funeral cards and a funeral votive with a picture of Lori, her wispy blonde feathered layers circling her thin, smiling face. On the wooden bookcase shelves, a business sign reading "Lori's Flowers" sits behind a photo of Lori holding their black-and-white Chihuahua. In another, she hugs Jenna before her daughter started wearing all black and dyeing her hair with streaks of red. On the refrigerator, a magnet declares it "Lori's kitchen," while other magnets support curling photos of Lori and the children in sepia tones of reds and oranges, where the family is playing in inflatable pools and holding up homemade crayon artwork.

A dry-erase board proclaims in blue marker "We love you daddy!" and "We miss you mom!"

Today, May 14, a day shy of Mother's Day, Lori would have been fifty-one years old. Each year, Najera holds a birthday party to honor Lori's life.

Lori's father sits at the small kitchen table, drinking a beer. Jenna watches TV. Kelly snacks on pretzels with her boyfriend. Kristen brought Najera's granddaughter for a short time, and left.

On the deck, Najera works the grill, flipping the frozen burger patties, wearing a white Harley-Davidson T-shirt, just one in his extensive collection. A Native American choker encircles his neck. The thick strings are beaded in tan and blue, and a silver medallion hangs from the center by leather straps.

Most of the friends who know him as "Tonto" are absent. Three childhood friends—Capobianco, John Goodyear, and Walter Price—sip beers, pondering to themselves what an awkward event this is. Each one had reservations about coming. They want to support their friend, but they look at this event—meant to remember the good times—as a destructive attempt to live in the past.

A multi-colored "happy birthday" banner drapes above the dining room table, which is full of snacks, a birthday cake, and matching partyware of paper plates, napkins, and plastic cutlery in purple and blue, like a fresh bruise.

Yet, Lori isn't mentioned in the conversations. The agony of loss keeps Najera from revealing the things he loves most about Lori—the reasons that no other woman can be her, those moments of stolen glances and kisses, of personal jokes and shared laughter, favorite meals and favorite songs, pet nicknames, and simple routines. As difficult and painful as it is for him to discuss Lori's death, it's impossible for him to discuss their life. Instead, topics turn to family, the weather, the economy, and old memories, such as when Najera "learned to drink and drive" with Price, and when the two could split a six-pack and get so drunk they would throw up.

A few hours in, after most people have had their fill of food, Najera quiets the room. Kelly's boyfriend picks up a guitar, starts strumming slowly, and Kelly begins to sing a Beatles song.

"Blackbird singing in the dead of the night, take these broken wings and learn to fly . . ."

As Kelly sings, no one moves. Everyone knows the song is for her mother. Nearing the end, tears roll down Kelly's cheeks, until she bursts into a sob. People look sideways at Najera for a cue. He smiles, begins to clap, walks over, and gives Kelly a long hug.

Price leans over to Goodyear. "Well, it's an improvement. Last year, he showed the wedding video."

They are small steps, slow and far between. But Najera thinks he has progressed far in the past four years. He only visits the gravesite three or four times a year now, he says. He no longer "gets all pissed off" when he sees happy couples holding hands. He's tried reading a daily prayer book for those who have lost a loved one. He says Lori's death is becoming easier to deal with, because he believes he has "pushed it to the back file cabinet" of his mind.

But he still bargains with God, that if he could trade places with her, he would. He still waves at the cemetery each time he passes. He still sleeps in the basement. He still refuses to attend counseling, because "my loss wasn't a bunch of strangers' loss."

"This is my pain, my grief," he says. "I don't want to be medicated out of it." Najera's red eyes glaze over. He stares at his folded hands in his lap. "Every tear is a testament to how much I loved her. Still love her."

EVE MILLS ALLEN (NASH)

CHINA ROSE ON THE FLOOR

It never occurred to me I might be depressed. The first time I walked past the stray fragment of blue china on the floor without picking it up, it was a Tuesday afternoon and there was no sun. When I noticed it a week later, as the midmorning sun bounced in prisms off its tiny body, it dawned on me that I was probably in trouble.

"Where do you want the photographs?" the funeral director asked, as we all prepared for my granddaughter's wake.

"Near the entrance so people can look at them while they wait to line up for the viewing," I answered in my characteristically efficient manner. "It makes more sense, don't you think?"

I made sure everything was perfect. A new crisp pink linen dress covered the tiny body in the white satin casket. For my daughter, Evangeline, the child's mother, I had chosen an appropriate navy blue dress. I set myself upon the tasks at hand like a soldier deployed to a war-torn country. There was no time to think about what had *happened*, only time to make sure everything and everyone was all right.

At home, I cooked mountains of food that could be transported to my daughter's home—a large pot of chili—Evangeline's favorite comfort food—dozens of golden brown, flaky biscuits; chicken and beef casseroles and sweetbreads—banana and, of course, zucchini. Zucchini was my granddaughter's favorite. I insisted everyone should be with my daughter. She needed the support. I was fine, and I needed the peace and quiet.

Even at the funeral, I stood on guard, inspecting the reactions of family members, ever ready to comfort, offer a tissue or a hug. After the burial and reception, I went home. That's the day I accidentally dropped the small blue china cup. The tiny pink rose painted on the side fell on the floor intact as the cup split down the middle and rolled under the coffee table in front of my sofa. I thought about the morning my granddaughter, Sophia, had given me the cup—how she clapped her hands when she handed me the tiny box wrapped in silver paper tied with a bright pink bow while her mother stood quietly nearby.

"For you, nannie—for Grandma's Day!"

"But I don't think there is a Grandma's Day," I'd told her.

"Yes, I made one and you are the queen," she declared with a dimpled smile that lit up luminous brown eyes.

Could that have only been a month ago, I thought to myself, as my shoes gently slid the broken fragments further under the sofa so I wouldn't have to look at them.

The next day I went back to work.

"What are you doing here?" my supervisor asked.

"It is better for me to be working," I insisted, as I retrieved the file of my last client.

"You're one strong woman!" he replied, as he left me to my work.

And, for me, for a long time, life went on as if nothing had *happened*. Eventually, I swept up the pieces of broken china cup, except for the tiny fragment with the pink rose. For some reason, I didn't want to touch it so I gently nudged it back under the sofa as if it were a valuable talisman.

When my daughter started drinking to deal with her loss, I called a friend to talk to her, and set up a visit to a rehabilitation centre in another city. I buried myself in my work.

Then, one morning, a year after my granddaughter's death, I was unable to get out of bed. My bones felt like they had been replaced by steel weights. Even my head felt heavy. It was the first time I ever called in sick.

Three days later, I was still unable to work so I put in for two weeks of vacation, hoping it would pass with just some rest. Days moved by in slow motion. Most of the time, I felt like I was standing outside of myself watching some strange woman in a movie.

The morning I picked up the fragment of the broken china cup was the morning my life changed.

My tears ran like an escaped prisoner down my sunken cheeks and landed on the polished grey tiles where the broken gift had waited for me. As I lowered myself to the floor, I pressed the pink rose to my cheek and suddenly I remembered what else my granddaughter said to me when I opened the box and told her how beautiful the pink rose looked on the tiny blue cup.

"It's like when everything is blue and sad, the flowers still have to grow. Or else we'd have no flowers. Ah, nannie?"

I remembered telling her, "That's right, Sophia, we all have to keep growing no matter what. Especially, wild roses like you and me and your mommy."

That had made her laugh. Today, it made me cry. It was time for this rose to grow again. Time to say farewell to a wild rose who now bloomed somewhere else. Time to find my daughter while I still can.

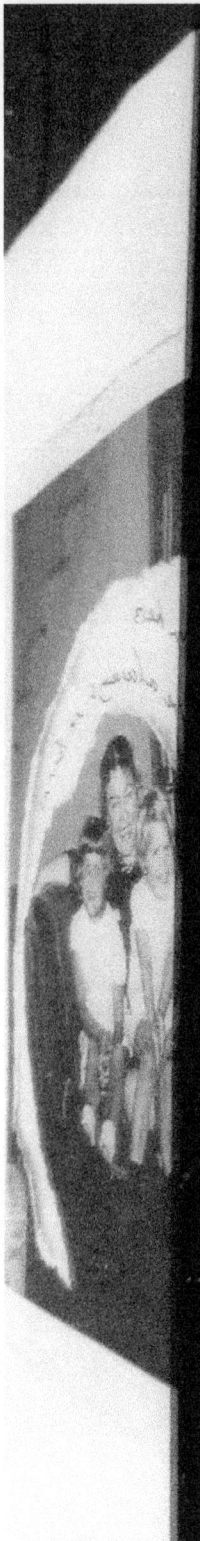

She delighted in my being a joy in hers.
And of love always returns.

WENDY BROWN-BÁEZ

A GOOD DAY

This is the beginning. It all starts here. The *cocinera* serves us cold salted cucumber slices, then brings a dish of dried red peppers instead of chili powder. Careful to add a few seeds at a time, the crisp explosion of salt and chili in my mouth is the best way I can describe our relationship. Not sweet, like you might expect with a gay guy. And not tender, like you might think a marriage should be. But salty and spicy. I like it that way, and not because I don't yearn for the sweet and tender as well. But I need the provocation.

I have returned to Mexico after four years of being a widow and on the first anniversary of my son's death. Mexico is also salty and spicy. Sweetness comes from a song drifting through the sultry air or a smile caught between me and a *señorita* on the bus or the lilting accents of the Spanish language. But all of the *"quiero"*s and *"mi corazon"*s won't change the past and I bite my tongue on the tears I am afraid could drown me.

Alejandro is a gorgeous macho Mexican male who would rather go to the dentist than caress me. He is the husband destiny has now chosen for me, and I will spend the rest of my life trying to figure out why.

Nevertheless, today it begins. No matter that the idea of *Sol y Luna* came to us on my birthday when Alejandro gave me a gold moon on a neckband to match his gold sun. No matter that we have searched for a place, drawn up budgets and made numerous phone calls. And no matter that we won't sign the lease until we return to town on Monday. Here in this small *pueblito* in the mountains, sleeping in a hotel room with a barrier between us as thick as steel bars, the taste of red pepper is wild in my mouth, and I finally know it will come true. *Sol y Luna*, a contemporary art gallery. More than that, despite my hesitation about staying in Mexico with Alejandro, I know I am not leaving. Even if we disagree about so many things, I know this much: I can't give up now.

We have come to this village in the mountains, San Sebastian del Oeste, to get out of the heat. The sticky humidity of Puerto Vallarta seems relentless at this point in mid-August. I don't know how anyone can stand it, unless you are on the beach or staying at a hotel with a pool. It makes me feel ill, and I can't get used to it. I don't think I ever will. It is so hot it hurts to wear lace next to my skin. My skin is covered in a sheen of sweat and behind my sunglasses, drops of sweat sting my eyes. Every day we find a way to get respite: shopping at Sam's Club, the movies, air-conditioned restaurants, trips to the river. And now this, a trip to San Sebastian, a town in the mountains reported to be unchanged for five hundred years.

Only 64 kilometers away, it takes an hour to make the turn-off and another half hour to drive the 9 kilometers to the town on a rocky dirt road. But forty minutes out of Puerto Vallarta, the air cools off, the vistas are green, and as we rise up the windy switch-back roads, the mountain is covered with pines instead of jungle plants.

I am a nervous passenger and the road curves dangerously close to the precipices, so I am relieved to park and find a hotel. In the Pabellon, the rooms surround a courtyard garden filled with trees, roses, benches, and potted plants that I have tried to grow with little success and that here are over three feet tall.

Will I ever learn enough Spanish not to feel awkward and tongue-tied? I hate the sensation of not knowing what I want to say nor how to say it. Most of all, I find myself answering questions I don't fully understand and the confusion expands exponentially. People chatter away at me. As I struggle to find the words I do know, I discover an amazing feature of Mexican communication: an answer is expected immediately. In a culture that has no respect for time—an 8:00 event means people come after 9:00, a morning appointment might not happen until the next day—to pause for translation is not permitted. Alejandro is a case in point. When we go out to eat, by the time I have read *la carta*, he has decided for both of us what to order. Usually I like it that way—not because I don't have preferences but because I like to put the reins in someone else's hands occasionally.

We share a room with adobe walls that enclose a silence with its own density, it is so thick. Of course he gets the double bed—he's my husband, after all! And I get the single. Ever since we got married, we hug and kiss as chastely as children. But tonight we will breathe the same air in our sleep, hear each other's dreams, and I awake in the pre-light of dawn to watch him sleep, curled up in his blankets like a baby. Wanting nothing more than to be alone so he can't see the tears streaming down my cheeks as I remember why I fled to Mexico.

I love my husband and I am not ashamed to admit it. No one enrages me like he does either. He leaves me to struggle through my fears and doubts and expects perfection. The sheer incompatibility of us both. And yet I can't live without him. The point is: who did I call at 3 a.m. when I found out that my son Sam had died? I woke up my older son who bowed his head to the counter like he had been punched. His wife was stunned into silence. The shattered dark. My grandson sleeping. The longest night of our lives. At the crack of dawn, who did I call? The sense of unreality: *I did this before, bearer of bad news. I don't know if I can bear to do it again.* I call my mom, and then I call Alejandro.

"How can I help?" he asks, and I unhesitatingly answer, "Drive up here."

But of course that is unrealistic. We have the cremation, the memorial, the many people who come to pay their respects, none who know him, and we won't have any time together. But to fly up later, to bring me home on the plane, when the initial shock wears off and I am paralyzed . . . this he offers to me. I call him because I want him to share the most horrible thing that has ever happened to me. I don't want to be held and comforted—not yet. That would soften me and I need to be strong. Others give me hugs and let me weep on their shoulders, and it is almost more than I can take. I need Alejandro to witness my life. To scold me into packing my suitcase. To hustle me into the taxi. To walk me down the corridors of the airport and steer me to the coffee counter. To tell me to buckle my seat belt. How will it be possible to place anyone else there? That's crazy.

I awaken to the sound of pouring rain. Alejandro is curled up in his bed. Spooky, our Akita dog, is nowhere in sight. Later she comes out from under the bed, where she hid when the thunder boomed. I think about the road we took to get here. In several places large rocks had slid down the hillside. In one patch before the bridge built over a chasm, the road was buried under the collapsing mountain and a dirt detour was created. Now it would be all mud. Are we able to go home?

A good day feels like this. The sound of rain, cool enough to be wrapped in blankets, wondering if I brought the right clothes. Someone near to me breathing, dreaming, privately but close. After Michael died, I had to learn to sleep by myself again, hugging my side of the bed for a year before I could stretch out. I loved the silence. It was healing after the cacophony of constant TV and constant complaints. I have forgotten the comfort of someone breathing in the same space as we sleep, knowing a warm living soul is there.

A good day is remembering and not falling apart, not thinking I can't go on, not sinking into shattering emptiness.

I am in Mexico, country of priests. What if I asked a priest to make confession? Are you allowed to confess if you are not Catholic? "Forgive me, Father, for I have sinned." Isn't that what you say? I could fake it. If I confessed that I was unable to keep my son safe, would it alleviate me? And do I want to be alleviated? Will it bring back Sam to carry this throbbing sword of guilt plunged into my heart? No, of course not. But I do not give it up. For the first time I understand self-flagellation. I understand putting on a terrorist suicide belt and I understand depression. I understand that a sorrow can be so deep, you can no longer stand to look at your own face in the mirror.

I get up, throw on some warm clothes, open the heavy floor-to-ceiling door, and go to find coffee. It is a good day. I can do this without a net to catch me—no schedule, no job, no support group, no therapist. No friends but the one asleep in his blankets, untouchable, but mine.

My provocateur. Keeping me afloat. I can't wait till he wakes up and shapes my day. Will we be trapped in a village where time has stopped? How many others have been trapped here as well? Five hundred years ago, before technology, before telephones and emails, before washing machines and trucks, a woman spent her life—her hands, her back, her arms, her heart—to take care of her family. The cycle of the day was repetitious and constant. The women had each other for gossip, for comfort, for solace. I read once about how women shared and gossiped as they sewed in quilting bees. Maybe that's what I need—a heart to heart girl talk. I know that many mothers have lost their sons. To famine, to war, to poverty, to crossing the border. But I am not yet ready to accept that. My loss is personal and mine alone.

It is peaceful in the dim cave of our room when I return with the coffee.

"*¡Que rico!*" Alejandro exclaims. "*Cafe de olla.*"

"I can't taste the cinnamon," I say.

"That's because you put cream in it."

Every morning we argue about the coffee. How I make it too strong and then add cream, killing the flavor. Just one of our many disagreements that make up the rich but fragile tapestry of our relationship. And yet, the love is also real and visible. Other people notice it and comment on it. Alejandro reminds the men he dates that he is married to me and won't give me up. He also makes it clear that we do not sleep together and never have, although few believe him and many are jealous of our affection, expressed by long gazes, shrugs, and asides in English since to hold me close would open his own wounds. He, too, has suffered deep loss: the suicide of his mother when he was becoming a young man. He doesn't talk about it and tells me to just move on, get over it. Words that set my teeth on edge, words I need to hear. I need strength, friction, challenge or I will deflate into depression. The dark night of the soul is a bottomless chasm into which I can continue to fall. Or I can grasp the hand that has reached out to me, someone who wants me by his side after others have broken his heart. After that first indelible heartbreak that he has never mourned fully, he hides the scars he carries from others and yet revealed them to me. This is the link between us: as strong as steel. As thick as blood. He is my life raft and in return, I believe in him, his dreams, his determination, his ability to force me to live. And yes, move on.

For a moment I think I would be content to live here for a while. But I know we'd get bored by the afternoon. We walked the entire town in an hour yesterday.

Did I ever ask Sam, "Hey, Sam, are you happy?"

He sounded happy the night he called to say he was getting married. Happy and intoxicated. I didn't know they had a drinking problem. She was the mother of his son. She adored him. I was worried but I thought, *who doesn't want to feel loved?*

The last time I talked to Sam, he came to my eldest son Shawn's house with Jason, my two-year-old grandson. I had arrived in Minneapolis from Santa Fe two days before and although I accepted his explanation that he was busy, that they couldn't host me because the house was still in a mess from moving, I sensed something, something not quite right. It was unlike him to not pick me up at the airport. But I thought I should accept the fact that my boys were grown-ups with responsibilities, with families, that they might not have free time to spend with their mom as they had when they were younger.

Shawn disapproved of Sam's choices and the tension was uncomfortable. Shawn, accountant and businessman, knew that the mortgage that Sam had taken on was not a good investment and the woman he was going to marry was unstable. I guessed that she had mental health issues, but I knew the attraction. Michael had been charming and generous and gregarious, too, when he wasn't depressed and unable to get out of bed. I knew well the desire to save someone, someone bent on self-destruction. But this night, the last night I would ever see Sam alive, we sat on the couch and Jason acted out Barney songs, making us laugh. Sam sat slumped beside me. "Are you ok?" I asked.

"I'm just really tired," he told me.

When he left, I said to Shawn, "He doesn't seem happy to me."

It was a mother's instinct. But I didn't have the sense to follow through, the intuition to insist that we talk, although I tried to convince him to meet me for coffee the next morning. And tried to invite myself to his house the following day. But I did not show up unexpectedly, which is what I should have done. *Should have, could have, if only, what if. . .* can become an endless litany of self-recrimination.

The next time I saw Sam, it was to anoint his corpse in a funeral home. He had shot himself in his own backyard. When I looked at his sweet, handsome face wrapped in white so we wouldn't see the bullet hole, the thought pierced me like a sword that it could have been me. That we were more similar than I had ever thought possible. That he had given up when I had persisted, had succumbed to helplessness whereas I had entered counseling, created support groups, let the rose-colored glasses smash on the rocks of reality and reached out for help.

After breakfast, we pack up to go back to Puerto Vallarta. The rain has stopped, the road is okay, we are told. On the bridge, a line of cars wait to cross. The gorge is deep, and Alejandro gets out of the car to look. "Do you want to come look at it?" he asks me. I shudder, remembering all the times Michael threatened to jump the Taos gorge. When he gets back in to the car, the other line has started to cross, the bridge shakes and he turns pale. "If we don't move soon, I'm going to turn around," he tells me. Later he says a man he met on the bridge told him it had been open only a month. "You were very nervous," I observe.

"It wouldn't be the first time a Mexican bridge collapsed," he frowns. "I was about to panic."

"I'm glad you didn't tell me when we were on it!"

A good day is to spend the entire day with someone you love and to cherish the silence instead of filling it up with the old tape: *Why didn't I? . . . I should have . . .* A good day is to be absorbed into the landscape, to reach out to be touched by the beauty of the sea, the green jungle, the changing cloud formations. A good day is to have a project to look forward to, to work on, to hope on. To leap with the fear in your throat that you might not make it, you might not have what it takes, but to leap anyway, as an act of faith. It will lead you somewhere, perhaps out of the bitterness, the sense of failure. My task right now is to regain confidence in myself, one tiny step at a time.

We are back in the heat but I know San Sebastian is there, just over the mountains, cool, misty, suspended in time. It has left a quiet oasis inside of me. When it gets unbearable, I can shift the direction of my sight. There, to the East. Still alive.

ELAINE J. TABER

GOODBYE AGAIN

Death rarely gives us
time enough to say
goodbye. And a
lifetime is never long
enough to tell another
all you have to say.

Gonna lay all my burdens down
Down by the riverside,
Down by the riverside

My husband was a
rugged man, most
comfortable when he was
in the garden or handling
home repairs. Although
he did appreciate
classical music and
reading his Bible.

Ain't gonna study war no more
Ain't gonna study war no more
Down by the riverside

He considered himself the
CEO of family life and took
responsibility for how the
family presented itself to the
world. He could tenderly change

a diaper, soothe a crying
infant or spoon-feed a
toddler.

Gonna lay down my sword and shield
Down by the riverside
Down by the riverside

But he could not
make peace with
a teenager or a wife.
Hierarchy was tradition.
Tiny tears in fabric
grew into rips that
refused to be mended.
I stumbled out of his world
and invented my own.
Years later, when death
became the equal of
forgiveness, I said
goodbye a second time.

Ain't gonna study war no more
Ain't gonna study war no more
Down by the riverside

When you start to run out
of experience and the past
becomes greater than the
future, you wonder why
you twisted so many knots
into the simple weaving
you were given to complete.

Gonna put on my long white gown
Down by the riverside
Down by the riverside

ISABELLE BRUDER SMITH

EGO

The day after you died I paid bills
bought two books of postage stamps
wandered through the grocery store

failed to notice anyone who was kind
walked the straightest path I could find

into cool woods over two short bridges
and gurgling streams good for fishing
searching for the slightest sense of order

to redirect my heart and mind
but all I felt was left behind.

I learned once to love without condition
but death gives the ego rare permission
to deny that letting go is an art
and the only way to hold a heart.

HERE

On the porch, Fourth of July.
Day lilies wave across the stone wall on the street
aching for light. Their blossoms compete

with rambling rose. A breeze unites their rhythm
with this rocking wicker chair.
The sound of driveway firecrackers ignites the air.

Dogs bark in protest. Cars speed past.
It's been almost a year since we spoke last.

In that time, beliefs have been shattered.
Worlds and lives have rearranged order.
Winter lingered. Spring was shorter.

I've traveled and returned to this home where
wind chimes are happy. Hundred-year-old maple shade
steadies the heart. Some days

are better or bearable or worse.
Less and less, acceptance is something I rehearse

and more of a habit
that saturates moments of unexpectedness.
That's the way it is, I guess.

Sparklers hiss as the neighbors cheer.
I'm cultivating gratitude to supplement tears.
On days when I'm able, I know you're here.

VI
EXPANDING INTO
THE HUMAN CONDITION

PARSING RESPONSIBILITY

ELIZABETH SWANN

PORT DESIRE

At twilight the crew drops anchor, waves
  slap the hull,
        and the solitary brig-sloop sways.

The *Beagle* has sailed seventeen days
          after giving up
the hunt for the flightless Lesser Rhea.

Darwin sits down to dinner, dark
  descending like a wing, and picks

      at the tender bird
          half-eaten on his plate, meat

warm in his belly with wine. He lifts
   his fork
            and stops mid-bite.

Sinking to his knees,
        frantic, he digs
   bones and feathers from the trash.

I've been there myself,
        anchored outside Port Desire,
love's breast
      essentially devoured—

  how easy
   it would have been to quit,

      throw the whole mess overboard.

PAUL HOSTOVSKY

GREENHOUSE

My Aunt Ellie lived in a greenhouse. This was in Irvington
New Jersey. A Jew alone
is a Jew in danger, her husband
said. Their daughter, my cousin,
wanted to go where she wanted
to go. They said it was a big
mistake. In a greenhouse you
cultivate certain delicate
non-indigenous plants. The house
was green and my cousin fell
deeply in love with a black man.
When she married him her father
sat *shiva* for her, meaning that
he mourned her for dead. But
she was only living over in East
Orange. She had two beautiful
daughters who never knew
their grandfather on their mother's
side. Because she was dead to him
until the day he died. That was the day
we all went over to Aunt Ellie's house
where she was sitting *shiva*. We met
my cousin's husband Toe, for the first time,
and their two daughters, Leah and Aleesha.
And we opened all the windows in
the greenhouse on that day, for outside
it was a beautiful spring day and we
broke out the expensive delicate china
from Germany which they kept locked up
in a glass breakfront in the hall.

LOVE THE MISTAKE

You are not the only mistake I have ever loved.
There have been others.
Just the other day in fact
when John kissed Billy goodbye—
his older brother Billy, who's retarded—
saying first, I love you, then kissing him
once on the mouth, so that Billy
stood up in the kitchen, rocking a little stiffly,
so that John reached up and fixed his collar—I saw
how all this time I have been mistaken
about John,
the hard, the vulgar
ex-cop, ex-Navy,
ironworker from the Bronx
who likes to say vehicle instead of car,
who likes to say fuck, who likes to hate
the enemy. And I loved
being wrong—I loved that I was wrong
about John
who isn't empty of love after all.
And I take his head now
from the square buzz-cut on top
down to the gash of the mouth,
and all the broken grammar of his face—
I take his head and I cradle it, saying: There.
There. Saying: Now.
Now.

WILLY CONLEY

SIFTING DIRT

Roger Folter leaned against the park's thick iron fence and crossed his right foot over his left. He was a few yards from the water's edge. In the middle of the Rancho La Brea pit was a gray mastodon stuck in tar; its massive trunk and tusks stabbed the sky in a frozen snarl. A squat pigeon rested on the mammoth's back, and down the sculpted shaggy sides were dried white dribbles of dung. As tar bubbles rose passively to the surface near the statue's legs, Roger envisioned his dirt-filled kitchen sink. The living room scene replayed in his head.

"You preach, still," said his wife Rhondee, standing in front of the anchorwoman on the eleven o'clock TV news. "Move please, she's talking about Bosnia now," said Roger.

"You preach, still," said Rhondee with stronger hand movements.

Roger leaned forward on the sofa to push her out of the way but she slapped his hand off her hip.

"Hey—can't you wait till this is over?" he asked.

"No, me saw you—you correct-correct him. Must stop now."

Roger sank back on the sofa.

"Correcting what?" he asked. He craned his neck to catch the news clip that flashed on the screen.

"You preach-preach English to him," she said.

Roger felt his gut tighten a little but he let it go.

The bubbles that bobbed up against the mastodon's leg released an oily film in the water. The pigeon fluttered its wings then settled down again on its haunches. Roger closed his eyes, trying to remember what happened next. He had been watching a closed-captioned newscast, reading fast scrolling lines of text at the bottom of the television screen, when Rhondee stepped in. It was a chore to read the news at a frantic pace especially when the captions were fraught with misspellings, but he kept at it knowing that it would pay off in the long run.

Roger looked around the pit to check on his son. On the other side Cody skimmed rocks across the water. The pigeon flew away. Roger crossed his left foot over his right and went back to the bubbles.

"I'm teaching English to Cody," said Roger. He emphasized teach with his hands, retrieving invisible information from his head and pushing it to an imaginary young boy next to him. "Now move—please?"

"You preach-preach!" The veins on Rhondee's neck and face began to surface.

Roger was proud of the way he preserved his emotions. He was a professional who sold his feelings; that's how actors work. Big emotional outbursts were all right for the stage, but the way Rhondee wasted her anger in their warm, serene living room was beyond him.

"Next year we're enrolling Cody in kindergarten, right?" Roger asked his wife.

"Right," she said. The interrupted lines of captions scrolled behind her.

"With deaf or hearing children?" he asked.

"Hearing children," she said with a bitter expression.

"Correct," said Roger. "Cody is hearing—we can't help that—he should be around other hearing children, right?"

Rhondee stared at the little scar on Roger's lower lip.

"And what language will these hearing kids be using?"

"English," said Rhondee. "What's the point?"

"Sign that again," Roger said.

Like a bored sign language student, she clasped one hand weakly over her wrist in a classic British pose.

"English."

"Right! And does Cody know English?"

"He knows enough," she said.

"Bathroom, me finish touch," Roger mimicked. "Me-know, me-know. Me-want, me-want. You call that English?"

Her eyes narrowed and her nostrils pinched. The unbuttoned pocket flaps on her blouse seemed to open and close as she took big breaths.

"What's—what's wrong—that?" Her hands trembled. "Before never bother-bother you, me not sit here watch-watch captions, improve my English."

"Nothing's wrong, if Cody's signing with us or other deaf people. But if he talks like that to his teachers and classmates, they're going to make fun of him."

"Give him time." Her index finger repeatedly jabbed her wristwatch. "Cody develop natural deaf language now. Dump two languages on little boy, age-four, can't. Later, English."

"I want to start now before it's too late," he said.

"Not now! First, what? he understand us, must!—you, me—our language—before too late."

"Do you want him to look stupid?"

She hit the palm of her hand with a firm karate chop in front of Roger's face. Roger flinched and thought she was going to slice his nose off.

"Stop!" she said.

The bubbles in the pit burst slowly, one after another. Roger felt something tug on his pants. Cody stretched his little french-fry fingers apart and pressed his thumb against his forehead.

"Daddy!"

"What's up?" Roger grimaced as he rubbed a stiffness in the back of his neck.

"Me hear bird. Talk funny."

"I hear a bird. It talks funny," Roger corrected.

"Can't. Hard," said Cody.

"Try it. You're a smart guy."

"Don't wanna."

"Do you want to go home now?" Roger asked. "I don't need to stay here."

"No, no, don't. Me want stay," cried Cody.

"Then you try harder."

"I hear bird. It talk funny," said Cody.

"That's better. Was that so hard?"

"Yeah."

"Ok. Where do you see this bird?"

"Not see bird but me can hear—says 'Hel-lo!' " said Cody. He fingerspelled the last word leaving the "O" formed in his hand.

"Oh, c'mon Code, you know birds can't talk."

"Come look-for," said Cody.

Roger hitched Cody up onto his shoulders; he smelled his light buttery scent that came from Rhondee, only hers was sharper. As he walked around the tar pit to a nearby construction site Cody gave him the signal, with a tap of his boot heel, to let him down. Cody ran up to a mound of excavated dirt and climbed up to the top. He had the look of a miniature cowboy scanning a prairie. Roger sat down at the bottom of the mound and scooped up a handful of moist dirt, slowly letting the finer pieces fall between his fingers. He looked over at the tar pit and studied the expression of rage on the mastodon's face.

In the living room, Rhondee still wouldn't budge from her position in front of the television set.

"Face it," said Roger, "we're living in a hearing world."

"Spittie," she said.

"What did you call me?"

"Spittie—pftht, pftht!"

"I don't need to watch that deaf bullshit," said Roger. "Get out of the way. I'm getting behind on world news, you mind?"

Rhondee stepped back and used the anchorwoman for a demonstration.

"You want act like hearing people, 'talk-talk-talk', spit fly out your mouth."

"Are you making fun of my work?" asked Roger.

"My life, you mock?" asked Rhondee.

There was a moment of stillness in the room except for the flickering images from the television.

"Me show what you look like on stage with other hearing actors." She stood erect, expressionless, one hand over her chest and the other behind her back. She imitated a bad actor's monologue, moving only her mouth in grotesque shapes: "Blah-blah-blah."

Roger took a minute to think while the anchorwoman signed off for a commercial break.

"I thought you supported the idea of me integrating with hearing people?"

"Too much," Rhondee said.

"What's that supposed to mean?"

"You leave behind sign language, deaf culture."

"I'm including it . . . expanding it. To see how far we can go with our potential."

"Uncle Tom," she said.

"You can't deny we live in a hearing world," said Roger overlapping her remark.

"Uncle T-O-M." Rhondee fingerspelled slow to catch his attention.

"Uncle Tom?"

"No, no, no; mistake me," she said. "Uncle Tom for blacks. Me mean Uncle R-O-G."

"What's wrong with you, Rhondee?"

"Everything! Thought me married *Deaf* man."

She stared at him, breathing hard. When he couldn't hold the glare, she backed up and left the room. The anchorwoman returned and continued her cool delivery. He went back to the news and absently read the captions. He couldn't translate their meanings.

A few minutes later Rhondee returned with her arms full of potted aloes from around the house. Dirt spilled on the floor behind her, some stuck to the sweat on her arms. She dumped the pots upside down and filled the sink with black soil. Roger watched from the corners of his eyes keeping his head in the direction of the television. She grabbed a bunch of aloes and plucked apart the fleshy, finger-like leaves one by one. The leaves were piled up on top of the butcher block next to the toaster. For an absurd second Roger imagined her making a salad. She took a fork from the drawer and methodically mashed the juices out of the leaves. When she was finished, the clear liquid oozed over the block and onto the counter.

From the far end of the sofa Roger sat with his mouth hung open. He thought of what he should be feeling but nothing appropriate registered. Her actions surprised him. There was no cue for her next move. She was going to sneer at him, he anticipated, and sign, "Now you know how me feel!" Instead, his wife walked over to the television, unplugged the wires from the closed-captioning device, and wrapped them around the machine. The television image shrank to a dot where the anchorwoman's lips were and disappeared. Rhondee snatched her keys off the top of the microwave oven and left by the front door with her captioning device under her arm. Roger waited for the vibrations to rock across the hardwood floor when the door slammed, but nothing happened. She left the door open.

Roger looked back at the television and saw that his wife left behind her muddy handprints all over the screen. He slowly got up to look in the sink. It smelled like a freshly-turned garden. He wondered which two of the leaves were the original ones that Rhondee gave him at the start of their relationship, before it had grown wild and out of proportion. Roger padded down the hall to peek into his son's room. Cody had slept through another silent argument.

Roger was still looking at the mastodon when Cody jumped on his back and knocked the remaining dirt out of his hands.

"Daddy! Me saw balloon man. He make-make balloon, like this . . ." Cody showed his father how the man blew a long, narrow balloon and twisted it into different shapes.

"Well, let's go buy a balloon. You know what kind of animal you want?"

"Yep!"

"Good. And, let's buy one for your mother. You know what kind of animal she wants?" Roger was thinking that Rhondee probably drove over to her mother's to cool off from the fight.

"Don't-know," said Cody. "Have idea—we tell balloon man make-make talking bird."

Roger raised his right hand to correct him but restrained himself. He lifted his left hand and signed, "Okay, and then, we'll go over to your grandmother's."

R.E. HAYES

GAIT

In the time of the half-remembered Korean War, army brass assigned young Victor Kittle to graves registration duty. On bloodstained burned hills, amid hell-on-earth battlefield chaos, he had risked all to bring out the KIAs and the wounded, often with vital organs exposed, dangling from grotesquely sundered flesh.

Decades later Kittle became the government über boss in the corner office, the director. Everyone on the staff at some point had heard his sermon regarding army combat medics. How, in anticipation of a dying GI's last breath, doctors had shrouded the soldier's face in gauze and waited out his final minutes on earth. Kittle always concluded with: "Sulfa killed infections, plasma saved lives, morphine stopped the screams." He relished the role of motivator-in-chief and was in his element linking this dying with work, with productivity, with "not spinning your wheels."

Cal Harris was a federal labor lawyer in the Chicago regional office. Earlier today, Kittle sent him a memo warning he might get passed over for third-year promotion, the big one.

Alone now in his small windowless office, Harris stared blankly at the memo thinking how heartsick Ellen and Justin would feel gazing down at his gauze draped, walnut-brown face.

Six months ago, Kittle evaluated Harris's gait. Said he had observed him walking with "greater determination," which in Kittle's rheumy eyes meant he could expect better productivity in the future, all monthly caseload time targets met.

Kittle was a paternalistic Boston liberal, and Harris did not intuit mean-spiritedness from the old man. But with only two and a half black lawyers on the staff of twenty-seven, the remark was demeaning, he thought, straight out of *Gone With the Wind*. As if finally he had learned to serve silver goblets of frosty mint juleps on the veranda without spilling a drop—and just how do white lawyers walk?

Later as daylight slipped away, Harris moved out onto the second floor patio overlooking the condo parking area, free of his coat and tie, clutching a chilled can of Old Style beer. Once before, he remembered, on a day like this when coils of gold, purple and crimson shimmered in the unstirred September air, he had lived a far better life and a pretty girl said, "Let's go to the carnival and win something."

He took a seat on one of the canvas director's chairs to wait for Ellen. Justin was dribbling a basketball up and down the driveway so Harris watched for cars. Last week someone turned in too fast and almost hit a kid. "We need speed bumps," he'd said to the air. On the Internet, he learned Brits in the U.K. call speed bumps "sleeping policemen." And though he remembered Ellen's throaty laughter when he laid this gem on her, even a playful memory did nothing now to halt his self-pitying slide. Soon, everyone in the office would suspect Harris was just spinning his wheels.

Yesterday's newspaper lay open on his lap and he'd read about a former beauty queen who confessed she'd boinked some bigwig politician before he achieved worldwide acclaim. She felt obligated to apologize publicly to his wife. "What I did was wrong and I feel terrible about it now. My behavior was inappropriate," the paper reported. The ex-beauty queen said she had come forward because she wanted the world to understand the sex was consensual. "He didn't force himself on me in the back seat of a limo," she said.

I should apologize to Kittle. The way I walk is inappropriate. Losing those two cases was inappropriate. Maybe that's what he wants to hear.

Music of the Kenny G variety issued faintly from someone's stereo, one-dimensional keening that the tin-eared call smooth jazz, anesthetizing ghost notes floating over on a quicksilver breeze. Soon he was nodding and drifting, transported to the Door County woods where Ellen was bending over a massive felled oak, polka dot sundress hiked up wickedly in back, a Marilyn Monroe dress, he says. "Let's do it this way, magic man." He needed no cajoling. Never before had he performed outdoors, thrusting and keeping time with a cool rhythmic breeze, the dance with no steps, his mind overflowing with Beethoven's Ninth, wanting to make it last, this Ode to Joy.

He bolted up straight and looked around remembering where he was, flinging the newspaper to the floor as if that dismissive gesture would settle his blood. Justin was now dribbling in front of the patio, and Harris smiled down on the eight year old when he tried a Kobe Bryant between-the-legs move. "Keep using your left, gotta use both hands," he said. The boy dribbled left, unsteadily, before switching back to right where he seemed more confident.

"When's Ellen coming home?"

"Soon, I hope. Hungry?"

"Uh huh, I'm so hungry I could ride a horse."

"You mean eat a horse, don't you son?"

"Daddy, did you ever eat a horse's meat?"

"Maybe. If I did, I didn't know. People don't usually eat horses, son. But when you're hungry enough to eat a big horse, you're really really hungry. See what I mean jelly bean?"

With the ball tucked under a thin wispy arm, Justin gazed up, mouth breathing through parted lips, heart-shaped his mother used to say. In the waning daylight, soft brown floppy curls danced over his cinnamon-colored forehead. In Brazil, they'd call him *pardo,* neither black nor white. In happier times, Harris and ex-wife Sophia (she and Ellen, both white) liked the caressing bossa nova musical tone suggested by pardo and didn't like *mixed* or *light-skinned* as identifiers. Sophia hit on beige and it became their thing.

"I think you might have a prodigious appetite, like Fats Waller."

"What does that mean?"

"Appetite so big your eyes pop out like this."

"Daddy, is Fats somebody's real name?"

"Well, yes and no, son. Fats was famous, a large black man who played the piano and organ. My daddy used to talk about how he'd sing and say funny crazy stuff. His real name was Thomas, everybody liked him—but one never knows, do one?"

"Do one? That's not even correct Daddy."

"That's Fats talking, told you he was funny."

"Where's he now?"

"In heaven, I suppose, with plenty to eat and probably playing on a grand piano."

Harris and Sophia shared joint custody though the arrangement seldom worked smoothly. One week with him, one week with her. Typically, Justin would return on Sunday evening with less underwear and socks than when he departed, and he'd have little to say about his time with her and her guitar-plucking younger boyfriend. Sophia had taught him to not reveal what went on when he was with her; they kept secrets from Harris leading him to consider filing for sole custody. Encouraging the child to deceive his father, bouncing him back and forth, not a healthy way for a kid to grow up.

Justin's crazy about Ellen so Harris understood why a divorced man with a child would pay a fortune to have a woman like her in their life. When folks spotted the three of them together, they often assumed Ellen was the mother and he could tell it pleased her inner mom.

He drained the beer and headed off to the kitchen, returning with another can as Ellen pulled in. She angled the red Prelude into a space then reached down and retrieved a purse, briefcase and something in a plastic bag. The small brown-eyed belle waved and flashed a beguiling smile as she moved toward him, her smile growing wider as she drew closer. Justin carried her brief case, struggling to dribble the ball with control. A handmade girl, Harris liked to say, crooning in her ear, "rolled tighter than a fine Cuban cigar." And she would blush, loving every second.

He wrapped an arm around her waist, leaned over and planted a light kiss. Smiling, she grazed her fingers along his cheek.

"God, I'm beat," she said, falling onto the couch, removing small silvery earrings. "Right now, the office isn't busy, watching time turtle by is mentally exhausting."

He raised the can and took a swig showing little interest in management tempo at the department of public works, justifiably self-involved or so he thought, gazing vaguely over the can watching as she snared Justin in a squealing bear hug.

After dinner, he supervised Justin's bath and hustled him off to bed. He settled the boy inside the red, blue and yellow Chicago Cubs sleeping bag and took up the plastic Fisher-Price toy mouth organ from the nightstand. Harris placed his fingers on the small keys and then played taps, the bedtime routine begun two years ago and now obligatory. Afterwards, he leaned down, and kissed the waiting forehead.

Framed in the backlight from the hall, he paused at the door before casting the last daddy-assuring glance of the day then turned off the light. Only the nightlight, a green and white roosting owl, glowed softly near the head of the bed.

"Okay son, say good night. Say good night, night owl."

"Good night daddy, good night, night owl."

The owl's faint warm light cast a gentle shadow above the child's drowsy profile compelling Harris to hesitate a little more, stalling to freeze time and imprint the precious memory. He smiled before turning and closing the door, leaving it open a sliver the way Justin liked.

He returned to the living room while Ellen was still busy in the kitchen, water running, cabinets closing, the rippling and crinkling of Saran wrap covering leftovers. When she came to him, he stood blinking and scowling, empty inside as a cathedral after a High Mass.

"Cal, something's bothering you, I can tell."

At the living room picture window, he stared into the blackness, morosely oblivious to the showy stars, the risen moon or the pane of glass inches from his nose, coming to terms with his life wherein another man held sway over how he moved his feet. And why had God denied him the physical skill to spin a basketball on his fingertip for Justin?

"Kittle gave me a warning memo, says I might not get promoted."

"A warning memo, what? What do you mean?" She fluffed two throw pillows.

"I just told you what."

"Honey, don't get mad, sit by me. Talk to me. Hon-nee."

"I'm not gonna—"

She broke in. "Kittle said you may not get promoted?"

His heart jumped, sensing she didn't understand.

"From Kittle, yeah, but my ass-kissing supervisor—you-know-who—is in on it too."

Harris had been pacing like a jittery sentry. He stopped abruptly and plumped down on the arm of the new blackberry velvet sofa, raising the beer can to mouth, swallowing. Could she ever fully understand? Last year Ellen didn't understand the bank teller she'd spoken so fondly of, a woman with a similar Wisconsin background whom she liked. The teller's husband had accidentally killed himself, electrocuted while stringing TV cable 25 feet up on a utility pole. Terms of the settlement were supposed to remain confidential but she bitterly confided the amount to Ellen: $163,425.00, after taxes, after the "thieving lawyers."

Days later, while Harris and Ellen stood at the teller's window, her stupefied face morphed into a glob of lumpy oatmeal and stayed that way until they left. Ellen was crushed. But he had seen this pathetic one-act production before. Consider it your intro course in American Bigotry 101 he said in the parking lot, kissing away salty tears. "You passed with flying colors." Both were too upset to spot the unintended pun.

Now, on the end of the sofa he can barely sit still. "I'm going online."

"When?"

"What do you mean, *when*? You think I'm drunk?" He averted his gaze. Staring at his feet, two dead fish came to mind.

"Cal, please!" Both hands flew up fluttering the air.

"I'm not taking this lying down. When attacked, counterattack." He jumped to his feet, stretching both arms out, reaching for the ceiling.

Ellen choked on a laugh. "Goodness. You popped up like some kind of mad scientist." She had returned from the kitchen with an Old Style for herself.

Ellen had been divorced for two years when he met her on Match. com. He'd hesitated about bringing up Sophia and only did it so she would learn up front he had child-raising responsibilities. She said *Heart* was her favorite group, but she was no barracuda. He said he didn't have a favorite group, taking the path of least resistance. With two fingers under the table she had tugged his pants leg and held on until he named a group. *Earth, Wind and Fire*, he conceded, deciding right then that women who drank beer, and not some fluffy pink umbrella drink, were fascinating.

On the second date, they dined at a Thai restaurant on Lake Street in Oak Park. When she recommended a dish made with a peanut sauce, he said, "I only eat peanuts at ball games or in fudge." Ellen laughed into her menu and asked, "Sir, are you always so rigid?" An enthralling sheen of perspiration lined her upper lip like cake frosting, but with a flick of her pink tongue, it vanished. Later, waiting for the check, he reached across the table and rested a hand on back of hers. She moved and got to her feet and suddenly he was a man standing upright in a canoe with his pants down. "Whoa Nelly, don't look so *discomboobberated*," she said. "Only going to the ladies' room. Coming right back." Never before had he heard a word mispronounced so charmingly and quicker than a wink he'd fallen heart-deep into her engulfing brown eyes.

"Counterattack?" Ellen said, dropping down on the sofa and smiling, seeming to anticipate getting in on the joke. Studs Terkel's book, *Working*, lay on the coffee table. She brushed it aside and settled the can on a coaster. "Whom, no, no, who do you plan to counterattack?"

"I'm gonna blow the whistle. On Facebook . . . YouTube, whatever! Black lawyer disciplined for walking like a jive-ass, let's face it, that's what Kittle meant."

"What?"

He eyed her as if a courtroom adversary, giving nothing away with his face.

"Now stop it, Cal. I don't like you when you behave this way."

"Remember Larry, the summer intern? Kittle always found time to *chat* with him and he's gay for sure. A gay giggling brother and Kittle's eating it up. Now there's a pun for you and you know how I hate puns. Maybe I'll upload a video of me walking, showing my normal stride, see how many likes I get. They'll be calling this Kittle-g-a-i-t when I'm done. Get it?"

Her brow knitted as if deciding whether to sign papers immediately committing the man she loved.

"He never marries, vacations every year, alone, the Galapagos Islands, photographing giant turtles. Yeah right! Probably somewhere rendezvousing with a twelve-year-old boy."

"Cal, you're tired and lashing out. Do you hear what you're saying?"

She reached for the Studs Terkel book, bookmarked at an interview with Louis Hayward, a washroom attendant at the historic Palmer House hotel in Chicago. "What's this about? Don't worry, I won't lose your place."

She patted the cushion and Cal moved to her. He understood Ellen could not bear his envisioned act of cruelty, and he could not love her if she did. Days after she moved in, she had asked him to please take down the sign affixed to the dresser mirror which said: A bachelor is a man who never makes the same mistake once.

"Yes, come closer and cuddle up," she said.

"He was my dad," pointing to the page as if identifying a carjacking suspect. "Hayward's not his real name. Rhymes with wayward and that sure as hell fits. You really smell good!"

"You like? It's new, DKNY, do I smell divine?"

"Yeah, sweet, tutti-frutti." Instantly her scent produced in him an unexpected but welcomed frisson of hope. Hope: that priceless commodity valued universally. Later tonight, desire may again range within his grasp. Recoverable.

He related how his father had worked on the railroad as a Pullman porter until they fired him. Later he worked as a sub at the post office until they too fired him. After that, he landed at the Palmer House and remained until he became eligible for Social Security. Harris wasn't aware he was in the book until several years after they buried him.

"So neat. You're kinda famous." She gave him a loud smooch. "Why didn't you tell me?"

"Why didn't I tell you? A washroom attendant?"

"Honey, don't be sad. Heck, my dad was a *frotteur*, may still be."

"A what?"

"A frotteur, frotteurism. French, for one who rubs. Mom divorced Dad when I was eleven. Some good ole boy busted his nose at a Willie Nelson concert because he was rubbing up against his girlfriend's behind while my mom was standing next to him. Dad admitted in court he'd been doing kinky stuff since high school. Really upset Mom. Why didn't he rub against her, she's standing right next to him? We have the same nose only now his is pushed over to the side like this. Would you still love me if my nose was over here? Cal, I was funny, you can laugh."

"She divorced him for—for that?"

"Well, she loves Willie Nelson and she did miss most of the concert rushing him to the emergency room. But I still love him—what was your dad like?"

"Like?" He squinted, struggling to bring his father into focus, worry lines forming between the eyes. "Wow, it's all kinda blurry. Mostly I just remember the weird stuff. There was one record he used to play when he was half-crocked. A Chopin polonaise as I recall. He'd wave a five-dollar bill promising the money to the first one of us who learned to play it."

"A musical family, how wonderful."

"We weren't exactly the Cosby family but we did have a used upright piano. From kindergarten to eighth grade, I had the nuns . . . or they had me. Hard to believe—but I was an altar boy. I used to be holy. Ha! Didn't even know we were poor until old high-pockets got himself fired from the railroad."

"Honey, aren't you being a just bit disrespectful?"

"Told Studs Terkel he lost his job because of the decline in railroad travel. Not true. The union had him canned for non-payment of dues."

"They can do that?"

"They could in those days. But go on, read the last paragraph." He wiped his hands down over his face, rubbing his eyes. "That's what gets me. No one ever told me my grandmother was a writer who'd sold a couple of stories. I think something's been missing in my life, some connection. Spiritual, metaphysical, whatever—and I missed it. I coulda been a writer, coulda been a contender, I coulda been somebody."

"I know that movie. Wait, wait, don't tell me," she said, rubbing her shoulder against his, to and fro, like a contented cat.

"Maybe writing was my ticket to ride. Recognition, know what I mean?"

"You're a good lawyer, honey, and that ain't chopped liver."

He gazed tenderly and imagined seeing clear through to her heart. "For my writing is what I mean baby."

Ellen cradled the book to her breasts and looked up, nodding thoughtfully. "I understand honey, I do understand. Let's sleep on it and tomorrow we'll figure out something definitive that doesn't involve outing Mr. Kittle on the Internet. He's a decent man and you know it."

"Decent my royal behind," he said with a snort laugh. "White man speak with forked tongue."

"Chill out Cochise and help me straighten up. You know how I hate leaving a mess. Honey."

He stood and with a flourish, raised his empty beer can. "So here's to you, as good as you are. And here's to me, as bad as I am. But as good as you are, and as bad as I am, I'm as good as you are, as bad as I am."

"Yes, honey, you told that one before, it's your father's—"

"Toast. His three-sheets-to-the wind toast."

She rose to her feet brushing hair from her eyes, bending over the coffee table, plaid skirt taut against fetching hips, each fiber freighted with suggested sensuality discoverable only by him. He stopped short and then moved to her, but when she turned to face him he faltered, dimly aware he'd be unable to account for himself if called upon to do so.

Twice a car horn sounded nearby, impatiently, and twice again. He rubbed the base of his neck and frowned.

"Cal, now what's the matter?" She reached for him. "You're so tense. Tell me."

"Jeez, it's annoying. This time of night. Really rude."

She turned her face toward the irritant. "I know, I know."

"Right," he said. "Something definitive. You hit the head on the nail baby. By the way, it's Brando, *On the Waterfront*."

She smiled. "Oh, listen to you!"

Harris blinked twice and headed stiff-legged to the kitchen summoning X-rated images of the beauty queen cavorting freaky-deaky with the big shot politician. He pictured himself nuzzling the nape of Ellen's neck, reaching around to the front with both hands and getting things started.

Three, almost four beers, he thought, would the old black magic work again tonight? If he made a move and Ellen did the diaphragm thing, would anything come of it? She explained once why she wasn't on the pill, but now he couldn't remember. After Ellen inserted the device (she never let him watch) he'd sometimes put pressure on himself to meet or exceed expectations.

She glided past him to the bedroom. "Coming honey?"

If the Alka-Seltzer doesn't fizz, she'll understand.

"Daisy Mae Hamilton," he said to her backside gliding by. "My grandma, the writer."

"Pretty name."

He had never met Daisy Mae who died when his father was twelve. He wondered what she had written, who her audience was. In her shortened life he hoped her writing had provided some measure of fulfillment but harbored no illusions about his father's level of fulfillment. He had earned a diploma from Englewood High School in the 1940s, back when it meant something, back when Englewood was not the crime ridden national blight it later became. Books were his friends when he wasn't cleaning up after others, trolling for tips, or plastered. Harris lamented his father's crappy luck. What might he have become if life had dealt him a better hand, freed from menial labor which ultimately drained his resolve in ball-busting gin piss? "A horse! A horse! My kingdom for a horse," he'd rave, apropos of damn near anything, drunk on his bumptious ass.

He listened to Ellen, humming in the bedroom, opening and closing dresser drawers in squeaky syncopated rhythm. Through the fog of his bruised ego he was slowly coming to grips with Kittle's assessment, understanding it might be spot-on accurate, the venerable old man's crusty demeanor obscuring genuine concern for his career. Still, he felt put upon, his sense of self deeply wounded and in a way he couldn't articulate, it affected his innocent sleeping son.

If stinging tears came now, he would not be ashamed.

From the bedroom, Ellen called, "hon-nee."

He moved to the cabinet beneath the kitchen sink and then stooped down and brought up the can crusher, a handy gadget Ellen ordered from a Miles Kimball catalog. No longer would he stomp beer cans with his foot, which she declared absolutely primitive. He set the made-in-China metal contraption on the counter and stood an empty Old Style vertically on the base. Steadying the can, he readied it to apply just the right upward jerk of the lever to create vise-like compression. A sharp yank upwards generated a decisive downward smash. The second can in position, fingers safely out of the way, he executed another perfect smash.

Again from the bedroom Ellen called out, "Cal, honey, what's keeping you? Are you all right?"

He tossed one crushed can into the blue recycle container, the second one fell short.

"Close enough for government work," he mumbled before walking over to pick it up.

"Come to bed honey, who're you talking to?"

Harris stood and listened, defying any rude joker to honk again at this late hour. He studied his feet splayed over the black and white tile, long maligned feet in black socks. A good lawyer Ellen had said, but will Kittle ever notice he was moving in the hall with greater determination?

He stood motionless and in the brooding silence, his pulse was deafening.

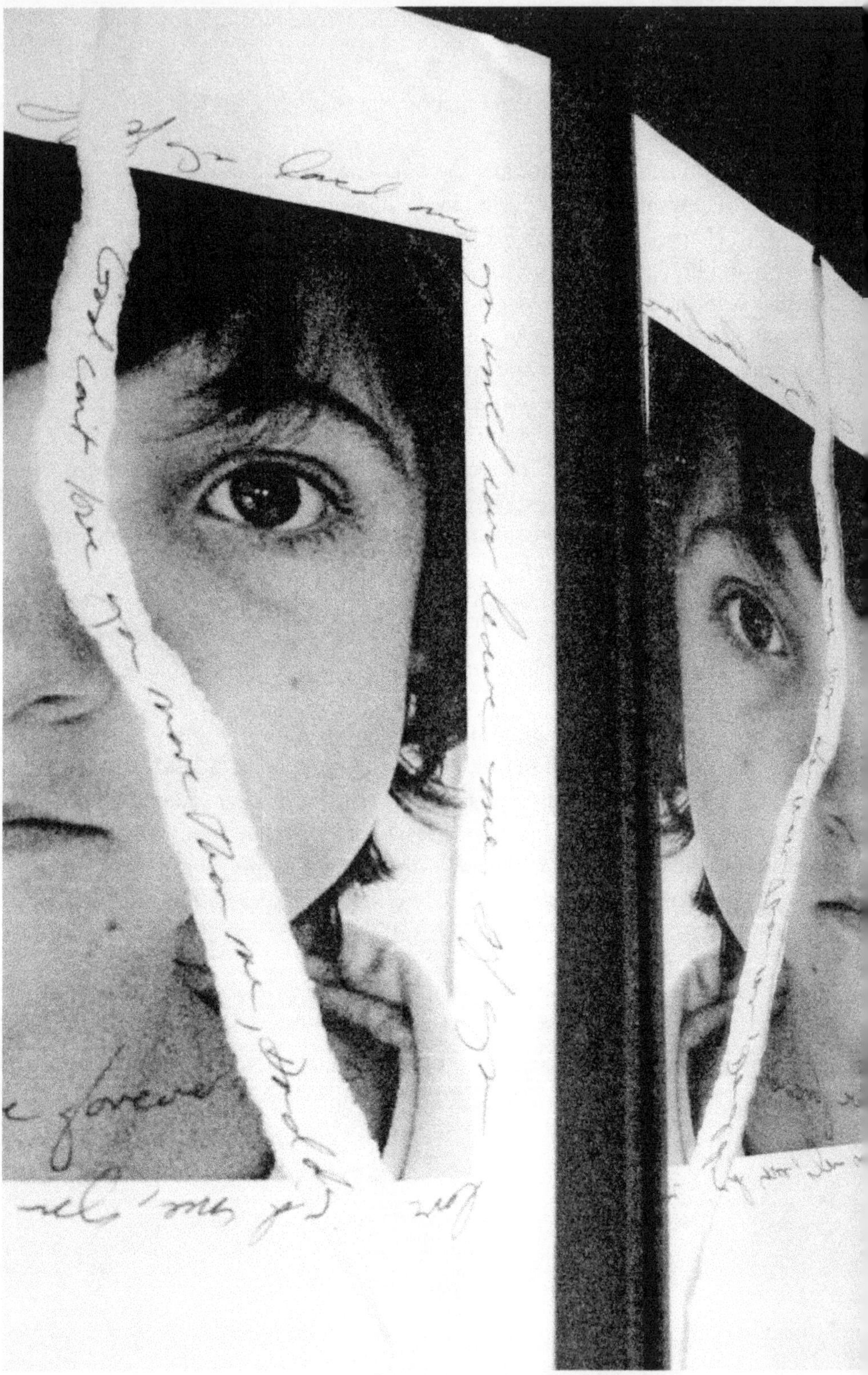

FRUITS OF ILLNESS

ANDY WEATHERWAX

POSSESSION

There are few words more ambiguous in meaning than possession.
The dictionary says possession is the act of having or taking into
        control.
In legal terms it can mean occupancy of property,
without regard for ownership, or without regard for legality
        as with drugs or weapons.

Possession can also refer to control of a ball or puck;
or domination by something, a spirit, a passion, an idea;
or a psychological state in which an individual's normal personality
is replaced by another.

But possession is most often associated with ownership,
though it need not refer to literal ownership.
Sure, we can speak of Bob's hat if Bob owns a hat,
but we can also speak of Bob's children even if Bob doesn't own them.

Which brings me to Parkinson's disease.

It's a funny name for it.
I have it, yet it is not mine.
Parkinson never had it, he just found it.
Now I have it, now it's my Parkinson's disease.

We would never speak of my Bob's hat,
just makes no sense.
Anyhow, that's not the point.
The point is, it's possessive.

That is exactly what it is.

MY TEACHER

I'd like to run with the boys,
cook dinner on an open flame,
and enjoy a glass of wine with friends and family

grasping at the past, I weep
an icy wall of anger and resentment builds
frozen, unable to break free from this frigid barrier
that holds hardened self-pity near and dear

I close my eyes and listen
to the sounds of the summer barbecue
the laughter of the boys
the chatter of friends and family

I close my eyes and breathe
letting the warm waters of gratitude rush in
thawing the raw grip of expectation
letting go of *I wish*, letting reality-as-it-is arise

I close my eyes and smile
it is what it is
and there is no way to escape it
I am of the nature to grow old, to fall ill, to die

everyone I love and all that I hold dear
is of the same nature
this I learn time and again
humbled by illness,
my great
teacher

THE GIFT

this is a gift
and I am ill with it

it bounces around my brain
slowly seizing my ability
to move
to speak
to think

this is a gift, I told my six-year-old son
not the type you wrap with a bow
not a gift you would wish upon anyone

there was a time when my musings strayed to madness,
my thoughts to terror

there was a time I would blame the moon
for its blurred reflection in turbulent waters

but gratitude's exquisite blossom now fills my heart
leaving fear no recourse
clarity returns and I can see the moon

this is a gift of understanding of the suffering
caused by illness, old age and death

this is a gift of compassion
putting self-pity in the past
the future is forever now

I breathe
the clear sky above my head
the vegetable garden at my feet

this is a gift
and I am alive with it

INDEED

He must have been 6'5" with broad shoulders and a menacing grin.
His jet-black skin glistened with sweat in the bright sunlight
on this sticky summer day.
Leaning on an umbrella, he flirted with two women.

Such was the scene directly in front of the entrance to the men's room
I so desperately needed to visit.
Anyone having to take a leak
would have to run this gauntlet.

He saw me shuffling toward them.
Our eyes met. He paused mid-sentence, and grinned.
After a moment he continued his chatter, all the while
keeping his gaze on me and grinning that menacing grin.

My unhurried advance became comical,
step after step, so slow to reach my destination.
When I was close enough to engage, he did,
"Looks like you're having a good ol' time bro!"

I don't bother to try to understand comments like that.
Some people think I'm drunk.
If they think me a drunk then I am a drunk.
"It's a beautiful day my man!" I replied.

I said hello to the two ladies and shuffled into the men's room.
He was waiting for me when I finally exited.
Through a hearty laugh he asked,
"You gonna make it bro?" The ladies giggled.

"Indeed I am!" I said as I shuffled past.
"Indeed?" he said in a mocking tone.
Turning to the ladies he pointed at me with his umbrella
"Listen to this guy! Indeed!"

I stumbled clumsily over nothing and froze.
He chuckled and the ladies giggled.
"Have you seen Muhammad Ali lately?"
I said with my back to them.

They fell silent.
"Yeah." He said with some apprehension.
"Well me and Ali . . . " I barked, turning quickly.
With both fists cocked
I lunged toward him.
He flinched.
" . . . we have a little something in common!"

Startled, he smiled a less menacing smile.
I smiled knowing he knew what I was talking about.

"Well, you have a good one bro; take care of yourself," he said,
with eyes down looking at the tip of his umbrella
as he tapped it on the ground.

"You too." I said looking back at the trio
"And be good. I don't wanna have to come back here and kick your ass!"

He chuckled "Indeed!"

RUSS ALLISON LOAR

COMPLETE HONESTY

I was an honest man when my father-in-law began to die.

It took me the first twenty-seven years of my life to become a consistently honest man, a scrupulously honest man. I was not a habitual liar, but I grew up wanting to stay out of trouble with my parents who were not of a forgiving nature, and so I lied. During my teenage years the fabrications multiplied as I tried my best to live free of parental rules and regulations. I didn't lie to get anything in particular, I lied to stay out of trouble.

> *Do you realize what time it is young man?*
> *I ran out of gas.*

I started lying for personal gain during the early years of my marriage when money was hard to come by and even harder to hold on to. I would tell any number of tall tales about automobile repairs and broken-down refrigerators to convince my wealthy yet retentive parents that their money, so painful for them to part with, was at least going to some practical use.

> *I need $150.*
> *What? More money? Again? We just gave you $400 to fix your car!*
> *The refrigerator stopped. The repair guy is here right now. I've got to get it fixed so the food won't spoil.*

Then, one day, the lies stopped.

I was no less impecunious, but something happened that changed my perspective. I became a father. I began to question just what kind of father I would be in the eyes of my son. I knew what kind of father I wanted to be, and so I set out to become that idealized person. I had many weaknesses to address and redress, but the first, most important task was to become a completely honest man. Honest in all things, at all times. I knew the foundation of morality, character and wisdom had to be honesty. Without honesty life is a house of cards, susceptible to the slightest breeze of truth.

I began to test myself. If a waiter forgot to charge me for some item of food, I insisted that it be added to my bill. If a cashier gave me too much change at a store, I returned it. In fact, I paid particular attention to the most trivial transactions and interactions. I had much to atone for. And I was tested. An inordinate number of people dropped money from pockets and purses whenever I was around.

Clerical errors in my favor abounded. The kind of happenstance I constantly wished for during my most poverty-stricken years now occurred with peculiar regularity. I still do not know if this was an odd coincidence, a divine test, or just the sort of thing that happens all the time, a normal state of affairs which I became acutely aware of only because of my near obsessive desire to make amends for a lifetime of ethical lapses.

> *You only charged me for three of these cookies, but I've got four.*
> *That's OK. We'll catch you next time.*
> *No, please, let me pay you for this other cookie.*
> *Don't worry about it. It's OK.*
> *I cannot leave here without paying you for this cookie.*

By the time I was forty-two, my honesty was habitual. A reflex. It must also be said that no being of human dimensions can achieve perfection, but I tried. I became prideful of the opportunity to display my honesty at every turn. In my professional life as a newspaper reporter, a career begun after my first son was born, I sought out dishonesty with a missionary zeal. I would recount the lies of various miscreants, their attempts to cover up their lies, their false claims of being misunderstood and quoted "out of context," and finally their apologies. I was instrumental in destroying their reputations and shaming their families. They were ultimately responsible for their own behavior, but I was merciless. There's no more fierce advocate for the truth than a reformed liar.

> *Former school superintendent Peter Snyder, convicted last year of embezzling $2.7 million from the Valley Unified School District, was stabbed to death in a San Diego County prison yesterday. "He was a good man who made a bad mistake," said ex-wife*

Theresa Snyder who divorced her husband two months after his conviction.

Does honesty have limits? Should an honest person lie to avoid hurting the feelings of friends and family? Does honesty require you to tell your mother her new outfit is forty years out of date and her hairdo makes her look like Bozo the Clown? Surely we are not required to voice every subjective opinion in order to fulfill the requirements of honesty. A reluctance to express opinions and preferences, after all, is not a masking of truth, it is a refusal to engage in momentary, subjective assessment.

> *You've changed your hair.*
> *How do you like it?*
> *I think it brings out the real you.*

And yet when it came to my personal beliefs, I never put the slightest tarnish on the truth. My late father-in-law, a physician, was a deeply religious man. Soon after I began dating his only daughter, I felt no reluctance in telling him just how medieval I thought his particular religion was.

> *How can you actually believe your religion is the only true religion?*
> *We trust in the teachings of our church.*
> *Did it ever occur to you that your self-serving religious leaders just might be wrong?*
> *We have no reason to doubt them.*

My wife and I were subsequently married without her parents' blessings, and only over the course of years did my relationship with the two godly souls that were her parents soften. Most of the softening came with the birth of my first son, their first grandchild. And so were we all changed by the miracle that is a newborn child. I learned to hold my tongue while simultaneously developing a genuine interest in the weather as a topic of conversation.

I returned to college and majored in journalism, a profession which is supposed to be about the truth. My father-in-law admired my determination to finish college while working odd jobs to support my family. He had entered medical school late in life after serving in the Army and knew only too well how hard it was to attend classes, study, be an attentive father and still earn some kind of living. My second son was born three years later, between semesters, and the bond between our families grew stronger. Religion was not a subject for conversation, but in all other matters, our relations became cordial.

About five years later, Grandpa Doc, as my father-in-law became known to our sons, retired from medical practice. He was a kind man who left many broken-hearted patients behind when he moved to the small Northern California town of Paradise. Yes, it's actually named Paradise. Moving was his wife's idea, for she was the font of all religious discipline in the family and believed the big cities would soon fall into chaos, what with the Second Coming nearly here. The small town of Paradise was indeed a beautiful, if not remote, place to live, but it left him bereft of friends and familiar landmarks. It was a cold turkey retirement. And a few years later, his isolation grew as his mental faculties failed.

And so Grandpa Doc traveled between comprehension and confusion, never fully surrendering to confusion, always fighting his way back for a while. I watched his struggle; only during our last visit did he ask me The Question. He was in the hospital and we were alone together. His wife had left the small, sterile room to get a drink of water, and my wife went with her. He was lying flat on his back with only a small pillow under his head, confused, but not scared. He looked at me and smiled with the same unassuming manner that had always been his way with patients, especially when broaching the subject of bad news.

How does it look? Do you think I'm going to pull through?

He was counting on my honesty, asking me to confide in him. As a physician, he was only too aware of the fiction of reassuring words from friends, family and medical professionals who have decided the patient is no longer in a sufficient state of mind to process factual information. But this was one of Grandpa Doc's clear moments and he wanted to know the truth. He figured I was the most likely person to give it to him—straight.

And what was the truth? Could I really predict the future? Was I medically qualified to give any kind of diagnosis, much less prognosis, to this man so cruelly cast adrift by old age? Of course, we all knew that his condition was not reversible. But how could I tell this religious man there would be no miracle for him?

Torn between the obvious and the miraculous, given this grave honor of rendering some kind of truthful information to a man momentarily clear enough to want to know what was really happening, I put my hand on his shoulder, smiled, and summoned my best imitation of the offhand remark, my best imitation of his own reassuring beside manner.

You're doing OK. You'll pull out of this. You'll be going home soon.

He looked into my eyes and at least for a moment, he knew the truth.

EVELYN SHARENOV

DELIVERANCE

Let me tell you about myself. I live alone and although that's a recent development, I'm settled with that. I consider myself average; well, maybe not average but not special or chosen in any way. I must add that I don't say this as an apology for any past hubris or explanation for my current station in life.

My son is healthy and intelligent. I usually enjoy good health although just now I'm down with the flu. I haven't moved from this bed in days, haven't showered or shaved or dressed. I'm perfectly comfortable. My son's cat is on the bed with me, basking in a square of sunlight, her pleasure principle undisturbed by my growing pains. I miss my son, suddenly and completely, my son of ten years ago, who would have fallen asleep in my lap. But he'll be home from college for spring break and then he'll be back for the summer. I reach over and scratch the cat under her chin; she stretches, then rolls onto her back. The cat, abandoned when my son went off to college, has adopted me and we sleep together in Eric's bed, keeping it warm for him in his absence.

Things average out. I like to think I am in the exact middle of my life, with as much ahead as has gone before. I have a small but respectable law practice. It has become more lucrative as the economy sinks into the Pacific Ocean and people sue each other not out of acrimony or greed but to survive. I like to think I am doing some good for my clients.

My wife's departure is not my first taste of loss. I've always felt as if something were missing, as if everything always turns out to be less than I expected—marriage, kids, life. When I was a kid I became obsessed with the plate-twirler on the Ed Sullivan show, the man who ran across the stage giving a twist to this pole or that plate, in an effort to keep them all spinning; I kept waiting for a single plate to fall and shatter but I can't recall that it ever happened while I was watching. My parents were mesmerized by animal acts or Elvis, but I waited impatiently for the man with the plates. Some of my plates have crashed but others are still twirling.

Leslie earned her freedom, raising our son and putting me through law school. Sometimes it seems to me our entire marriage was a preparation for her leaving, all our years together an accumulating process, leverage gathered like storm clouds. But that leaving, although I figure I contributed to it, is still a loss.

So, even though it's a hot sunny afternoon, perfect for a walk or nine holes of golf, even though I feel better, you'll understand if I take a nap. When I waken, my son's room is in shade. I step outside into a wall of heat and putter in my yard a bit. We used to have a gardener, but that seems like a foolish luxury now.

The winter rains have ended; the hot Santa Ana winds have cleared the air and fooled the lawns into thinking it is an early summer. We are on the cusp. As winter leaves, it clears the way for spring. That first hot day, when cats scratch at the screen to get out, when pale legs emerge in shorts, when winter's ballast appears curbside for garage sales and recycling, the lawnmowers growl and the barbecue grills are fired up. Confusion of seasons is over. The sky is broad and high and the air is tight and oppressive on my skin. The stubble of newly planted lawns appears as a five o'clock shadow of green. I assess the year's casualties: the neighbors disfigured by divorce, maimed by illness, the defections, infidelities, deaths. Those who remain standing, even if not quite upright, are survivors. I'm one of them.

My next-door neighbor's lawn is overgrown and brown. I offered to mow it myself, but he turned me down. Last autumn his son committed suicide, perhaps in anticipation of his father's reaction to the announcement he was gay. Now their dog sits quietly all day and watches me do yard work. He shyly wanders over and sets a tennis ball at my feet, hoping for a game of catch. I spend the remainder of the afternoon playing ball with the dog while the kids come home from school, screen doors slam, dinners are cooked, dates are made and broken. There's yelling up and down the block. The neighborhood is transformed.

The phone's ringing somewhere deep inside my house and I debate whether to answer it. I've dismantled the answering machine. I leave the dog on the porch with a bowl of water and his tennis ball. At first I don't recognize the voice; it's been a while. Then I have a rush of brains to my head.

"How've you been?" I ask Stuart, my oldest friend in the world. And more to the point, "Where've you been?"

It's been about six years since we've spoken. He was banished from our home by Leslie for his lifestyle choice—he did a lot of drugs and periodically called me to bail him out of jail, a bad influence. I'm glad to hear his voice. I wondered why I didn't call him the day Leslie moved out of the house.

"I've been around, here and there, you know. How're Leslie and Eric?"

"Leslie left me and Eric's fine. He's away at college."

"Les is gone? I'd of thought you were in it for the duration."

"She's living with some guy. So what's new with you? You want to come over and have some dinner?" I move to safer ground.

"I have to tell you something first."

"So tell me." But I already know what he's going to say.

"I have AIDS," he says.

I think about this for a moment. "Well, duh," is all I can come up with to say, so I don't say it. The wages of stupidity shouldn't be death.

"Come over anyway. I promise I won't kiss you," is what I finally say.

Through the heat and tranquility of dusk, I'm chilled. Certain things seem timeless and immutable and for this I'm grateful. The children still gather in the shade of a serious tree to play and giggle and share what they've learned about sex. When Eric was young—six or seven—I would take my telescope outside on hot summer nights and set it up on the sidewalk. Steady as Polaris, I would find the planets. Word got around and soon the children on the block lined up to take turns looking through the telescope. I gathered them in, myself a star, the children a nebula around me. Until city lights obscured the stars, until gravity and earthly hungers called me back. Leslie behind the screen door needing me.

It's difficult seeing Stuart like this. Did I say difficult? It breaks my heart. He's thin; his skin is ashen gray and he has a cough. He denies he's in pain, but I don't believe him. I hold him for a moment in the doorway; it's like hugging a skeleton. I feel his shoulder blades like wing buds through his shirt. I order in a pizza. Stuart eats very little. I have no appetite but make a show of eating.

"So where are you staying?" I ask.

"I don't really have an address at the moment. Sort of between residences." He stops. "Look it, here's the thing. I don't have a home to go to anymore. I have no money. I have no medical insurance. It took all my strength to call you." Stuart starts crying. I stifle my impulse to put my arms around him.

When we were kids, Stuart and I used to sleep over at each other's house. I knew his parents as well as I knew my own. I dated his sister a couple of times when we were fifteen and again when we were twenty, before I met Leslie. Stuart was always wilder than me, took more chances, pushed the envelope; I hung back. Stuart said danger made him feel alive. Maybe not so much now, I guessed.

I weigh the offer I'm about to make because Eric will be home soon. "Come stay with me. For as long as you need. Until . . ."

Stuart moves in that night. Next day I take him to see my doctor. I fill his prescriptions for him. And I learn to cook.

A week later I drive past my parents' house. They don't know that Stuart is staying with me. I don't know if they would approve and I haven't entirely stopped caring. Their house is old; it needs paint. They've lived there since they were first married. My father just retired from his only job. I'm fashioned of the same stuff. Their trees are overgrown; they made my room a cool dark cave when I was a boy. An old flat tire swing is suspended from a low hanging branch, awaiting my son's children to come ride it.

I remember Eric when he was three, laughing and begging me to push him higher, giddy with sensation, joyous in his freedom from gravity. Les and I took him on a picnic that year, to Point Fermin. We bought sodas at Walker's diner. Bikers held court in the dark cool interior. Their motorcycles were lined up outside, a chorus line of gleaming chrome and black lacquer. Those were the days before weekend Hondas warred with weekday Harleys.

I hiked down to the beach with Eric. Leslie rested on our blanket under a tree. The sea was wild and I chased Eric as he ran, heedless of the tides, strong winds at his back. I yelled after him, but Eric didn't hear. He was under a spell, dazzled by brightly colored human birds, hang gliders who perched on the cliffs above the beach, then swooped and hovered above the ocean before landing on the sand. It frightened me, the enchantment that pulled Eric from me. But Eric was guided by an unseen hand, as if god or nature looked his way, and I was able to grab him before he ran into the sea.

Arguing before a jury was simple compared to being a father. Having Eric sharpened my taste for the kill. Everything came easily to me—verdicts, money, women. These days I'm worn out by the show of material wealth around me. I haven't had a good night's sleep in years. I want that time back, before I became successful, when there was less outside and more inside, before there was so much to lose.

Eric comes home at the end of March; he plans to spend the entire two weeks of spring break with me. He'll have dinner with Leslie and David once or twice but will sleep in his old room. He seems unaffected by his freshman year at Berkeley. He's overjoyed to see Stuart and the three of us fall into an easy rhythm.

Stuart's talkative, happy even; he reminds me of when he was a teenager. He hasn't changed an iota. He doesn't know the meaning of accountability. It's all the fault of the system. His parents and his ex-wife threw him out. His parents relented and offered to let him stay in an RV they had parked in their driveway. Stuart called me first. He tells me he hasn't got the support system that gay men with AIDS have, that he has the *good* kind of AIDS, whatever that is, but I know what he means because I know how he thinks. He's a loser and when we get drunk together, I tell him so. Eric is with his mother that night.

"So you think you're doing so well? How come Leslie left you?" It's a challenge. I cringe.

In the last quiet days before my marriage ended I was able to kid myself that Leslie would stay with me. She was seeing someone; I knew that. She was a nurse and met a lot of people. This is what I tell Stuart.

But I know what really happened. At best I was tepid, at worst cold. She found someone she thought loved her more than I did—a married doctor—who took care of her. I never gave her an appliance for Valentine's Day or our anniversary. I was a good provider and father. In the absence of a core, I thought this was enough.

So Les moved in with her lover and now she's waiting for him to make sense of their lives. The truth is I miss her. But it's the way I miss her that made her leave. I don't know if Stuart is capable of understanding any of this. And sometimes there's just no explaining the choices we make.

On our last morning in bed together—this is what's so weird—I could still have asked her to stay but I didn't. It was like she had already gone through our divorce in her mind, had done her grieving, and I hadn't even started. We knew she was moving out on June 30th and we slept together until that day. We got up and made breakfast and ate together as if nothing awful were happening. And then the movers came and she was gone.

There are times I think I see her—on a street or at the market—and I feel that same excitement as the first time we met. And there are nights when the last image in my mind before sleep is Leslie going down on me in my car, her wild dark hair spread over my lap, caressing my thighs.

It's hot and sunny through Eric's spring break. We're happy, the three of us together, in a strange and timeless way. I barbecue on Easter Sunday. Steaks, potatoes and corn-on-the-cob. The briquettes are ashen and ready. A drop of fat catches fire and billows of rising smoke make my eyes tear. Eric is stretched out on a chaise near me; he's reading *Return of the Native*.

"This is a great book, Dad. Have you read it?" I say I haven't. "Well, you should." Eric loves college. He reads thick novels. He tells me he's dating a senior who will visit in August. I've already told him she can stay with us during the summer. She's majoring in literature and I'm certain has an influence on his current tastes in reading. I want him to major in something sensible, but there's time for that discussion.

I watch Eric through the smoke. His long tan limbs are comfortable at rest. He is at ease, energy and potential. Last year he was amorphous, half boy, half man. This year he favors man. He wears his hair in a peculiar cut I recognize from the kids who work at the Starbucks next to my office, short, black, spiky.

Stuart carries out three Coronas, with a slice of lime in each, perched precariously on a tray. His balance is a little off and his hands tremble. We sit quietly as the evening cools down and a light breeze comes up. Eric sleeps in his chair, his novel face down in the grass.

It was a night like this last summer that Leslie told me she was leaving. We were getting ready to grill. Leslie carried out a platter of raw dismembered chicken and a bowl of barbecue sauce. I held long handled tongs and a brush, expertly turned and basted each piece until they were evenly done. We ate in silence. It was easy to believe we were alone in the universe. The charcoals were a dim nightlight, quickly dying to embers. The veil of summer humidity parted briefly then closed again.

"I'm moving out," Leslie said. Her voice was flat and practiced. She shivered and hugged her slim bare legs in the Adirondack chair.

I just sat there, silent, expectant. I heard the insects pick up their instruments again, as if the world had taken a deep breath and moved on.

Leslie began to cry. "I have to start over," she said. "Do you understand?"

I did and I didn't. I wanted to warn her not to get hurt. I wanted to protect her. I didn't tell her that I hoped she would change her mind. I moved to put my arms around her, but stopped, as if offering comfort late was worse than never offering it at all. She swiped at her eyes. In bed that night she moved up against me.

"They'll be lining up with homemade stew for you," she said.

Imminent separation makes me feel a tenderness I do not otherwise experience. One night years ago Leslie stayed up with our dying cat. I watched her, overwhelmed by an ache that was almost physical longing. She didn't limit her caring to people. The cat had arrived on our doorstep hungry and lost years ago and now went through its death throes in Leslie's arms. I buried it in the back yard under a tree. Eric cried and put flowers on the small gravesite every Sunday for months. Leslie brought him home another kitty six months later, when Eric was over the loss of our first cat.

Leslie always said it was the little things that mattered, that gave life its grace, the universe its karma. It was the little things, she said, the day-in day-out that were the glue. I was the master of the grand gesture. For her thirty-fifth birthday I surprised her with a 1970 Jaguar XKE roadster. She loved it. She looked great in it, speeding up the Coast Highway on a hot summer night, with her hair billowing on dusk winds. But this was not what she was about. She hated arguments and loud voices, so she never raised hers. She didn't expect thanks for putting me through school. It was part of an overwhelming commitment to me. She loved her work. Leslie is competent, substantial; I could always lean on her, depend on her reactions to things. I just don't love the way she does.

When Stuart moves in I learn about the little things.

When Eric returns to school, I set up his room for Stuart. I move back into the bedroom I shared with Leslie. In May, my second television goes out. My first stopped working the week Leslie moved out. I don't bother to repair them. I stack one on top of the other for Stuart; one has no picture, the other no sound. I turn them both on.

"Pathetic." Stuart comments on my hospitality.

I get a call at my office one afternoon. You can see the ocean from my windows and on a clear day when the Santa Ana winds blow you can just make out the topography of Catalina. This is such a day and I'm enjoying the view, relaxing for a few moments without worrying about my caseload. The police have arrested Stuart for beating up a vagrant on the main drag of the fashionable beach community at the other end of town. He's told them his sad story and they don't want to keep him. Will I take responsibility for him? Yes, I will.

"You're worse than a child," I tell Stuart when I retrieve him from the police station.

"He threw trash at me." Stuart is enraged. I know the guy Stuart is talking about. He's a homeless schizophrenic who wanders the shoreline muttering about Jesus and fornication; his trousers are stained where he pisses in them and he smells of urine and shit. He favors wealthy neighborhoods for hanging out.

"So you hit him?"

"First I yelled at him. He got lucid in a hurry and ran away. He didn't start talking to himself again for a few blocks. I ran after him. And then I hit him."

I take Stuart home.

"Stay put. Stay out of trouble. Just because you're dying, you don't get to beat people up."

"Yes I do. I can do what I want. What difference does it make?"

"You know, right now I'm trying very hard to like you. It isn't easy. So, you can do what you want. But if you make any more trouble, you don't have a place to live or die."

I call him later to apologize. He *is* dying; there's no getting around that. And while he tries my patience, someday soon I'll miss Stuart as surely as I miss Leslie.

During early summer I mow my neighbor's lawn. Such simple and familiar acts give my life its meaning these days. Their dog shows up with his tennis ball. My neighbor, shocked into silence by his son's senseless death, is mute with grief. He is in the middle of his mourning. He walks slowly; step by labored step moves him past tragedy. One morning I find a basket of home grown tomatoes on my porch with a note of thanks from his wife. I inherit the dog. His name, I learn, is Phooey. He befriends Eric's cat and tempts her with his ball. They sleep with me on the bed at night.

In July Stuart wakes me one morning with his screams.

"I can't see."

He's petrified and grabs for my hand, which he can't find. I take his hand in mine and call the doctor. Apparently this is one of the opportunistic diseases that afflict AIDS patients. More and more medications find their way onto Stuarts's nightstand. None of them change or slow the steady downward progression of his T cells. But Stuart adjusts quickly to his new disability. After all, he doesn't have a lot of time.

I hear him banging around the house; he sports new bruises daily. I'm told he may lose his memory as well. I think this would be for the best.

In July Eric comes home with his girlfriend. I'm taken aback at first. I knew she was a senior, but I didn't know she was at least ten years older than Eric. Eric is obviously smitten; he hangs on her every word. In truth, I'm a little jealous. Lisa is beautiful and funny.

She grills fresh fish for us, or prepares pasta with meat sauce from scratch, or eggplant that doesn't taste or look like eggplant.

"Um, um, um," Stuart says after each meal. "What do you look like?" he asks her. "Blond or brunette?"

"Red hair," Lisa says. "Green eyes."

"Freckles?"

"Peaches and cream." She smiles. She's covered in freckles.

"Um, um, um."

Eric and Lisa giggle conspiratorially and for a month this summer the house is noisy and happy, scented with her perfume; there's lacy underwear hanging to dry in one of the bathrooms and summer dresses hang in Eric's closet. She's already been admitted to a graduate program for a doctorate in literature. In the fall, they'll take an apartment together. Eric says that sharing expenses will be cheaper than living separately. Leslie calls to tell me she really likes Lisa.

Stuart asks if it's serious between them.

"It's serious. Eric did good."

"I love red hair," he says.

He sounds wistful. I can read his mind, that he'll never have another woman.

In September Stuart is admitted to Memorial Medical Center, to a respiratory unit with the pneumonia that AIDS patients get. He survives but he's very weak. The hospital wants to send him to a nursing home or one of those places where the dying go to die. I visit Stuart often.

"I'm afraid of dying," he says one night.

"I know." I am too, but I'm uncomfortable discussing it and I'm glad he can't see my face. After that, he doesn't bring it up again.

Leslie advises that Stuart be transferred to an extended care facility. She feels I'll be taking on too much if I try to care for him at home. So Stuart goes to a nursing home for a couple of weeks, then back to my house. In October he forgets my name and where he is and that he's sick. He develops diarrhea and doesn't make it to the bathroom in time. I'm afraid that if I take him to the hospital, he won't come out again.

His doctor puts in an IV that goes into the big veins that go into the heart. Stuart will get antibiotics this way—and morphine and fluids. When I look at the array of bottles and bags of medicines, I'm intimidated and almost change my mind. My hands are too clumsy for sterile technique and anyway, I can't see the purpose. After all, Stuart is already glowing in the dark with fever.

I call Leslie. I realize that I'm calling Leslie an awful lot these days. She doesn't seem to mind. She needs to be needed and now I need her. She arranges for a hospice nurse to come to the house to bathe Stuart and help with the medications. A hospital bed with side rails come with the deal so Stuart won't fall on the floor. Eric's bedroom is a miniature hospital room now.

I watch the hospice nurse bathe Stuart, gently holding each limb, carefully soaping and rinsing his skin, shampooing his hair, changing the water in her blue basin, drying him with soft cloths. She inspects and changes the sterile dressing around the IV line in his chest and disposes of her equipment in a red bag. These seem like acts of tenderness for her, more than just her job.

Stuart's parents and ex-wife don't visit. My parents and Leslie come a couple of times a week.

In the evening I sit at Stuart's bedside and read to him from the newspaper. I doubt he understands but I'm told he knows I'm there and it makes me feel better. At least he's not alone. Mercifully he slips into a coma. Sometimes he seems to acknowledge me; there's a smile on his face, like a baby with gas. He's not in any pain. When he stops breathing, I'm in the room with him, my feet up on his bed, my eyes closed. I wait a while before making any calls, hoping he might start breathing again.

This is not weather for dying. The insects continue their music well into autumn. The air is benign and warm; the nights lengthen but the day sky remains high and blue. It seems unfair that anyone should die in such perfect weather. This is what I think during those first weeks after Stuart is gone. The clouds arrive finally, but are rainless. I throw out the broken television sets and blast old rock instead. One warm night I go down to the shore to one of the local hangouts for a beer and some Mexican food; I figure maybe I'll meet someone. But I'm closed in by the heat and the crowd of people. I can't get out of there fast enough and walk down to the beach.

The vagrant who accosted Stuart is stretched out on the warm cement strand. I give him a twenty-dollar bill thinking that Stuart would have been disgusted. He looks hungry, pathetic, like a lost animal.

Karma or grand gesture? I don't care. It just seems like the right thing to do.

I walk out onto the beach, remove my shoes, dig my toes in; it's cool and damp. I'm alone out here, but I don't feel particularly lonely. I sit in the sand and watch a full harvest moon rise slowly above the beach. When the hot autumn sun comes up next morning, it's treated to the sight of me, curled on my side, fully clothed, asleep on the sand.

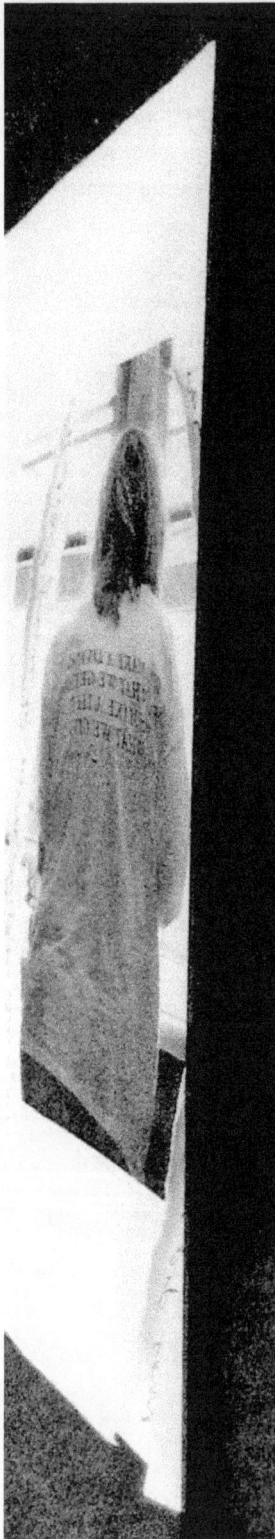

What did you give me that I want to cover?

If I can't forgive me, will my daughter forgive me?

SOCIAL CURRENTS, INNER SELVES

MARY KAY RUMMEL

SURFACING

That summer we wore a path
around the lake as if around
a clock whose hands kept time
and us in its tight loop.

Sundays we took the children
in the boat, with coffee and papers,
looking whole to others,
no one knowing how we talked
in circles, grim, accusing.

We watched maples turn,
and lose every leaf,
crushed and broken underfoot.

When fire had dulled again to dun,
when we had seen
each other's hurts perfected,
magnified like barren boughs reflected
upside-down in water, no birds
except crows kept their black watch.

The clouds massed, muffled us in snow.
Wordless winter nights each wished
the other gone.

We were digital clocks, numbers flicking
into place, tarnished coins
in the time bank, a room of months.

We were entrenched in battles
at the back of an island.

With spring we knew, despite the thaw
nothing would grow again from us;
no paths cut through cambered flesh
of clover, wild carrot.

We didn't see white cirrus fingers
drift above us. Didn't know how
love returned to change
the shape of the house we'd made,
unraveling the year of our exile.

Without the help of words, words grew,
welled up as wild honeysuckle
turning clockwise,
swaying there, between us.

SOMETIMES AN ANGEL

Rain pounds through the palm fronds—we are all
looking for an ark. There was a time I was holy
and a time I was not. In the rain, a stranger
resembles my seventh grade teacher—
small intense grey-haired nun who refused to talk to me.

Have you forgiven me for leaving you, for writing about it?
In dreams I enter a church built like a ship where she waits
at the altar, her face lit up as if she were one of those angels
who are all fire, arms opening the tight knot at the breast.

*   *   *

Rain pounds earth, ancient repeating rhythms—
we are all in need of forgiveness.
There was a time when I was free and a time I wasn't.
It was summer, riding through the Appalachians
toward Cumberland Gap with my husband and his brother.

I held myself off the backseat as we bounced over ruts,
afraid for the child, the passenger in my womb.
That narrow potholed road, oak and pine draped
with kudzu on both sides—a border dividing my life

into a time when I held a red bowl offering love,
reclaiming it whenever I wanted and a time
when I became a well—a wild good plumbing deep—
love always there for taking and I in its thrall.

PAINTING THE WALLS

"Life is a fall down a well"
-A Buddhist monk

My mother's fingers never stopped twisting
for sons in Korea, Vietnam, or somewhere
in the streets. We prayed and sang in stadiums,
not churches, each night counting the dead.

Through that violent winter, we argued
over draft-cards, afraid of prison, batons, not knowing
who we were, how to find our voices, how to love
in a world that war was ending.

Our children gone, we are alone again
and again young ones die.
Neil Young sings our past, our present
Helpless, helpless, helpless, helpless. . . .

History forgets to remember
the stumbling walk of the sun across water,
wind that keeps grieving around the corners
of the black monument.

Forget your angry voice, my exhausted
dreams, how time is life in reverse.
What can we do but hold hands as we fall?
And leave messages on walls
for those who might remember.

THE ROAD

When Anne Marie drove us through Normandy,
we stopped at the American Cemetery
and walked acres of crosses—
this century's bared teeth—
ground dense with spirits
whose air I breathed as an infant.

The French in the north—they're still grateful
to the Americans for what they did in the war,
Anne Marie said.
My parents lived just down the road on a farm.
They loved the Americans when they came.
German soldiers stayed in the village
but they were kind to my parents.
My mother and father don't hate Germans.
They tried to keep on farming.

I excuse myself from war, a poet wrote
but I can't do that.
My mother stopped sleeping
when my brothers were fighting—
in Korea, in Vietnam.
My brothers still scream at night.

I live with the pain in my brothers' eyes.
What else is there to do?
Be like the artist who hangs a print of an oven
in her living room, the American sculptor

and Polish women who crochet rosettes
in Potsdam and turn a tank into a garden,
my friend, Carol, who writes stories
of women she knew in political prison.

Face darkness while building
strong houses for light.

ADRIENNE ROSS SCANLAN

DROPS OF WATER

When I was twenty-three, I knew more about first-strike capacity than I did my heart's desires. It was the early 1980s. The world was filled with terrifying inventions of death. Trident submarines. Pershing missiles. Cruise missiles. Neutron bombs. Like many, I feared the Cold War's escalating hostility between the U. S. and the Soviet Union would spark a pre-emptive "first strike" of nuclear warheads that could eventually engulf the world. England and Western Europe were reeling with protests and peace encampments over America's missile deployments against the Soviet Union. In America, the nuclear freeze movement was spreading. One night, driving home along upstate New York's country roads, I pulled my Dodge Dart over and stared as I mistook a meteor shower for falling missiles. And so, I helped create an Albany household dedicated to opposing Knolls Atomic Power Laboratory sites critical to the Trident's development: a GE laboratory in Niskayuna and a Navy site in West Milton where sailors trained to operate the submarines. It seemed petty to hear my half-voiced dream of becoming a writer. Believing I had no story worth telling, lacking the experience that births voice, my silence felt more immovable than changing the world.

My housemates and I lived with cars parked in front of our house, the motors left running, and men wearing sunglasses sitting inside scribbling notes. We organized non-violent civil disobediences, teach-ins and concerts, shared ideological battles and broken hearts over dinners of barley mushroom soup and tofu enchiladas. I remember black-bearded Clay's hands stabbing the air as he praised pacifism. There was Nancy, home after an arrest at the Pentagon, her brown curls bobbing as she canned tomatoes. Cate had married, divorced, and traveled much of Australia before joining our house and organizing battered women's shelters. I remember Siobhan's blue eyes, ready laugh, and amazing ability to bake cheesecakes from scratch. Pony-tailed Reuben filled his room with teddy bears and had a political meeting, affinity group, or organizing committee to attend almost every night. Mike slept on the floor alongside books by Thomas Merton. And myself.

I grew up in bone-dry suburban boredom where I saw photographs of Martin Luther King, Jr. looking off at a mountain top while standing on a Memphis balcony, evening news shots of body bags shipped from Vietnam and stacked on glimmering tarmacs, Bobby Kennedy's open eyes watching his death. My father was becoming paralyzed from Parkinson's disease. I watched in terror over the injustice done to him, in guilt and anger over my powerlessness, and in hope that there was something I could do if not for him then for the world. After college I was adrift, eager for experience, lonely and failing at jobs. And so, I joined a community dedicated to peace and non-violence. I wanted a refuge of friends, an identity, and a more passionate life than one I thought capable of creating. I couldn't hope to call myself a writer, but even then I knew when I needed raw material.

We worked as graduate assistants, community organizers and human service workers, and filled our home with golden pothos, posters of Nelson Mandela and Steven Biko, second-hand sofas, bickering cats, and creaking bookcases filled with well-thumbed volumes of Marx, Millet, Zora Neale Hurston, and Martin Luther King Jr. We turned the backyard into a garden of sweet peas, cauliflower, cucumbers, a lifetime supply of zucchini. A calendar hung on the avocado green refrigerator, its date squares showing who pulled chef's duty and each night's non-violence training, war tax resisters' potluck, affinity group meeting, draft registration counseling session, teach-in, or disarmament meeting.

Every Monday, Nancy or Siobhan used the onion scraps, carrot peelings and other remnants of a week's cooking to make a brown, bitter soup served with cornbread. The money saved by Simple Meal was donated to food banks or shelters. We knew that being white and middle class made Simple Meal a choice not a necessity, yet like growing our food and turning off lights, it was a way of replacing the fear of nuclear annihilation with a daily life infused with meaning. Even small actions could disavow the insatiable materialism driving America's need for a military capable of securing third world resources. Yet instead of guilt, a calm fell over the house on Monday nights. As we sat crossed legged on the dining room's wood floor, our chipped plates atop a door-sized board laid across cinder blocks, our voices were softer, our jokes less rapid, our political disputes silenced. I never felt the sustenance of matching principles to action. I just felt hungry.

Tuesday nights we gathered for house meetings, never to be interrupted, especially by the tapped hall phone. It could be days before a workshop, demonstration or civil disobedience, and the black rotary phone would start ringing, only to go dead if we picked it up, and once the receiver was set down, start ringing and ringing and ringing grating on nerves stretched from in-house romances gone sour and the inevitable clashes of seven iconoclastic people. Listening through memory, as though still sipping ruby mist tea and sitting cross-legged on the wood floor, I can hear how we argued whether we should have a Thanksgiving dinner with its celebration of imperialism (and if we did, should we have a turkey?), whether we should squish the cabbage worms chewing holes in our broccoli or follow St. Francis and let all creatures share the bounty, whether violence was justified even after Nancy and I were attacked in a park. Siobhan would darn socks as we tried to determine if it was ethical to work in an economic system where the bulk of our tax dollars went to the military. Yet how could we reach the Knolls sailors and scientists if our lives were so different from theirs?

Right and wrong answers stalked whether I walked snow-covered streets or carpooled to a meeting, whether Malvina Reynolds croaked *We Don't Need the Men* or *Walls to Rose* played on the stereo. There was never a moment I could be myself (whoever that was) rather than a reflection of my politics. Call it raising consciousness. Or idealism. Or self-censorship. I bellowed certainties where every twenty-three year old deserves to have questions. Poems and stories withered. Journal entries rambled into angry, unfinished paragraphs.

Thursday nights were quiet. At 5:30 a.m. every Friday, Siobhan and I drove north on highways and back roads past dairy farms and apple orchards. We reached the West Milton site in time to leaflet sailors starting their morning shift. Meanwhile, Reuben, Clay and Cate gathered with other activists to leaflet the Niskayuna site's physicists, engineers and office workers. At our height, we were leafleting 450-500 sailors or Knolls workers weekly.

Siobhan and I took our places along an intersection of white houses and trimmed lawns. Atomic Project Road veered into a dirt road ending at a chain link fence and barbed wire. A guard would drive up, exchange "hello"s and weather forecasts, write down our license plate number and ask for a leaflet. Some weeks Siobhan selected articles on disarmament or U.S.-Soviet relations from *Bulletin of the Atomic Scientists*. Other weeks it was writings from Martin Luther King or Andre Sakharov, news clips or reports on economic conversion to a peacetime economy, radiation safety, or fact-sheets (*"At the moment of an explosion of a medium sized nuclear bomb the initial wave of radiation can kill unprotected human beings in an area of 6 square miles . . . "*) With a wave and "See you next week" the guard would drive away.

In summer, I shivered in the dawn. In winter, I shook under long johns, blue jeans, a green wool sweater beneath a tan wool sweater beneath a beige wool sweater, a double-lined coat, and a wool hat. Siobhan would be muffled under layers of long-johns, Icelandic wool sweaters, and a black muffler, her blonde braid swaying to the knees of her corduroy pants as she stamped booted feet on icy ground. I heard her laugh with the joyful grace of doing one's proper work.

Sailors drove up on Harley's, in red Fords or blue Chevy pick-ups. They would take a leaflet with a soft-spoken "Thank you ma'am" or flirtatious invitations for a beer at the local bar. I heard flat mid-western voices, southern drawls, New Englanders' elongated vowels. "We're all going to die one day, sweetheart," said one beefy, middle-aged lifer as he patted my hand while taking a leaflet. "It's nothing to be afraid of." Other sailors were disillusioned, and Clay and Siobhan helped several secure conscientious objector discharges.

I was desperate to leave after twenty minutes. I returned every week for almost three years. I loved the morning's first light gleaming against the trees, the unmoving donkey in a pasture of ice-frosted grass, the squeals of children in snowsuits running to reach the school bus. All could be gone in a flash. No matter how loudly I grumbled during the morning drive, I never questioned that each leaflet's message was more important than sleep, warmth, putting my pen to paper.

I trusted the power of other people's words. What significance could my words have compared to saving the world? But did the world want to be saved? I didn't understand that saving the world is like doing the housework: dust is always gathering in the corner; another shirt is always dropped on the floor. I learned (eventually) to be reasonably good at leafleting, meeting, phoning, organizing, planting and picking kale. I respect its importance thirty years later. But was this the work I was meant to do? What if I had something to say that had nothing to do with what I was supposed to believe? What if I had lessons to learn about power, evil, and idealism that had everything and nothing to do with social change? And what was the point of saving the world, anyway, if all it brought me was a nagging itch left unscratched: my life as a writer.

I thought speaking truth to power would magically change the world and me along with it. What I know now is that social change, like writing, requires the daily work of moving beyond inspiration to finishing the imperfect attempt, practicing craft, revising, coming to the imperfect conclusion and using that as material to try again to create something beautiful. Those West Milton mornings were an initiation into honoring the difficult, necessary dream. They remain a sustaining grace when I send out an essay or story to an inevitable volley of rejections and a rare, vital publication.

Siobhan would have the heat on full blast when we drove home comparing sailor's comments, or the controversies and romances coursing through the peace and justice community. Some days I never lost a chill beneath my skin.

Eventually the house ripped apart. Arrests at the Pentagon. Arrests at Knolls. Court appearances. Broken romances. The gut-kick of Reagan's presidency. The exhaustion of organizing rallies, concerts, civil disobediences, teach-ins, the weekly leaflets, the next series of meetings. Slowly, we went our own ways, and when we did, others arrived to take up leafleting and other actions at Knolls well into the mid-1990's.

For the next decade, I lobbied legislators, staffed information booths, and slammed bulging files atop calendars scribbled with meetings. Sometimes a beam of light would break across my cluttered desk. I'd glimpse in the shimmering gold and silver motes the halting first lines of a haiku, a sestina, a short story. Instead I wrote newsletters, position papers, grants. What was my life in the face of disarmament, violence against women, other struggles? What did I have to say? I banked my small stories like embers between black coals.

Exhausted by thirty, a cross-country road trip gave much needed solitude. The only voice I heard was mine as I drove under western skies or up a foggy coast. Writing classes eased out meetings as I settled in my new Seattle home. Then the legislature passed a law I'd fought for that created funding for battered women's shelters and stricter penalties for abuse. I was thirty-four, and a black and white suit with shoulder pads had long since replaced blue jeans by the time I attended the governor's bill-signing ceremony. But a rebel pounded within my heartbeat.

The next Saturday I sat in the armchair of a Whidbey Island retreat center. I wrote down every lecture series, concert, phone bank or rally organized, every information booth staffed, every politician lobbied, every political action I could remember from fifteen years as an activist. I wrote through a rainstorm, cups of tea, and a croissant and yogurt lunch. By late afternoon I looked at my list. I had changed the world. Not completely. Far from it. Perhaps hardly at all. But just enough. In that newfound freedom was one last barricade to topple. I gave myself permission to write.

Gingerly, I took up my pen. Afternoon darkened to evening. A crescent moon cut the rain clouds. British grandmothers sipped tea as they shared stories of spirit guides. Silence fell as strangers went to their beds. I stayed in my chair, my fingers sore as I wrote.

These days I live a few hours from a Trident base. Sometimes when I cross the Hood Canal Bridge I see a submarine gliding dark, silent, deadly. We are both still here. Did those long-ago meetings and leaflets matter? I keep my faith in the small, cumulative acts of ordinary people. Without those soft persistent drops of water upon a stone the world would be far worse.

I've not given up trying to change the world. I turn off lights in empty rooms, eat low on the food chain, vote in every election and volunteer at get-out-the-vote drives, write elected officials, and make a living raising money largely for environmental and social change organizations. I can't attend political meetings without becoming claustrophobic. But I don't see my politics as being opposed to my writing, as if each was located on the Grand Canyon's opposite rims. After decades navigating both landscapes, I've found a wild, shared river carrying the power of imagination and the capacity to transform. If politics flows downstream to an estuary of agendas and answers, then creativity flows upstream to headwaters of questions. These days, I try to keep my creative writing close to my blood and bone. I trust that unseen ripples of change flow from my words.

I'm sure the woman I was then would be appalled by the woman I am now were we to meet in a ground beyond time and space. Perhaps I would envy her passion while abhorring her certainties. Perhaps she would abhor my commitment to creativity while envying the freedom that comes from growing a true self rather than being a correct one.

On my writing desk there's a note that reads: *Do the work you were meant to do, no matter how small and humble, no matter how exciting someone else's work looks, no matter how glamorous the work you could be doing.* I don't know who first wrote those words. Sometimes I wonder if I did.

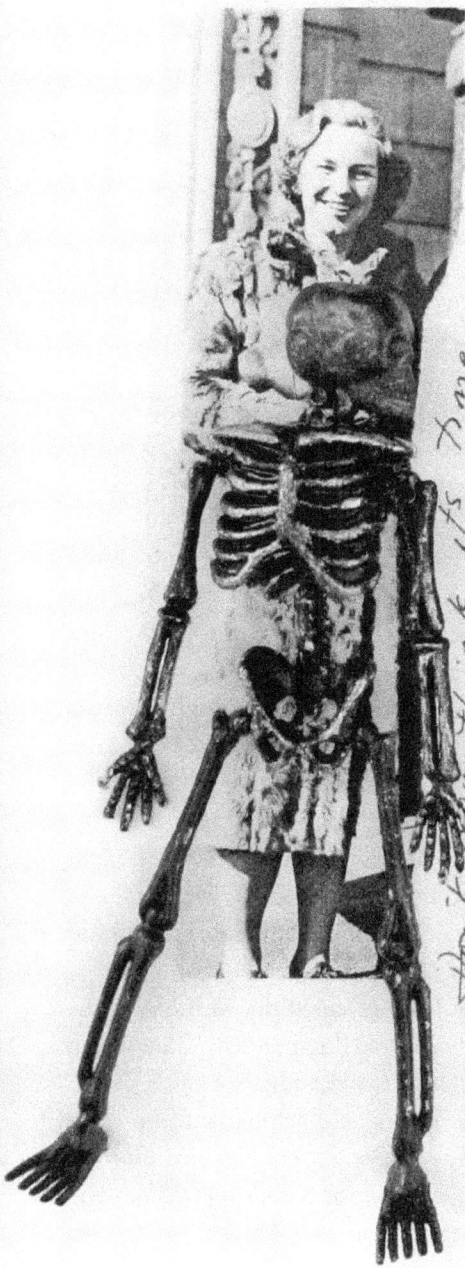

Don't you think it's time we said we're sorry?

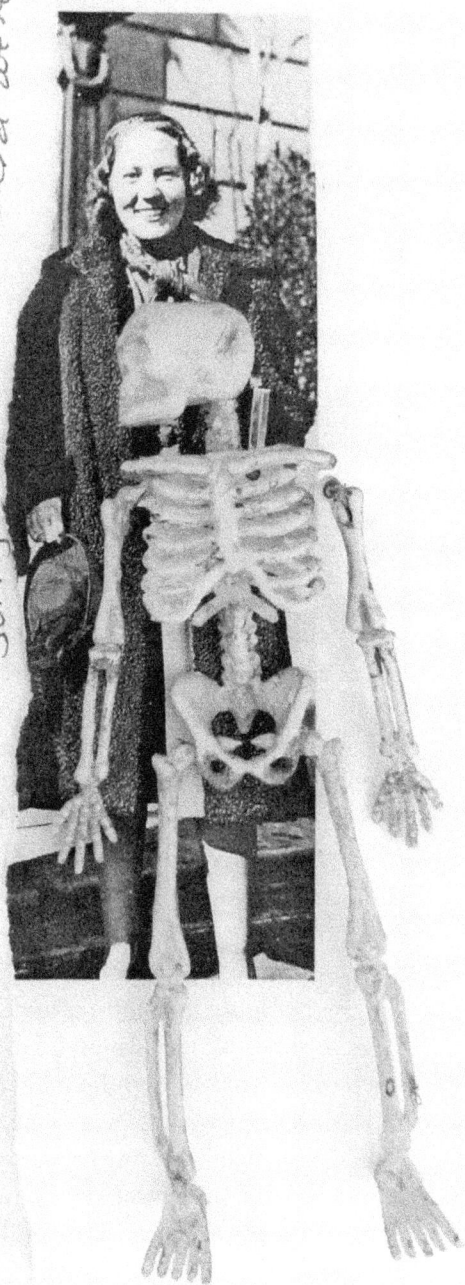

DIANE MIERZWIK

SUNSET RED

Roe v Wade, 1973
   The Supreme Court establishes a woman's right to safe and legal abortion, overriding the anti-abortion laws of many states.

"You're so ugly, you're the reason there's adoption," one of my students joked with another while we stood on the blacktop awaiting the all clear signal for the latest bomb threat on the campus.

"Hey, I'm adopted!" I interjected.

Both boys looked stunned, too young to remember so many unwed pregnant girls in a disapproving society. Keeping a child out of wedlock was so unacceptable in the United States, young families were recruited to adopt babies born out of the free love movement. Abortion was illegal.

Though I am two generations older than my students, I have no memory of when abortion was illegal, or when adopting a healthy baby did not cost thousands of dollars. Still, I have always believed that giving a child up for adoption is the kinder, more difficult decision.

"If you knew a woman who was pregnant, who already had eight kids, three who were deaf, two who were blind, one mentally retarded, and the woman had syphilis—would you suggest an abortion?" a college professor asked as a way of shaking my convictions.

He could then inform me I had just prevented the world from the pleasure of Beethoven's genius, if I fell into his trap. I responded, "That would be up to the woman, who should be in charge of her body. Not me."

When I was teaching persuasive writing and helping students draft counter arguments, a young female student listened as I gave reasons abortion should be legal, prompting the students who were anti-abortion to come up with arguments to defend their position. This was easy for me, since I was pro-choice.

I began with the argument of an unwanted child born to a destructive household. All the students were quiet, save Tanesha who said quietly, "It's better than being dead," as if she knew more than me, and she probably did.

Silenced, I grappled with the idea that if abortion had been legal, I would most likely never have been born, let alone put up for adoption.

Corning Glass Works v. *Brennan*, 1974

The Equal Credit Opportunity Act prohibits discrimination in consumer credit practices on the basis of sex, race, marital status, religion, national origin, age, or receipt of public assistance.

Bill and I arrived at the carpet store to meet with their credit specialist. Buying carpet for our second home, I had visited the store earlier in the week, found the carpet I wanted, and filled out the credit application. Today, we just needed to sign the papers and set up an appointment for installation.

Bill and I sat in chairs opposite a squat, balding man who pushed the papers our way. I perused the first page and asked, "Why is my name listed second?"

The man rubbed his chin and looked confused.

"When I filled out the financing paperwork, I put my name as the borrower and my husband's as the co-borrower. It's been switched here." I pushed the paper back toward him.

"It's just our company. That's the way they do things."

"But, it clearly showed in the paperwork that I make more money than my husband."

Bill sat quietly beside me, still.

"It's just our company; that's the way they do things. If you'll just sign."

I pushed back my chair and announced, "I refuse to do business with a company so clearly sexist in how it handles its customers." Marching from the building, I said to Bill, "Come on."

I strode from the store and didn't wait to see if Bill had followed me until we were in the parking lot, where I allowed him to unlock my car door and open it for me.

Meritor Savings Bank v. Vinson, 1986
    The Supreme Court finds that sexual harassment is a form of illegal job discrimination.

Teaching has traditionally been a female profession, but teaching secondary public school is a mixed bag, with equal parts male teachers and female teachers.

Part of a team of teachers who all shared the same students, we met once a week: the math teacher, Ron; the science teacher, Edward; the social studies teacher, Julie; the art teacher, Rachel; and me, the English teacher.

As we gathered in the staff lounge, I positioned myself in my favorite seat, the one facing the window so I could stare outside at the trees and field beyond the school buildings. Julie sat beside me and asked how I was feeling, being six months pregnant and all. Edward hovered over me while Ron sat on the top of a nearby table, placing his feet on a chair, and Rachel got a soda from the machine. Not sure what Edward was doing, I ignored him until I felt something mussing my hair. I turned to find Edward gently lifting a lock of my hair to his nose and breathing in deeply.

"Divine," he stated with his eyes closed.

"Edward, sit down," I commanded, jerking my head so my hair yanked out of his caressing possession. When he made eye contact, I scowled at him disapprovingly while he pretended to not understand why I was upset, shaking his head slightly and feigning perplexity.

The meeting began and I imperceptibly moved further and further away from Edward throughout the meeting so that, finally, Julie nudged my elbow and nodded toward all the space between me and Edward and the lack of distance between her and me. I scooted my chair back over, but tensed up, ready.

The talk turned to a young student, Joseph, who was giving us all a run for our money. All, that is, except for Ron.

"He's good for me. Maybe it's because I'm a man."

"If I only had a penis, then I could teach Joseph. Is that what you're saying?" I asked.

Ron shrugged his shoulders. "I'm just saying he doesn't give me any trouble."

I left the meeting looking forward to my impending due date and the year off I would have to raise my son.

Kolstad v. American Dental Association, 1999
   The Supreme Court rules that a woman can sue for punitive damages for sex discrimination if the anti-discrimination law was violated with malice or indifference to the law, even if that conduct was not especially severe.

"Whoa there, Diane. Stop to say hello."
   Though I was distracted by the game of tag I was playing with his kids and my sister, I stopped briefly to bask in his adult adoration. Gaylon had me swirl around in my skirt while my dad looked on, both beaming.
   "Bob, you have one adorable little girl there," he told my dad.
   I stood still, waiting to be released from the spell they had cast on me, one of being loved simply for how I looked. Too easy.
   "Run along," my dad finally said.
   Mrs. Branscum, my sixth grade teacher, announced to my mom at a parent-teacher conference that I was lucky—with my looks life would be so much easier. My mother scowled and we never, ever mentioned it—like I imagined the whole thing.
   My best friend and I walked up and down the boulevard filling out applications the summer we were both sixteen. We both got callbacks from Thrifty Drug Store to take a math test. Later that night, Jeanette asked me how I did.
   "I missed two."
   "I got 100 percent," she told me. I assumed she would get the job, until I got a call later that week to come in and sign the paperwork. The manager admitted they were looking for a cashier people would enjoy seeing day after day. Jeanette later got a job at a pizza parlor, pulling pizza from the ovens.
   The day my mom came into the store to buy hair dye, I told her, "You earned those gray hairs. You should be proud of them."
   But my mom ignored my entreaty and continued to wear dresses and heels and even a bra. I refused, choosing instead to be clad in blue jeans and T-shirts with no make-up.

In my thirties, I gave up on not wearing a bra, after a teenage boy commented as I strode past him on the sidewalk, "Jell-O jiggles like that."

With my underwire, contouring bra, whenever I talked to men, their eyes wandered . . . up to my graying hairline. I kept wanting to say, "Hey, fella, I'm here, down here! No! Not that far!"

Then I picked up my son from a local skate park and the cute guy behind the counter looked right through me. I had become invisible to young, good-looking men.

I made an appointment the next day to have my hair dyed, my nails done, my lip waxed and my face facialed. Finally, I wasn't being judged by how I looked. Finally I could make an impression with my personality. Instead people looked right through me or focused on the anomalies of my aging appearance.

Jackson v. Birmingham Board of Education, 2005
The Supreme Court rules that Title IX, which prohibits discrimination based on sex, also inherently prohibits disciplining someone for complaining about sex-based discrimination. It further holds that this is the case even when the person complaining is not among those being discriminated against.

I am quite the fan of Comedy Central, unless it's after 9 p.m., when every other commercial is for "Girls Gone Wild." I'd like to be insufferably outraged. Instead I am unabashedly ashamed of myself.

Twenty-five years ago, I flashed boys on boats out of arms' reach, picked fights with girls eyeing my man, danced suggestively at concerts and did other things I barely remember because I was sloppy drunk. Lucky for me, videotaping had not been invented.

I remember when my body was a tool: to get a job, to get a free drink, to get attention. I wore miniskirts to job interviews. I went braless to bars. I flaunted my bare midriff in formal situations.

Now I hide my saggy arms, camouflage my accordion-folded stomach and always wear a bra in public. Late at night, when my boobs become just one more roll on my torso and my face has been washed down the sink, I look away from the "Girls Gone Wild" commercials. I try not to remember how I used to act and wish those girls well while they have beautiful bodies, gorgeous long hair and smooth taut skin.

Mierzwik v. The World, 2009
Taking a brief legal look at the treatment of woman throughout history, I invent myself as one woman among many.

In second grade I got third place in an art competition. I still have the piece I made and the white ribbon. Astonished, I assumed the judges had made a mistake. I hadn't even tried.

That same week, I got an invitation to Debbie Hunsucker's birthday slumber party.

On Friday night in Debbie's living room, we all sat around in our pajamas and discussed appropriately applying make-up. None of us were allowed to wear it yet, but were intensely interested in blush and mascara and eye shadow and lipgloss. Mrs. Hunsucker was in the nearby kitchen, apparently eavesdropping because when she brought us a plate of freshly baked sugar cookies she chimed in that I was SO pretty, I didn't need to wear make-up.

"What about me?" Debbie asked.

"Oh, you know us Hunsuckers. We need all the help we can get."

None of us reached for cookies as we watched Debbie's face register her mother's answer then fake a smile. "Oh well, I did get *first* place in the art competition this week."

Now, so many decades later, I wonder who I might have been had I thought of myself as an artist rather than as the pretty girl everyone invites to their parties.

So today I arrive at an art store and splurge on a box of 128 colored pencils. When I get home, the pencils sit on my desk and taunt me. I have never even taken an art class. I should spend my time doing sit-ups and getting facials, not drawing worthless pictures.

I wander into the bathroom and check my make-up under the severe lights. I apply more black eyeliner and peach lipstick. Two basic colors I have perfected creating my face with, rather than 128 to recreate the world I live in.

I find it difficult to distinguish between sunrise red and sunset red.

WEIHUA ZHANG

MAMA'S HAIR

"Tell me more about Grandma," my daughter Feifei pleaded with me, her face tilted upward, her tearful eyes trying to hook mine. Her voice was not sad, though, but full of longing, which surprised me. It was April 1996. Feifei had just turned ten in March. I tried my best to gently break the news to her that Grandma had died of a massive heart attack on January 6, more than three months before.

Not knowing where to start, I bent down and hugged Feifei tightly, letting the hot tears roll down my cheeks, which dropped on her straight, thick, black hair. "Grandma had hair just like yours," I said to Feifei between sobs, attempting to hold off my own tears. Nevertheless, thinking of Mama's hair brought a faint smile to my face.

For as long as I can remember, I have always loved Mama's lustrous black hair. I remember seeing a picture of her in the family album. Her long hair was braided into two thick pigtails and tied with thin ribbons at both ends. In that picture, she was very young, probably in her early twenties, and breathtakingly beautiful. She had big black eyes with double lids; her refined, elegant face was anchored by a straight nose; her sensual lips were full and firm. When I was in first grade, I had pigtails too, though mine were not thick like Mama's, and much shorter; they barely reached my narrow shoulders. Many a morning, Mama would stand behind me braiding my hair while I sat on a stool eating breakfast of rice porridge and pickled vegetables. Some mornings, Mama tied my hair with red or pink ribbons, my two favorite colors; on other days, she put bright clips on my hair. With her tender loving touch, Mama made me feel as if I were the prettiest girl in my class.

When I was still a little girl, Mama seemed magical to me. She would hum to herself while doing chores; her thick black hair dangled loosely behind her back. Her magical voice, chirpy like a lark, soothing like a balm, enchanting like a dream, often took me to a faraway land. When Feifei was just a baby, Mama used to sing her the same lullaby she sang to me:

The wind has stopped blowing,
the trees are no longer swaying,
the birds have ceased their chattering.
My little darling,
close your eyes tightly,
and start dreaming.

Mama possessed a pair of magical hands too. She could peel an apple with a pocketknife in a blink of an eye. We kids jostled one another to get in position to catch the long spiral peel before it fell to the floor. We pulled it long ways and sideways, as if we were playing an accordion. And those paper-cuts Mama did! A line of little girls holding hands; dogs; butterflies; fish; roses—you name it and she could pull it off right in front of your unblinking eyes.

As I grew older, however, I started noticing that Mama's songs and magic could go missing for days and even weeks. Those were the "silent war" days when Mama and Father stopped speaking to one another, when fear hung heavily in the air of our apartment. I dreaded these days and had resigned myself to their intermittent occurrences. All I could do was to wait for the heaviness to dissipate and for Mama's singing to return.

Until one day I was stupefied with a shocking revelation: what if Mama's singing would never return? I was only nine at the time. My parents were at "silent war" again. It was an overcast October day. We were living in Changchun then, the capital city of Jilin Province, located in northeastern China. That chilly morning, I followed Mama to the People's Square, a public plaza nearby, some five-minute walk from our apartment. Oblivious to the people who gathered at the square to practice Tai Chi, or the ones who hurried to get to their jobs, Mama sat on one of the wooden benches in the square. Her face blank and pensive, her motionless eyes looked at nothing in particular. I sat next to her timidly. I knew when not to disturb her. But I was scared, scared to death. For some reason, my young mind was obsessed with the fear that Mama was going to kill herself. If I were to leave her then and there, I would come back finding her gone. Gone forever.

On that chilly October morning many years ago, we sat there, mother and daughter, for maybe an hour. Mama did not utter a single word. She kept looking in front of her, at nothing and nobody in particular, her shoulder-length, jet-black hair tucked neatly behind her ears. I sat close to her, but made sure that my body did not touch hers. Now and then I would cast anxious glances at her, but dared not to make any eye contact. What if I saw tears in her eyes? Would I be able to hold mine? Just like her, I remained silent the whole time. Fear and sadness filled my heart as I waited for her to acknowledge my presence. I found it hard to breathe and tried in vain to shake off this heaviness sitting on my chest. Finally, after what seemed an eternity, Mama said in a barely audible voice, "Go on to school. Don't worry about me."

It was much later—I was already in college—when I finally was able to piece together the causes of Mama's unhappiness, her strained relationship with Father, her emotional demands on her children, and her entangled fate with China's history.

My parents were married in 1948, shortly after the liberation of northeastern China, or Manchuria, a former Japanese occupied territory. Their union was not out of the ordinary. Mama was a young assistant at the district government's office and seventeen at the time. Father was twenty-eight, a seasoned revolutionary. At seventeen, he had run away from home to join the Red Army, shortly after Japan's full-scale invasion of China on July 7, 1937. Father pledged not to return home until he had killed every single Japanese soldier. The Sino-Japanese War lasted eight years. Father proved to be a brave soldier and later a shrewd commander in the army. He had seen battles big and small, close to a hundred in total.

After the war, Father left the army and assumed the Chief of Public Security position (sort of the combination of police chief and sheriff in the States) in Hailin District, where Mama lived with her parents and three younger siblings. That was how their lives' paths intersected. Father must have been smitten by Mama's youth, beauty, and brains. He followed her to her parents' house, trying to woo her. When he was too busy to go, he sent his bodyguard to accompany her home and do the talking for him. He even asked his superior to put in a good word on his behalf. Mama acquiesced after a year, succumbing to the pressure. "I didn't want your Grandpa to lose his job," she later told me.

In September 1948, my parents were reassigned to Liaoyuan Coal Mining Company, thus started their life-long careers in the coal industry. In time, my siblings and I were born. First came Sister in 1949, then Big Brother in 1953, followed by Second Brother in 1955, and me in 1957 to bring up the rear. By then, my parents had been transferred again, this time to Beipiao Coal Mining Bureau, where I was born. I'd like to think that in our unique ways, each of us kids brightened our parents' lives. Yet deep in my heart, I am saddened and troubled by an unspoken fact, a coincidence perhaps, that my birth in 1957 signaled the beginning of Mama's long suffering. Of course, no one ever hinted at that. It is just my gut feeling.

The year 1957 saw Chairman Mao launch the Anti-Rightist Movement. As if to mark my grand entry into the world, Mao chose the month of July for the launch. The Anti-Rightist Movement served as a countermovement against the Hundred Flowers Campaign, endorsed by Mao himself, just a year prior. The Double-Hundred Campaign—"Let a hundred flowers bloom; let a hundred schools of thought contend"—called for pluralism of artistic expressions and public critiques of the government. When hundreds of thousands of letters and suggestions poured in, offering candid criticism of the central government, Mao sensed a public dissatisfaction and potential threat to the new republic, and to his reign. He pulled the plug. The Anti-Rightist Movement targeted particularly those outspoken critics of the central government. In a short two-year period, some 550,000 people were affected nationwide, with close to ninety percent of them intellectuals. Among the charges: anti-Communist Party sentiments, opposition to the socialist system, counter-revolutionary activities and views, subversion, advocating capitalist ideology, and instigating social unrest. Their punishments: demotion, dismissal, forced labor camps, imprisonment, torture, and even death. In September of that year, Mama was removed from her position as Director of Education. Her offence: displaying "Pro-Rightist inclination." I was just two months old.

One could only imagine the shock and anger I later felt when I found out the truth of Mama's 1957 downfall. She had actually taken the political fall for Father. A couple of Father's fellow managers had become very disgruntled with him, the no-nonsense guy, who led by examples, not words; who upheld integrity, frowned at corruption. They could do nothing to Father, a decorated veteran and highly capable manager of the company. They plotted against Mama, the young, beautiful, ass-kicking Director of Education, who was full of herself and consulted no one for personnel decisions in her own department. Mama was only twenty-six then, passionate for life, adored by her children, admired by her friends, and revered by her colleagues. Sadly, her life, her career, and her happiness were put on hold. Though Mama had never told me so, I suspected that her strained relationship with Father was caused largely by this tragic turn of fate. Perhaps in her heart, she blamed Father for having failed to come to her defense, to prove his love with action; or perhaps she saw this inaction as an act of betrayal.

I was barely one year old when the entire country was mobilized to answer Chairman Mao's call for modernization. The Great Leap Forward in 1958-59, aimed at overtaking Great Britain and the U.S., proved too giant a leap. It backfired and shattered the country's fragile economic foundations. Then the three-year Great Famine followed in 1959-1961. Millions of people were displaced from their homes. The death toll is staggering no matter which figure you choose to use: 15 million by the Chinese government's estimate or 30-45 million according to studies done by western scholars.

My family survived the Great Famine with minimal sufferings, thanks largely to Father's leadership position at work and his past distinguished service in the Chinese Liberation Army. Faced with a scarcity of food and daily necessities such as rice, flour, meat, cooking oil, sugar, matches, clothing items, and the like, Father's special monthly food rations at least kept our stomachs full. Almost full. Mama was the distributor-in-chief. She would divide rice porridge, steamed buns, and the occasional treats that Father brought home from his business trips—candies, cookies, sometimes, fresh fruit—into four roughly equal portions. Being the youngest child, I always got to pick first. Unlike Kong Rong (153-208 A.D.), the renowned literary scholar in the late East Han Dynasty (25-220 A.D.), who, at the age of four, chose to pick the smallest pear on the plate and saved the bigger ones for his older brothers, I always went for the largest portions. I would follow Mama's hand back and forth when she ladled rice porridge into our bowls, making sure I got the same amount as my older sister and two brothers did. I'd hide the leftovers somewhere in the house and nibble on them later. I was not ready to share the rice porridge, the treats, or Mama, *especially* Mama, with my siblings. It meant nothing to me that Kong Rong went down in Chinese history as the model of a courteous child. For this four-year old, going down in history as a courteous child was the least concern on her mind.

Growing up, I was always afraid of Father and carefully stayed out of his way. Truth be told, none of us children was close to Father. Second Brother and I were especially nervous around him, tiptoeing in the house whenever Father was home. Years later, Mama shed light on our fear of Father: During the Great Famine, Father often lamented over meals that there were two children too many in our household. One day, Mama decided that she had heard it enough. She raised a meat cleaver and calmly asked Father, "Just tell me which two you don't want." Father shut up right then and there. That was Mama, like a fiercely protective hen, she had us safely tucked under her warm, comforting wings.

But Mama's wings could be heavy, even suffocating, at times. Many a time, I wanted to break loose from her wings. Yet Mama saw no wrong in her control of me, her youngest and meekest child, and dictated her terms. I started high school in 1972. By then, after more than two decades of isolation from the western world, China slowly opened herself up. Some girls in my school started having perms and wearing fancy-looking clothes sent to them by their overseas relatives. I wanted to be just like them. Mama dismissed it as a fad. She considered this attention to one's appearance—hairdos, trendy clothes, makeup, and high heels—a distraction. "You are not going to get your teachers' attention and respect just because you wear fashionable clothes or have fancy hairdos every day. They like you when you can correctly answer all the questions. They like you even more when your clothes are plain but neat, when your eyes are buried in the textbooks, and when your hairdo does not overshadow your character." Mama even picked out a new hairstyle for me. Short, athletic cut, just like this movie character had in *Woman Basketball Player No. 5*. No bangs. "You don't want bangs blocking your vision. You need to see clearly every word your teachers have written on the blackboard," she added adamantly.

I had never watched the popular Chinese movie *Woman Basketball Player No. 5* and I wondered why. A quick Internet search yielded a possible explanation of Mama's insistence on my having short hair: That movie was released in 1957; in that same year Mama *released* me into the world. I fancied that Mama, amid her fight against the "Pro-Rightist inclination" accusation, was still full of hopes for her new born, her baby girl. She wished that I would grow up just like the basketball player No. 5 in the popular movie. Xiao Jie, at eighteen, is the youngest player on the team; she is also the best. I happened to be the youngest on Mama's team, the youngest of her four children; but was I the best?

Over the years, while the political battles were no longer being waged in the nation, the many "silent wars" inevitably ripped my parents apart.

Though they remained married till Mama's death in 1996, they hardly had anything to offer one another except a few terse exchanges. Mama turned increasingly to her children for emotional support. Her ever-growing need to demand and secure her children's unconditional love was like a minefield: one hesitant step, one wrong turn, one careless move, you could become a casualty and did not even know it, until it was too late. Being the youngest and last one to leave home, I bore the brunt of her demands. Simple things like a salutation in letters home could trip you. I quickly learned my lesson while attending graduate school in Nankai University during the early 1980s. "Dear Mother and Father" was rewarded with a quick, warm return letter from Mama; "Dear Father and Mother," however, was met with her deafening silence.

Years later the location had changed—I had moved to the U.S. in 1989 to pursue my passion for American Literature—but this tug-of-war prolonged, and went up a notch in intensity, more like a thousand-fold in intensity. For well over a year from mid-1989 to the end of 1990, I got no letters from Mama. Two months into this cold war, I knew damn well I hadn't learned my lesson after all. What was I thinking, acting like I-know-your-problem-and-I-have-the-solution-for-you, telling Mama to either divorce Father or reconcile with him, just because I saw some middle-aged American couples holding hands, taking a stroll? Now more than twenty years later, I still hold onto her twenty-page tirade—the mockery of my newfound independence—that had started our year-long war of silence. She simply ignored my subsequent letters of beseeching and reasoning to highlight my betrayal. Yes, betrayal. You either love Mama always, or you do not love her at all.

The news of Mama's death funneled its way to me in a self-revealing dream, some 12,000 miles away on this side of the world, three months too late. In that dream, I was having a conversation with Father. Mama was conspicuously absent. Upon waking up, I called Second Brother. My mind went blank when his mumbled words came via the deep-sea cable, "Short pain . . . better than long pain . . . you will find out eventually . . . Mama passed away on Jan. 6 . . . Massive heart attack." "But I just spoke with her on the phone on New Year's Day! How could that be possible?" I screamed at the receiver.

Father made the decision to withhold the news of Mama's death from me in the name of love. I did not appreciate his kind gesture, though I did understand his reasoning: my husband, daughter, and I had just visited them in China six months prior to Mama's sudden death; the trip had wiped out our savings; I had been desperately trying to complete my dissertation; I had been dispiritedly looking for a job. Still, his decision left me helpless, angry, anguished, guilty, empty, and numb. Like a broken kite, I was aimless, freefalling onto no man's land. Not having been able to say goodbye to Mama tops the list of my regrets.

Ironically or fittingly, Father was the only one at Mama's side when she wrestled with death. I often wonder what was going through each of their minds when death came to claim Mama. Father recounted to me the last moment of Mama's life: "Your mother grasped my hand tightly and wanted to say something. But by then, she was not able to speak. I put my ear close to her mouth, but could not make out what she was trying to say. Then, she let go." Could it be possible that Mama wanted to tell Father that she had forgiven him; that she loved him in spite of all the "silent wars," sufferings, and betrayals; that she wanted to see her little daughter one last time?

"You know what?" I gazed at Feifei's large, innocent eyes, and gently ran my fingers through her thick black hair. "When you were born, the doctor handed you over to Grandma. She held you up in her arms, marveling at your hair. For a newborn, you sure had a head of almost inch-long black hair. 'She has my hair,' Grandma proudly announced. She was right."

I hugged Feifei again, more tightly this time, feeling her thick hair caressing my face. In that moment, I felt Mama's presence in Feifei's steady heartbeats, and in that unmistakable hair of theirs.

What's this? Why does everyone ask us to smile?
It's not my birthday! Why do I have to share?
Old MacDonald had a farm

AMENDS & MISMITZVAHS

SUSAN KAY CHERNILO

WHEN TRYING IS ALL YOU CAN DO

Rebecca always cringed when she entered the lobby of Jamilah's building. She restrained from peering down the cul-de-sac on the other side of the elevator, into which two raggedy characters had disappeared, took a breath and pressed the elevator button. When it landed she bravely stepped inside.

It stunk of urine and several kinds of smoke and God knew what else, and entering was an act of faith because you could never be certain it was going to make it all the way up to the fifth floor. Two home visits ago, it got stuck between floors 3 and 4 for twenty minutes. People got on and off, some speaking Spanish and a teenage boy with pants down to his knees. But she couldn't knock the conditions really, now could she, when it was her agency that placed Jamilah in this building? They were supposed to place clients in buildings that were drug free and not in desperate need of repair. But, the fact was, there were no buildings in their section of Brooklyn in 1994 that fit those criteria. Like everyone else, they did what they could.

Entering Jamilah's apartment, though, was like entering another world. Jamilah welcomed her, sat her down, went for some snacks while Rebecca once again admired what she'd done with it: the peach colored walls that Jamilah herself had painted, the cheerful pictures and posters.

The child was being so quiet, it took a few moments before Rebecca noticed her: a little girl, about six, enrapt coloring a picture, pigtails, anointed with bright beads, cascading from her head. "My grandbaby's with me this week," Jamilah explained, setting the tray down. "Ebonette say hello to the lady," Jamilah instructed, "Rebecca. She my case manager." Ebonette blinked, said hello, and turned back to her drawing.

"She's lovely," Rebecca said. "How's it going?"

"Oh, I like having the baby with me! Me and her, we get along just fine."

"What is your daughter doing for the week?"

Jamilah's face dropped. "Lord knows," she said. "Truth is, Keisha dropped her off for me to babysit for a few hours. That was five days ago!"

"My God!" Rebecca said.

"Aren't you gonna have some of that?" Jamilah nodded toward the juice and cookies.

"Of course," Rebecca said. But it was too late. She'd hesitated.

"You know that's not how it spreads!" Jamilah scolded.

"I was just taking my time," Rebecca lied, "admiring your apartment again." But she was already busted. She felt so ashamed that after months working with people with AIDS, visiting their homes, and having the head knowledge about this stuff, she still felt such squeamishness.

So she swallowed and dug in. The cookies that Jamilah herself made were delicious, and Rebecca cooed their praises, hoping to overlay her faux pas. Then she settled into their conversation. She always enjoyed talking to Jamilah the best. Some of the clients just wanted to cover the basics, the logistics of survival and health care, but with Jamilah they always got deep, in this case, exploring the ins and outs of the unexpected granddaughter landing in her lap.

Jamilah stuffed carrot after carrot into the machine, watching the orange, life-giving juice spurt out. Her kitchen was almost the same color, a little more yellow. She filled a quart, then washed the thing out and sat down to enjoy a glass. Her friend, Habibah, had offered to take Ebonette for some hours, so she had some time alone.

Not that the child was any kind of a problem, really. She was plenty good at keeping herself entertained if Jamilah was praying or otherwise occupied. She did like to get read to. They were going to have to take a trip to the library soon because Jamilah did not have children's books. They went through the one book Ebonette came with in a day. After that Ebonette had dumped another onto Jamilah's lap, and scooted herself up next to her on the couch, looking up expectantly. "I don't think *HIV in Minority Communities* is for you," Jamilah had laughed. She went through her shelves and dug one up about Harriet Tubman, which kept Ebonette enthralled even though it was way over her head. But they were just about done with that one too.

Jamilah couldn't help being proud that the dance of generations had led to this, that some part of her had gone into producing someone with as much intelligence and good plain common sense as Ebonette. It was truly a miracle, a true flowering through concrete, that in spite of all her hard living in the past, and whatever mess Keisha was in now, they had this girl. And Jamilah was going to do whatever it took, to keep her from sinking into the same muck as the rest of them. It was as if Allah was giving them another chance to start over fresh.

The buzzer startled her. "Who is it?" Jamilah said into the intercom. She was stalling for time. It was too early for Habibah to be back with the girl and she knew it was just a matter of time before Keisha came to, looked around and noticed her daughter wasn't with her.

"I come to pick up my baby!" she heard Keisha say.

"You six days late, baby girl!" Jamilah said.

"Look," Keisha said, "some unexpected things happened."

"So unexpected you couldn't pick up a phone?"

"I'm sorry, Mom. Okay. Will you quit playing games and let me in?"

"I ain't playing, Keisha. Ebonette is staying with me."

The intercom went dead and Jamilah held her breath. Soon the pounding started. Keisha had obviously snuck into the building, and was camped outside the apartment now. "Bitch," she was screaming. "You can't kidnap my daughter!" This was accompanied by a head throbbing pounding. And it wasn't just her fist either, or it'd be broken by then. Jamilah was just glad the child wasn't there to hear it.

"I'm going to call the police," Jamilah heard the shouts of a neighbor, "if you don't stop that racket!"

Fine, Jamilah thought, *let the cops settle it.* But her heart softened. Besides, it wasn't right to annoy the neighbors. Plus, if her door got banged in, she couldn't count on Damone, the housing manager, to get it fixed. "Put whatever you got away," Jamilah called, "I'm opening the door, and I don't want to get hit!"

She found Keisha on the floor with a Walkman, a blanket, a thermos and yes, a bat. "She's not here," Jamilah said, as Keisha scrambled up and pushed herself inside, looking around like a fox on the scent.

"You're lying. Where you got her hid?"

"I'm not lying."

"All right then, what you done to her?"

"Nothing. My friend took her to a museum."

"Okay fine," Keisha made herself at home on Jamilah's couch, and unscrewed the thermos. "It's more comfortable in here, anyway. I'll just wait 'til she come back."

"Even if you take her now," Jamilah said. "It'll be just temporary. I'm going to go for custody."

Keisha slammed the thermos down and the poor table shook. "You can't do this to me, Mama!"

"This is not about you. I just want what's best for Ebonette."

Keisha blinked and picked up her thermos. Jamilah followed suit with her juice. "What's that crap you're drinking?" Keisha asked. "That look nasty!"

"Fresh juice?" Jamilah said. "This keeps me alive. I just hope what you're drinking is as good for you as mine is for me."

"Oh it good for me!" Keisha said. "This is my medicine."

"Um-hm!" Jamilah grunted.

Keisha swallowed noisily. "It's a little late for you to be thinking about the best interest of the children," she said, "don't you think, Mama?"

Jamilah sighed and looked up at the poster she'd put up, set perfectly in the midst of the peachy cream wall. It had Arabic writing on it, which she couldn't read, but she knew it meant: *may the peace of Allah be with you.* "I know I made my mistakes," she said. "But that's no reason for Ebonette to suffer." Jamilah was still only three years, five months and seventeen days sober. She still went regularly to her Islamic twelve-step group, reporting her successes every few months or so. But she had learned too much from her own sorry life. There had to be a point where you said, the buck stops here, and this was it!

"No, Mama, you have no idea about it. To you, your mistakes is just something you throw around in those meetings you go to. Something to make you feel holy . . ."

"No. I know there are amends to be made."

"Amends! Give me a break, Mama. There are things that don't get amended!" Keisha got up to use the bathroom. Jamilah knew that growing up as she did with the dealers and the fly-by night "daddies," not to mention the months in foster care, Keisha had good reason to be angry. But that did not mean that she was a fit mother for Ebonette now.

But would the child be better off with her? That was the question. True, so far, by the grace of Allah (and her juicer), she was mostly keeping that nasty virus at bay. But it did win some rounds, knocked her out from time to time and it slowed her way down, often to stopping. It made resting an active verb in her life. When other people partied, she stayed home and rested; it was something she lived her life around. When her kids said, "what are you doing Mom?" and she said, "resting," she meant she was doing something.

Rebecca had asked if loneliness was impacting her decision, and Jamilah had thought about it. She hadn't given up on men completely, but she'd been through so many losers. If there was still some decent man out there for her, Allah was just going to have to deliver him up to her door; she no longer had the strength to look. And true too, a part of her longed to feel her hands on child-flesh, day after day, now that she was sober enough to enjoy it, to finally do it right. But as Rebecca helped her sort out, that wasn't what this was about. All that mattered was what was best for Ebonette.

Rebecca was a good case manager, Jamilah thought, and she was grateful to have her. Habibah told her she was a fool to trust a white woman. "When push comes to shove," she'd said, "you'll see which side she's on."

But Jamilah knew how special it was to have a person of any race, creed or color listen to your innermost thoughts. "Maybe you haven't noticed," she'd responded, "but push has already come to shove for me a long time ago. That's why I take a good look around to see who it is that's really on my side." Still, Jamilah knew that a young Jewish social worker from Park Slope wasn't the same thing as a friend. But everyone had their limits. And there were all kinds of black folks messing with the devil's playground, as far as that went. No, Allah was the only one who was going to come through one hundred percent and that was just the way that it was.

"I guess you know your toilet don't work," Keisha said, coming back into the room.

"It does. You just have to do a jiggling thing with the jigger there."

"It supposed to go down by itself!"

"I know," Jamilah said. "I told my case manager, and she's told the housing manager who is calling my landlord."

"So with everyone telling everybody else, it still broke!"

"They have a lot of apartments they tend to," Jamilah said. She was grateful for the apartment, but she did wonder what Damone and his crew did riding around in their van all day, 'stead of fixing what they were supposed to fix.

"Well no one's gonna give you a child living in this dump!" Keisha said. "That elevator stink so much, I had to walk up the stairs."

Jamilah flinched. She knew the building was a mess but she was proud of what she'd done with her apartment. It had taken weeks to roll herself around the walls with the paint, but she figured she wasn't going anywhere quick. Weeks could go by, with the same ugly walls. In this case they went by, and she had beautiful rooms (and yes, a tired old back; but some nice colors to look at when she was ready to give it its due of rest) at the end of them. "You look like the exercise could do you good," Jamilah said. Keisha was still her beautiful girl, but things sagged on her that ought not to, not on a young thing like her. And her hair was just tacked up to her head, like she didn't want to bother with any plan of design or action. It was good for Keisha what she was doing, too, Jamilah thought. That girl needed to have an ounce of reality knocked into her. "Anyway," Jamilah said. "She's staying with me whatever you think of this place. If you leave her for an hour, and don't come back for days, what do you think is going to happen?"

"It's not like I left her on a street corner; I left her with you! I assume you think you're a safe place for a child. Even with your screwed up toilet . . . "

"Praise to Allah for that!" Jamilah said. "But who knows what you're going to do next. You lost track of six days!"

"It was Raphael, Mama. He had some deal going on down in Phillie and he talked me into going down with him. I figured Ebonette was safer with you. Don't you understand; I was trying to protect her?"

"Well you're right. She was better off with me. But she still is. I don't want to know what that fool boy was doing down there; but whatever it was, I don't want my granddaughter anywhere near it!" Jamilah held her breath. She'd learned to say "NO!" one temptation at a time but this was one of the hardest, to her own daughter. It almost took her breath away and her breath was precious scarce those days, still recovering as she was from the last bout of pneumonia.

"Okay, you're right about one thing," Keisha said. "Raphael, he can be nasty. That's why I need Ebonette. She's all I have Mama, don't you see? Please. Don't do this!"

"You have me."

"No I don't. And if you think they gonna give her to an old lady with AIDS on a platter, you crazy. They gonna give her away to some white folks. Or rich blacks. You're just gonna get her set afloat with strangers who don't know anything about who she is."

"Well maybe strangers would be better for her, if they treat her right."

Keisha stood up, and started pacing. "See," she said. "That's what I'm talking about. I don't have a mother. My Mama would never say a nasty thing like that to me!"

One afternoon Rebecca combed through the tangle of streets in downtown Brooklyn. She could see the bridge and Manhattan in the distance; then it all got eclipsed by the massive courthouse. "Do you think I should do this?" Jamilah asked when Rebecca found her upstairs waiting.

"I can't answer that for you," Rebecca said. "I'm here to support whatever you decide."

"I don't know how I can judge her," Jamilah said. "Not with my history."

"It's not about judging," Rebecca reminded, "It's about doing what's best for your granddaughter."

Rebecca glanced up at the huge clock as it ticked away the minutes of her afternoon. "They're always late," Jamilah said. "They don't care about our time, believe me."

Rebecca had a thousand things to do back in the office, including a staff meeting. It was too bad to miss it too, because she had a bunch of things to talk to the housing manager about, and that communication always went better when other people were around. But she couldn't be in two places at once so she might as well relax. And she liked being with Jamilah. It wasn't always easy between them; they did have their client/case manager struggles. Jamilah had come into the office a couple months ago yelling her head off because her food stamps had been cut off. Rebecca had simply said, "I understand your frustration," and got on the stick making phone calls. After the problem was solved, Jamilah came repentantly into the office. "Sorry I yelled at you," she'd said. "I know it isn't your fault." "And I understand not having food is infuriating," Rebecca had replied.

"Always?" Rebecca echoed back to Jamilah at the courthouse.

"You can imagine this isn't my first time," Jamilah admitted. She wore a long skirt and her hair was bound with a head piece of African design. "It does bring up some memories."

"I'm not surprised."

"Do you want to know what for?" Jamilah said.

"Do you want to tell me?"

"Well," Jamilah hesitated only a moment, "why not? We got time to kill. Okay. I got into some trouble for forging checks. That's what drugs will do to you. Some of it fed the habit; some kept my kids off the streets."

"I see." Rebecca thought about her own daughter, home by herself during school vacation just then. She wondered what risks she'd take to keep her needs met. "So what happened?"

"I went to jail. Fifteen months and my kids were put in foster care. That's when I started to turn my life around. Course it took the diagnosis and turning my life to Allah for it to clinch."

"Well good for you," Rebecca said. "That you succeeded! What a survivor you are!"

"No," Jamilah said. "It was the Higher Power that pulled me through. I'm still one day at a time. Praise be to Allah!"

"Okay," Rebecca said. "I stand corrected. But I have to admit I'm a little impressed too. I mean, obviously stealing and addiction are wrong. But you lived by your wits and you found a way to get your kids fed." Jamilah was endlessly humble, but Rebecca couldn't help blaming the circumstances of her life. What could this smart and caring woman have accomplished if she'd had a better start in life?

Suddenly Jamilah was crying. "You're right," she said. "It's good to look at our faults but sometimes you could overdo it. I did love my kids, Rebecca. And Keisha, she was my favorite. I hate to see what she's doing to herself!"

"Maybe there's something you could do for her too," Rebecca said.

"Yes, I'll think on it."

A name was called and repeated. "That's us," Jamilah said, scurrying up. Rebecca followed her into the awesome chambers of the King's County Courthouse, and watched Jamilah handle herself like a queen.

Rebecca came back into the office one afternoon during the next week, after a trip down to a food stamp office with one of her clients. Damone was standing on a chair in the big room, his head reaching to the ceiling. One or the other of them was often in the field, so she hadn't seen him in a while. "Uh, hi, I've been wanting to talk to you," she called up at him.

"You see I'm busy," he said. "I'll get back to you when I'm through!" But he finished fixing the light in just another minute, jumped down, and looked at her.

"I just want to remind you about some things still broken in clients' apartments; there's Marco's front door, and Jamilah's toilet."

"You been on my case for a while," Damone said. His eyes glistened and his near shaven scalp shone with a dark layer of peach fuzz.

"Well, these problems have been going on for some time." The fact was she'd given him a list a month ago that included, besides what she mentioned, inadequate heating, broken furniture, clogged sinks, and a stove that didn't work. Meanwhile the maintenance crew took off in their van day after day. It was anybody's guess what they were doing.

"Speaking of Jamilah," he said, "how's the custody case going?"

"We're waiting to hear. Meanwhile, the child is with her mother."

"Do you really think a grandmother with AIDS can raise a child?" he said. "And with no resources except what we and the state give her?"

Rebecca thought a moment. "I think if Jamilah thinks she can, then she can," she said.

"Pretty naive," he said. Rebecca bridled. Some people at the agency liked to call her that and she hated it. Maybe her life wasn't as hard as the people they served, but she'd had her own struggles that they knew nothing about. And if she was naive in some ways, she was working hard and learning an awful lot really fast!

"Well, so," she returned to the main point. "Do you think you could get over and fix these things?"

"Look! Why don't you attend to what concerns you," Damone said. "You do your job and I'll do mine!"

"Making sure the clients are adequately housed is part of my job," Rebecca said. "And we're supposed to be working together!"

"They're lucky they get these apartments for a song and dance," he said, "I don't know what they have to complain so much about!"

"Actually," Rebecca said. "We're contracted to keep the apartments in decent condition. It isn't legal for there to be so much disrepair."

"You want me to lose my job, don't you?" he snapped. "It's because I'm black isn't it? I know about white bitch social workers like you!"

"Look," Rebecca said, "our clients are every color of the rainbow, and I'm just trying to get them served."

She reeled into her little office and closed the door. It was really too small to be considered an office or even a room. It was a closet, a cubicle. The walls were an ugly, metallic shade of blue and scratched beyond repair. The only window faced a brick wall, and the walls had only two ugly and depressing posters warning people about HIV. Every day she swore she was going to fix it up but there were always crises to deal with and she never had time.

Tears welled up inside her just behind her eyelids. It wasn't professional to cry on the job. But her job was to validate and respond to needs and feelings; didn't her own count? No they didn't, she answered herself. Not on this job. She didn't have time to fix up her office, let alone indulge in her own feelings. Maybe it was just too hard. Maybe it was time to give notice, and take her husband up on his insistence that she develop a private practice from home. "Knock, knock!" The voice was accompanied by the door being pushed open a crack.

"Come in," Rebecca said, relieved to see it was Jamilah interrupting her privacy.

"I was in the neighborhood," she said. "And I wanted to tell you, I have Ebonette again, but it's temporary." Jamilah was draped in layers of colorful, flowing material. "I'm dropping the case against my daughter."

"All right," Rebecca said, "but tell me why."

"We made a deal. She left that fool boyfriend she been running with. And she got her behind into a recovery program."

"Great. But can we be sure she's not going to relapse and put Ebonette in jeopardy again?"

"I got that covered too!" Jamilah said, her bright face shining beneath the colorful scarf. "Folks at her program are also watching out. Any backsliding, they tell me and the custody case is on again. Keisha knows this."

"How do you feel about it?" Rebecca asked.

"Good," she said. "Keisha deserves a chance to see what she can pull together, by herself just like I did. She's my child too, and she's Ebonette's mother."

"You're a good mother," Rebecca said.

"No. That ship sailed a long time ago," Jamilah shook her head. "No, sank. Now I just get to pick up some broken pieces and dry them off."

"I think there's more that was salvaged from that wreck than you think," Rebecca said.

"I'm just grateful to Allah for helping me through this," Jamilah said, gathering her things. "And you too," she added, turning back to face Rebecca.

"My pleasure," Rebecca said.

"Are you okay?" Jamilah asked.

Feeling her eyes scanning her face, Rebecca was stunned by the sudden attention. She was too close to crying to lie, and it felt good to be seen. "I had a run-in with Damone," she said.

"I'm sure whatever you said, he had it coming. And then some. That boy don't do a darn thing. He just sit on his behind soaking up the pay check."

"He said I was on his case because I'm white." Rebecca said.

Jamilah burst into laughter. "That fool. He gonna blame anyone but himself for the mess he's making!"

"Thank you," Rebecca said. "Good luck with your family."

"And thanks too," Jamilah said, "for trying to get the toilet fixed!"

"Trying is all I can do."

"I got news for you; trying is all any of us can do!"

"But we do have to try," Rebecca said. Sometimes she bridled at Jamilah's insistence that everything was up to God. Her Rabbi liked to say that people are meant to be co-creators, responsible to help repair the world, and she thought that an interesting idea.

"Sure," Jamilah nodded. "Don't hurt to try. Trying means you're giving God a chance." Then she let the door close behind her. The room seemed to hold the afterglow of her presence. Rebecca was impressed at the way Jamilah had figured her way through this difficult problem, and came up with such a good solution.

But it was her triumph too, Rebecca thought; hadn't she helped walk her through it, trying all the while to build up her confidence? And surely such a success was worth taking a few knocks over. Didn't all the clients do that, living with the reality of what the virus was doing to their bodies as well as the stigma attached, not to mention the poverty they lived in? Rebecca packed up her things and went out of the room. Damone looked up at her from the desk where he sat. "Calling it a day, Ms. Garetsky?" he said.

"Yes," she said.

"Look. I'm sorry about what I said before. There was no call for that."

"It's OK," Rebecca said, a bit stunned. "I'm sorry too if I seemed to disrespect your job. I know you're under a lot of pressure."

"That's for sure," he said. "We can never catch up. Something's always falling apart!"

"It must get overwhelming."

"And it falls on me and my crew to fix it all; we don't get to just sit around and talk to the clients!"

Rebecca noted the dig but let it slide. "We just have to all do what we can," she said. "One day at a time."

"Yes, that's correct, Ms. Garetsky. Well, see you tomorrow."

"All right," Rebecca said. "Have a good night."

The anonymity of the Brooklyn streets was comforting, the darkness an accepting, protective cloak, and she hurried over to the subway. She didn't know if Damone was totally irresponsible like Jamilah thought or trying his darndest to fix things. She should talk to the director about it; it was his responsibility after all.

The subway doors closed behind her and the rattling train whisked her away, back to her own neighborhood. It was time for her to put her own family on the front burner of her mind, and she appreciated what an opportunity and privilege she had to give her daughter a good home. But she'd be back in the morning to face another day. Certainly she had to see how Jamilah's plan was going to work out.

Trying was all they could do, Jamilah said, but sometimes, a little push made amazing things happen. Sometimes trying was enough.

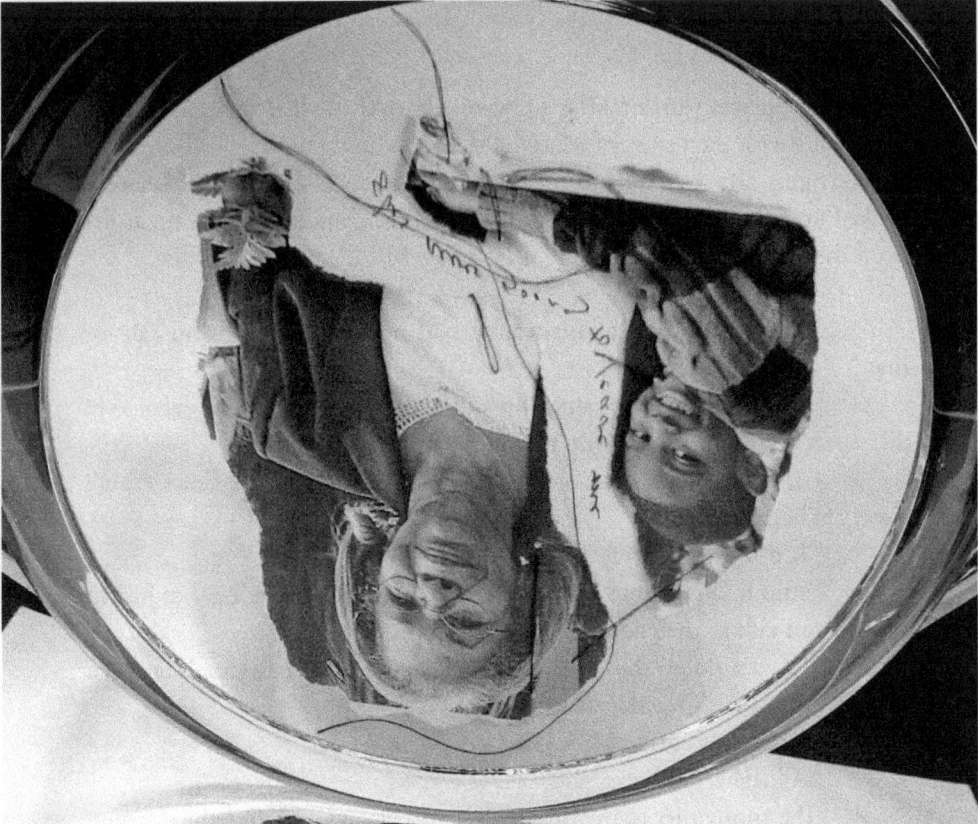

JIM PAHZ

GOOD INTENTIONS

I first met Angelina in the beginning of her sophomore year. One day she just showed up at our door. She was a pleasant-looking individual, somewhat overweight, and appeared a little sad. I could sense she was nervous. She explained that she was a friend of a friend and mentioned some names I didn't recognize. "And," she said, hesitating, "well . . . I heard you had horses. I was wondering if you might let me come sometime and brush them. I'm not asking to ride the horses, I just want to groom them. I've had experience, I've been around horses all my life. I know this is an unusual request, and I apologize for making it. I have rehearsed this speech because I wanted to get it right. I practiced. I wasn't sure I could do this but I was told you and your wife were nice people and that you taught at the university. I hope you understand. I really like horses. I like being around them. They make me feel good."

I didn't know what to say. This girl was a stranger. There was something so pitiful about her that I was genuinely moved. I thought of my father and how he used to tell me to try and cultivate a *gracious spirit*. Those words were important to him. It was his version of the golden rule: treat others as you yourself would like to be treated.

I called Hannah into the room and introduced her to Angelina. I knew Hannah had a gracious spirit. Angelina stood with her head bent, eyes downcast, and repeated her request. Then Hannah reached for her hand and in a soft, motherly voice said to the young lady, "Sure you can. Come, Angelina, would you like to meet our horses?"

That was the beginning of a relationship that would last through Angelina's college career. At first we didn't pay much attention when she came and spent thirty or forty minutes in the barn. Then one day after Angelina had been coming for about five weeks we noticed her car had been parked outside the barn for a long time. "I better go check on her," I said, "and make sure everything is all right." When I got to the barn I found Angelina sitting on a bale of straw weeping. I was alarmed and immediately thought there had been an accident. Maybe a horse had stepped on her. Worse, maybe she had been kicked. Our horses were gentle and well trained. I didn't think such an accident likely, but horses are unpredictable. They are large, heavy animals and any sudden movement or noise can startle them. Even the best horsemen have been known to be seriously injured. The actor, Christopher Reeve, who played *Superman*, immediately came to mind.

"Angelina," I asked, "Are you okay? Did something happen? Are you hurt?"

"Oh no. Thank you for your concern, but I'm fine. I just needed to cry. Sometimes when I'm not feeling so well I start to cry. I've been known to cry for hours. It's nothing to worry about, and when I'm done I feel much better."

"Okay," I said. "I'm glad to see that nothing bad happened. I guess I'll just leave you then." I started walking but then turned around, "Angelina," I said, "you did say you had experience with horses—right?"

"Oh yes," Angelina said between sobs. "I have been around them all my life. I had a mare named *Sahara*, but I was forced to sell her to help my parents pay for college." Then she started crying even louder. The last thing I heard as I walked from the barn was, "I loved *Sahara* so much. My parents should never have sold her."

When I got back into the house I looked at Hannah and said, "Something's wrong with that girl."

Over time, Hannah and I came to believe that Angelina had *issues*. Despite feeling that way, we allowed her to keep coming to the barn to brush the horses and have her cry. We suggested she should take advantage of the counseling center at the university. Because she was a student, the service was free. She thanked us and promised to go and see a counselor, but I doubt if she ever did. Throughout her sophomore year Angelina continued to come to the farm once a week, usually on Fridays, a day when she didn't have classes. She came almost every week, and she cried.

By her junior year, Angelina, Hannah and I had developed a sort of friendship. We recognized the girl was a wee bit strange, maybe neurotic, but she was pleasant company when she wasn't crying and the horses had never looked so clean.

One day Angelina came to the farm with a baby pig. It was a tiny thing and she explained it had been the runt of the litter. A farmer gave it to her to raise as a pet. "Otherwise," she said, "he would have had to kill it. I named the pig Madelyn. Isn't she precious?" Angelina's request was simple. "You have empty stalls; can't we use one of them for Madelyn? I will come out every day to feed her. I'll take really good care of her. I promise."

Once again I was at a loss to know what to do. Angelina was so animated she reminded me of a small child. I looked at Hannah, but she just rolled her eyes and shrugged her shoulders. The best I could come up with was, "Angelina, you know Madelyn won't stay a baby forever. She will grow up. Pigs get big."

"Oh I know, Daniel, but I've always believed in taking one step at a time. Right now Madelyn needs love and care. She's so helpless and since I live in the dormitory, I can't raise her there. That's why I'm asking. I'll try to find another home for her as soon as I can. Please. She won't be here long. Please, please?"

I think Hannah and I were thinking the same thing. We had often talked with each other about Angelina's sadness and speculated on why she came to our barn to cry every week. Angelina had told us she had preferred the company of animals to people. We assumed she was lonely, and didn't have many, if any, friends. So when she made, what seemed to us, this simple request, we both thought, what harm can it do? Maybe it will make her feel better. It might give her a sense of purpose and raise her self-esteem at the same time she was raising her piglet.

Hannah and I relented, and Madelyn became a fixture at our little farm. And just as I predicted, Madelyn didn't stay a baby for long. Day by day, she grew. Maybe it was because of her diet. In our town there was a commercial bakery named *Aunt Millie's Enriched Breads*. The products that were not sold when the bread was fresh were made available as animal feed. Angelina bought the baked goods by the barrel, and brought them home for Madelyn. The pig's diet consisted of bread loaves, sweet rolls, cinnamon buns, croissants, and doughnuts. Occasionally, Angelina threw in some cracked corn, and we provided the table scraps from lunch and dinners.

Angelina would walk that pig on a leash, just like it was a dog. And pigs being extremely smart creatures, Madelyn learned the routine well. She was litter trained and always did her *necessaries* in the same area. Hannah and I noticed that Angelina stopped crying in the barn once she began to take care of Madelyn. Hannah and I claimed the credit for that accomplishment and complimented each other on our insightfulness.

"We should enter the counseling profession," I said. "I think we have an intuitive insight into human nature."

"It's amazing," Hannah responded, "She isn't melancholy anymore. I think we cured her."

All the while Hannah and I kept complimenting one another, Madelyn continued to grow. Soon, she was so big that Angelina wasn't walking her at all. Rather, the pig was pulling Angelina along and going wherever the animal wanted to go. It began to root up our lawn and frighten the horses. Both Hannah and I realized it was time for Madelyn to leave.

On several occasions I approached Angelina. "Angelina," I said, "Madelyn is too big. She is scaring our guests and frightening the animals. And, she is tearing up our yard. Have you seen what she has done to the front lawn? Madelyn is not that cute little piggie anymore. You promised to take her elsewhere and it has been more than one year."

"Oh, I will," Angelina promised again, "just as soon as I can find a place to put her."

But she never found that place. She broke promise after promise. As time passed, Hannah and I got angry. Angelina's attitude towards us began to change also. She tried to avoid our company. When we did run into one another, she was belligerent. In private I began to refer to Angelina by the derogatory term *the pig lady*. It wasn't a nice thing to say, but it was my way of expressing my frustration.

One day, Hannah said, "I guess we weren't so smart, after all. I thought we were helping that girl, but she is obsessed with that animal and being completely unreasonable. No matter how many times you or I ask her to move Madelyn, she ignores our requests. I don't know what more we can do. I'm at my wits' end."

"I think I know what to do," I said. My anger too had reached a crescendo. I got into my car and drove to an attorney's office.

The following week Angelina received a registered letter from the lawyer. The letter said that as of this date Angelina would be billed for board for Madelyn at a rate of ten dollars per day. If she didn't pay promptly by the first of the month a judgment would be rendered against her and her parents, and the university authorities would be notified.

When I next saw Angelina she was livid. Her yellow Volkswagen was parked at the barn, and she was trying to entice Madelyn to climb into the back seat. She refused to speak to me when I addressed her. The problem was Madelyn was almost as large as the automobile. That intelligent pig refused to enter the car. I think it was at that moment that I realized that Madelyn had more sense than Angelina, who I believed now was certifiably nuts. No right-thinking person or pig would attempt such a ridiculous maneuver.

"Angelina," I said. "Madelyn isn't going to fit into your car. She knows that. That's why she won't get in. Even if you did somehow manage to squeeze her in there, she would destroy the vehicle if she panicked and started to thrash around. Let me help you. We can use my truck and horse trailer to move her to her new home."

Angelina started to cry. She began to protest but realized that my solution was the only reasonable one. "Couldn't we . . . " she began to plead.

"No, I won't negotiate on this," I said firmly. "You have been asked numerous times and promised repeatedly. Madelyn has got to leave. It's just as simple as that."

Finally Angelina relented. Later that afternoon we coaxed Madelyn into the horse trailer with a dozen donuts and a few English muffins. We hauled her to a farm that Angelina knew of. I was expecting some words of gratitude for the trouble I went to getting Madelyn to her new home. But I was wrong. The last thing Angelina said to me was, "Well, Daniel, now Madelyn isn't your problem and you can just go to hell!" And following those words, Angelina, a.k.a., *the pig lady*, walked out of our lives.

I have to admit, my feelings were hurt. I regretted ever getting involved with Angelina. What is it some say, "no good deed goes unpunished."

"It was a mismitzvah," Hannah said.

"A what?"

"A good deed gone bad. The Yiddish word, mitzvah means good dead. Well I changed it. My word has to do with intentions and unforeseen consequences. You were trying to be helpful to Angelina when you agreed to let her keep Madelyn here. You were doing a good deed. But it didn't work out. Your good intentions were for naught. Thus, it wasn't so much a good deed as it was a good deed gone wrong—a mismitzvah. Understand?"

"I think so," I said and nodded my head.

We stopped talking about Angelina and in time the memory faded. About five years later Hannah and I received a letter from Angelina. She informed us she had graduated college, attended nursing school, and now lived in St. Petersburg, Florida. In her letter she wrote,

> I want to apologize to you for the grief I put you through with Madelyn. I had no right to be so intrusive into your lives and I am truly sorry. I was selfish and inconsiderate. Madelyn lived for two years after she moved from your farm. She became morbidly obese and eventually couldn't stand by herself. A veterinarian advised me to *put her down*, which I did. Needless to say, my heart was broken. I will always remember her as my little princess. She was so cute and cuddly when she was a baby.
>
> I want to thank the both of you for the kindness you showed during my college years. I have been in therapy now for more than two years and I have learned a lot about myself. I was diagnosed with a condition referred to as *severe premenstrual syndrome*. That is why I was depressed all of the time. My hormones were out of whack and it affected me in many strange ways. Crying made me feel better.
>
> I hope when you think of me you can find it in your hearts to forgive. Please understand that when I was with you I was sick. I couldn't help myself. I especially want to apologize for the terrible things I said to Daniel when you were kind enough to deliver Madelyn to her new home. What I said was inexcusable and I am ashamed of myself. Both of you had always been kind to me and didn't deserve to be abused by me.
>
> I am writing this letter in an attempt to make amends. I want you to know that I will be forever grateful for your kindness. God bless you both.
>
> Sincerely,
>
> Angelina

We never heard from Angelina again. It's been years. I sometimes think about her and wonder how she is doing. In my mind, I try to picture her as a nurse. I wonder if she cares about patients half as much as she did about that pig. If so, the sick people will be in good hands. Sometimes I think about Angelina's letter and the *kindness* she said we showed her. For a long time Hannah and I had regretted ever getting involved with Angelina. But I don't feel that way now. When I reflect on those days, I smile. And although the episode had turned sour and didn't end as anticipated, in retrospect it wasn't so bad. Madelyn was so cute at the beginning and so bizarre at the end—Hogzilla on a leash. She was almost the size of a hippopotamus. Like a locomotive out of control she dragged Angelina around the farm. It was a comical sight.

I have wondered if the whole episode wasn't a mistake from the start. Beginnings, it seems, are easy. We get into situations with our eyes half closed, never stopping to anticipate what the outcomes might be. It is the endings that are difficult—the extraction—the break up. This is true for people and giant pigs. So, what's the lesson? Should we never attempt to be kind to people? Is it better to keep others at arm's length and remain islands unto ourselves? I don't think so. Life is complicated, and it's not always easy to know what to do. Mismitzvahs happen. As for me, I guess I'll just try to remember my father's advice about cultivating a *gracious spirit*. My dad was usually correct.

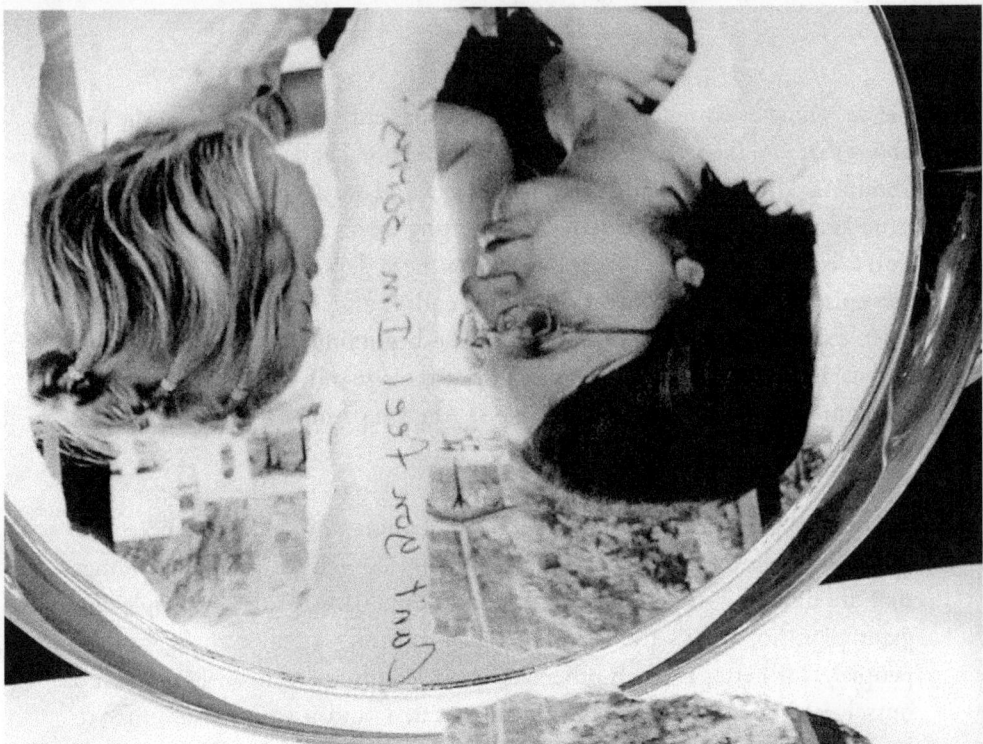

ACKNOWLEDGEMENTS

Marian Mathews Clark's "Getting There" was previously published in *Persimmon Tree* (Fall, 2008).

Willy Conley's "Shifting Dirt" first appeared in *The Tactile Mind* (Winter, 2002-2003).

A portion of William Henderson's "Scar Tissue" originally appeared in the online journal *Zouch Magazine.*

Paul Hostovsky's poems "Greenhouse," "Love the Mistake," "Ladders," and "Visitation" are reprinted from his book *Bending the Notes* (Main Street Rag, 2008).

Caridad Moro's "Coming Out to Mami" first appeared in *Fifth Wednesday Journal* (Spring, 2008).

Mary Kay Rummel's "Surfacing" was previously published in her book *What's Left Is The Singing* (Blue Light Press, 2010).

Adrienne Ross Scanlan's "Drops of Water" originally appeared in *Under The Sun* (Summer, 2011).

Don Thackrey's "Coming To Know Pa" was first published in *The Lyric* (Summer, 2009).

Carol Tufts's "Correspondents" previously appeared in *The Panhandler.*

Photographs by Heather Tosteson, who thanks all those, including friends, neighbors, and family both living and dead, who yet again generously donated images of themselves to art with no idea what words or ideas they would be brought into association with.

We are very grateful to Kathleen Housley, Kerry Langan, and Debra Gingerich, members of the Wising Up Press Writers Collective, for so generously and scrupulously reading the manuscript in part or in totality and so ably sharing their skills as editors and engaged and thoughtful readers.

CONTRIBUTORS

Eve Mills Allen (Nash) has a passion for storytelling. She teaches therapeutic writing through the College of Extended Learning at the University of New Brunswick. Her memoir, *Little White Squaw: A Story of Abuse, Addiction and Reconciliation*, co-authored by Kenneth J. Harvey, was released in 2002. She has an MA in Creative Writing and MEd in Counseling Psychology from UNB.

Patricia Barone published a novella, *The Wind*, with New Rivers Press. Her short stories have appeared in anthologies from Wising Up Press, Plume/Penguin, Prentice Hall, Prentice/Merrill, and Peter Lang; and in the periodicals, *West Wind Review* and *American Writing*. She received a Loft-McKnight Award of Distinction in poetry and a Lake Superior Contemporary Writers Award for a short story.

Bari Benjamin, LCSW, BCD, is a former English teacher turned psychotherapist with a private practice in Pittsburgh, PA. Her essays have been published in *Adoption Today* and *StepMom* magazines, as well as *Chicken Soup for the Soul* books. She is currently working on a memoir book of letters to her adopted daughter.

Wendy Brown-Báez is a writer, teacher, performance poet and installation artist. She is the author of *Ceremonies of the Spirit* and *transparencies of light,* and her prose and poetry have appeared in dozens of literary journals as well as in Wising Up Press anthologies. She has received McKnight and Minnesota State Arts Board grants to present writing workshops to at-risk youth and in non-profits.

Caitlin Buckley is a recent graduate from Emmanuel College in Boston with a major in English Literature and Writing and is currently pursuing a career in writing. This is her first published story.

Rose Burke is a retired parole officer who writes from the heart. Her writing credits include book reviews, an article in the York-Sunbury Historical Society's *Officer's Quarters* and a children's story, "Tricksters," that was shortlisted in the 2012 Atlantic Writing Competition. Her current focus is on recreating her mother's life as a WW II Dutch war bride to Canada.

Susan Kay Chernilo has recently completed her novel, *The Liberation Diaries*, the first in a series about women searching for personal wholeness as they attempt to mend the world. She is also an experienced counselor and adult educator, currently teaching fiction and memoir writing at Cambridge Center for Adult Education. She lives in Brookline, MA with her husband, Michael.

Arhm Choi is a poet from Ann Arbor, MI, with an MFA from Sarah Lawrence College. She has competed nationally at the Brave New Voices Poetry Slam, and has been published by *Split this Rock, Two Hawk Quarterly, Peal, Otoliths,* and *Scholars & Rogues.* She has taught writing workshops at the Neutral Zone, the YWCA, and many other schools and organizations.

Marian Mathews Clark grew up in Mist, OR but also feels at home in Iowa that's nurtured her for forty years. A graduate of the Iowa Writers' Workshop, she's published fiction in *Story* and *The Sun* and nonfiction in various anthologies. Recently retired from The University of Iowa, she's working on an essay collection, *Solo, Sixty and Stupefied—in Iowa: Sorting it Out.*

Willy Conley's writings have appeared in *Deaf American Prose, Urbanite, Kaleidoscope, American Theatre, The Deaf Way II Anthology, Deaf World, The Baltimore Sun, The Washington Post, The Tactile Mind,* and *No Walls of Stone.* His most recent book was *Vignettes of the Deaf Character and Other Plays.* He is currently a professor of Theatre Arts at Gallaudet University in Washington, DC.

Terry Cox-Joseph is a member of the Poetry Society of Virginia and has been published in *Chiron Review, The Poet's Domain, Avocet* and *Prairie Poetry* among others. She is a former newspaper reporter and editor and has had one book of nonfiction published, *Adjustments* (Hampton Roads, 1993). From 1994-2004 she coordinatedthe Christopher Newport University Writers' Conference.

Bill Denham, as a southern boy growing up in the middle of the last century, learned to love the soft sounds and rhythms of the words he heard around him—a love of language that now, decades later, is evident when he speaks the poems he has taken in, learned by heart. He is a 1963 graduate of Davidson College with an MA from the University of California. His first book of poems, *Looking for Matthew*, will be published later this year.

Martha Gies is an Oregon author whose short stories and literary essays appear widely in literary quarterlies, including *Orion, The Sun* and *Zyzzyva*, and in various anthologies. She teaches creative writing in Portland and abroad, and is an activist for low-income housing and human rights.

Judith Goedeke began wondering about things at the age of four during a bit of a tantrum and has been trying to make sense of life ever since. After five decades of writing while working at more practical things, she recently began submitting. Her work appeared in the 2011 Maryland Writers' Association Poetry Anthology. She practices acupuncture in Laurel, MD.

Janet Lunder Hanafin grew up on a South Dakota farm, transplanted herself to St. Paul, MN for college, and grew deep roots. Her writing has appeared in local and metro-wide publications including the *St. Paul Almanac*. She and her husband have two children and three grandchildren (all above average) and enjoy the companionship of two very fine cats.

R.E. Hayes has published fiction in a variety of magazines and journals including *Crab Orchard Review, Evening Street Review* and *OASIS Journal 2010*. He is a labor lawyer and was, in an earlier life, a machine gunner in the Marines.

William Henderson is a Boston-based writer who blogs about love and tweets about everything else. He writes for *The Good Men Project* and *The Huffington Post* and is included in *Best Gay Writing 2012*. "Scar Tissue" is adapted from his forthcoming memoir, *House of Cards*.

Paul Hostovsky is the author of four books of poetry, most recently *Hurt Into Beauty* (FutureCycle Press, 2012). His poems have won a Pushcart Prize and been featured on *Poetry Daily, Verse Daily, The Writer's Almanac,* and *Best of the Net 2008* and *2009*. He was chosen as a featured poet for the Georgia Poetry Circuit 2012-2013.

Beth Lefebvre earned an MA in writing at Johns Hopkins University. She is a former newspaper reporter and editor, and currently works in public affairs in Washington, DC. Her recent work has appeared in *Baltimore Review, Cobalt Review,* and *Urbanite* magazine. She resides in Maryland.

Russ Allison Loar grew up in Southern California and was a musician and songwriter until returning to college to earn a journalism degree. He was a reporter for several newspapers including the *Los Angeles Times*. He lives in Claremont, CA where he writes poetry and prose, sporadically published in some of the nation's most obscure literary journals.

Michele Markarian is a Boston-based playwright, fiction writer and performer. Her plays have been published and performed in the U.S. and abroad. Michele is a member of the Dramatists Guild. Her fiction has been published in two prior Wising Up anthologies: *View From the Bed, View From the Bedside* and *Families: the Frontline of Pluralism*.

Diane Mierzwik is the author of four books, most recently *Weekly Affirmations for Pre-menopausal Women* (Rock Publishing) and was a 2011 Norman Mailer Writer's Colony Scholar.

Caridad Moro is the recipient of a Florida Individual Artist Fellowship in poetry and a Pushcart nominee. Her poetry has appeared in numerous journals including *The Comstock Review, The Crab Orchard Review, MiPoesias, The Seattle Review, Slipstream, CALYX, The Lavender Review* and others. Her award winning chapbook, *Visionware,* was published by Finishing Line Press. She resides in Miami, FL.

Tim Myers is a writer, songwriter, storyteller and university lecturer. He won a poetry contest judged by John Updike, and has published much other poetry, fiction, and nonfiction. His *Dear Beast Loveliness: Poems of the Body* will be coming out from BlazeVox while *Glad to Be Dad: A Call to Fatherhood* is out from Familius.com. He has also published eleven children's books.

Wendy Jones Nakanishi, an American by birth, has been resident in Japan since 1984, when she began full-time employment at a private Japanese university having earned a doctorate in English literature at Edinburgh University. She has published widely on English, American and Japanese literature as well as creative non-fiction stories about her life in America, Britain and Japan.

Sophia J. Nolan is the pseudonym of native Pennsylvanian author, Amanda L. Moritz. "No Reservations" is her first non-fiction publication. A science fiction novel, *Called to Midnight* (2009), was her first publication.

Jim Pahz is Professor Emeritus at Central Michigan University. He is the author of a collection of short stories, *Saving Turtles,* and has co-authored, with his wife, Cheryl, two novels, *McAngel* and *Almost Chosen . . . Nearly Saved.*

Rachel Raimondi has a BA in English from the State University of New York at New Paltz and an MA in Publishing from Pace University. Her first novel was published in 2005. She was also featured in the August 2011 online issue of *Epiphany* magazine.

Melanie Reitzel's poetry and prose has appeared in journals such as *ZYZZYVA*, *Poet Lore*, *Tulane Review*, *North American Review* (which nominated her personal essay for a Pushcart Prize), *The Prose-Poem Project* and *Berkeley Poetry Review*. She received her MFA in Creative Writing from San Francisco State University and works as a RN Lactation Consultant at Lucile Packard Children's Hospital at Stanford.

Lori Rottenberg is a writer and teacher who grew up in New York but now lives in Virginia with her husband and daughters. She has published poetry in a variety of literary journals and anthologies, and has served as a visiting poet for Arlington County Public Schools since 2007. She also works as an adult ESL instructor for Virginia Tech.

Mary Kay Rummel divides her time between California and Minnesota and teaches part time at California State University, Channel Islands. Her sixth book of poetry, *What's Left Is The Singing*, was published by Blue Light Press of San Francisco. Her short story, "Enough," appeared in *Double Lives: Reinvention and Those We Leave Behind* from Wising Up Press.

Adrienne Ross Scanlan's essays have been published in *Adventum Magazine*, *Tikkun*, *Under the Sun*, the *American Nature Writing* series, and other publications. She received a Seattle Arts Commission award, an Artist Trust Literature Fellowship, and her essay "Salvage" was listed as notable in the Best American Science and Nature Writing 2002. She is the *Blue Lyra Review's* nonfiction editor.

Evelyn Sharenov has contributed to *The New York Times*, *Glimmer Train*, *Fugue*, *Mediphors*, *Etude*, as well as numerous other literary journals, magazines and anthologies. She is a member of the NBCC and has written reviews for *The Oregonian*, *Bitch Magazine* and *Willamette Week*. She has been a notable in *Best American Short Stories*.

Isabelle Bruder Smith started writing at an early age. Her work has appeared in various anthologies, including *If I Had A Hammer: Women At Work* (Papier-Mache Press) and *So Wonderful As Thirst* (Road Publishers). Her first chapbook, *View From Here*, was co-authored with her mother, Florence. She lives in Connecticut with her husband, artist Tom Smith, and son, Andrew.

Thomas J. Stevenson never sought publication before 2011. While a graduate student at Oxford, a friend encouraged him to enter a university-wide poetry slam. Stevenson placed second. Then, his college awarded him the McKay Poetry Prize. Encouraged, he decided to actively share his work. The Studios of Key West and *Emerge* each published Stevenson's poems earlier this year.

Elizabeth Swann's poems have appeared in numerous journals and anthologies, including *Atlanta Review, Pinesong, Southern Poetry Review, storySouth, Liturgical Credo, Ruminate Magazine, Iodine Poetry Journal, Inkwell, Into the Teeth of the Wind,* and *Pine Mountain Sand & Gravel.* A high school English and journalism teacher, she earned her MFA in Creative Writing from Queens University in Charlotte, NC.

Elaine J. Taber has published a chapbook, *Secondhand Rain;* a poem, *In Silence,* in the anthology, *In The Cathedral;* and numerous nature poems in the periodical, *Life at Linden Ponds.*

Don Thackrey lives in the small town of Dexter, MI where he is retired from teaching and administering at the University of Michigan. Having grown up in rural Nebraska, he writes formal verse about the farm and ranch experience of many years ago.

Carol Tufts teaches in the English Department of Oberlin College. Her poems have appeared, or are forthcoming, in a number of literary magazines, including *Poetry, Poet Lore, Tribeca Poetry Review,* and *Poetica.* She is a recipient of an individual artists award.

Georgann Turner lives on Bainbridge Island, WA. She is an affiliate of Amherst Writers and Artists and leads *Healing Art* workshops. Her work was published in *under the gum tree,* and her poetry was chosen by Bainbridge Island Arts and Humanities Council for their annual Poetry Corners. She was a Pacific Northwest Writers Association literary contest finalist in 2012.

Marta Tveit has published two articles in the Tanzanian national newspaper *Daily News* and written several plays, one of which was produced at the Dutch amateur theatre festival Theater van Het Vat. She recently graduated from the University College Maastricht with a BA in Liberal Arts and hopes to go on to do an MFA in Creative Writing.

Andy Weatherwax began writing poetry after being diagnosed with early-onset Parkinson's disease. His work has been read at venues throughout New England and his first collection of poetry, *Renegade Pinky*, is soon to be published. A musician, sculptor and practicing Buddhist, Andy lives in the moment with his wife Josa, son Tyler and cats, Frank and Ruby, in East Hampton, CT.

Mary Wheeler has published educational books for teachers including *Nurturing Writers* and *You Said Yes*. She is an educator in Houston maximizing the empty-nest years with her husband and an assortment of pets. Mary is never without a journal to capture life and never without a book to keep her company. She restores her energy with daily exercise, creative cooking and painting.

Weihua Zhang is an English professor and scholar of African-American literature. A published writer and photographer, she lives in Savannah, GA.

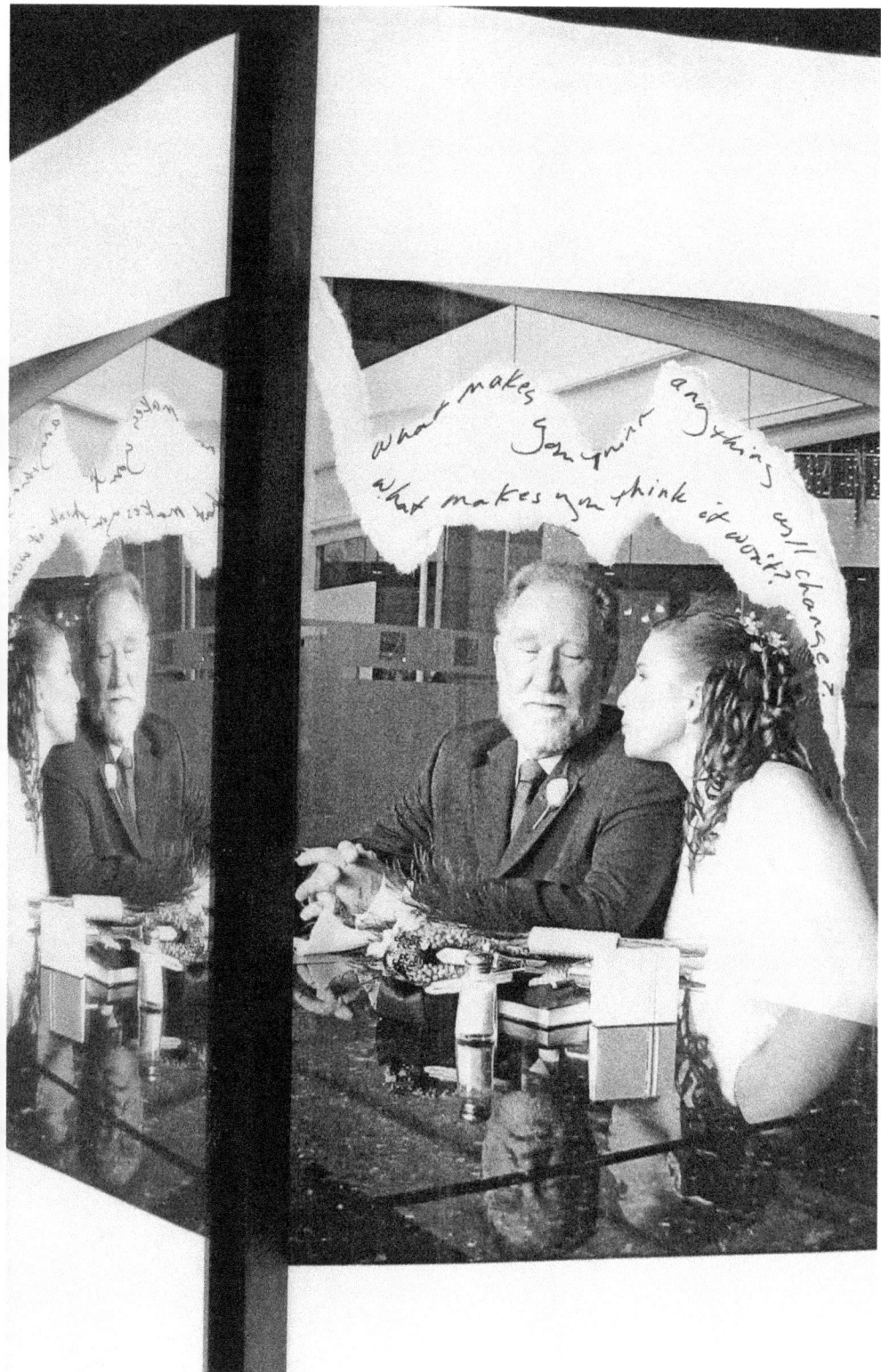

EDITORS/PUBLISHERS

HEATHER TOSTESON is the author of *The Sanctity of the Moment: Poems from Four Decades, Visible Signs, Hearts as Big as Fists* and *God Speaks My Language, Can You?* She has worked as executive editor of two public health journals and in health communications with a focus on communication across professional disciplines, racism, social trust, and how belief systems develop and change. She holds an MFA in Creative Writing (UNC-Greensboro) and PhD in English and Creative Writing (Ohio University). She is founder, with Charles Brockett, of Universal Table and Wising Up Press.

CHARLES BROCKETT has a PhD from UNC-Chapel Hill and is a recipient of several Fulbright and National Endowment for the Humanities awards. A retired political science professor, he has written two well-received books on Central America, *Land, Power, and Poverty* and *Political Movements and Violence*, and numerous social science journal articles.

See our booklist and calls for submissions for new anthologies
www.universaltable.org
wisingup@universaltable.org

Sometimes Stones Listen

better than People

www.ingramcontent.com/pod-product-compliance
Lightning Source LLC
Chambersburg PA
CBHW020604270326
41927CB00005B/163